DATE DUE

Sexual Coercion

A Sourcebook on Its Nature, Causes, and Prevention

Edited by

Elizabeth Grauerholz
Mary A. Koralewski
Purdue University

Lexington Books
D.C. Heath and Company/Lexington, Massachusetts/Toronto

Library of Congress Cataloging-in-Publication Data

Sexual coercion: a sourcebook on its nature, causes, and prevention / edited by Elizabeth Grauerholz, Mary Koralewski.
   p. cm.
  Includes bibliographical references and index.
  ISBN 0–669–21786–7
  1. Rape. 2. Child molesting. 3. Sexual harassment. 4. Prostitution. 5. Sex crimes—
Prevention. I. Grauerholz, Elizabeth, 1958– . II. Koralewski, Mary.
HV6558.S494 1991
364.1'532—dc20   90–43214
                           CIP

Published simultaneously in Canada
Printed in the United States of America
International Standard Series Number: 0–669-21786–7
Library of Congress Catalog Card Number: 90–43214

The paper used in this publication meets the minimum requirements of American National Standard for Information Sciences—Permanence of Paper for Printed Library Materials, ANSI Z39.48-1984. ⊗™

Year and number of this printing:

91 92 93 94 10 9 8 7 6 5 4 3 2 1

Contents

Preface and Acknowledgments

The fourteen chapters in this book address central concerns related to the nature, causes, and prevention of sexual coercion. The Introduction discusses the continuum of sexual violence and how sexual coercion is manifested. Part I explores the nature of rape, child sexual abuse, sexual harassment, and prostitution and provides a critical review of the research and theory in these areas. In part II, feminist, individual, and social psychological, and sociobiological theories are presented in order to understand better the occurrence of sexual coercion. Preventive strategies aimed at individual, interpersonal, and institutional levels are proposed in part III. The book concludes with a summary chapter on what is known and not known about sexual coercion.

We thank the authors of these chapters for sharing their time and expertise to help create this book. Special thanks go to David Wright, Kay Solomon, Candy Lawson, and Margaret Zusky for their assistance in preparing the manuscript for publication.

Introduction

While we were talking with a group of friends about this book recently, the conversation turned to the number of times and different ways during our lives that we had felt forced, tricked, or pressured into engaging in sexual acts. Some of the memories were acute and had occupied our thoughts over the years about how these experiences had shaped our feelings about being women, our sexuality, and our relationships, especially with men. Other experiences had been practically forgotten and were only brought to mind that day by something another had said. What struck us was not only how commonplace these events were but how similar the experiences were, even though the circumstances and actors varied, in terms of our feelings about them and the characteristics of the perpetrators.

Our experiences reflect what researchers have been suggesting for years: that sexual coercion—the act of being forced, tricked, or pressured to engage in a sexual act or acts—is relatively commonplace in American society and that for some, the experience is a familiar and ongoing one, beginning in early childhood and continuing into adulthood. Sexual coercion is manifested in different ways, but these various acts are similar and related in many ways. As one researcher states, "The basic common character underlying the many different forms of violence is the *abuse, intimidation, coercion, intrusion, threat and force men use to control women*" (Kelly 1988: 76). Leidig (1981) adds that all acts of sexual violence are under-reported, unidirectional (perpetrated by males against females), trivialized by society, involve victim blaming, and serve to control women's lives.

This book provides a closer look at the problem of sexual coercion. Drawing on the expertise of researchers across several disciplines—sociology, psychology, anthropology, women's studies, and biology—the chapters seek to answer three central questions concerning sexual coercion: What is the nature of sexual coercion (its prevalence, background, characteristics of victims and perpetrators, and consequences)? What are the possible social, psychological, and biological roots of sexual coercion? Can sexual coercion be prevented or eliminated, and if so, how?

The focus is on four types of sexually coercive acts: rape, child sexual abuse, sexual harassment, and prostitution. Although these acts tend to be the most researched, they are not inclusive of all forms of sexual coercion. Rather than explore the entire range of sexual violence, we focus here on four acts that involve coercion (physical, financial, or psychological) and explicit sexual behavior (although nonsexual violence may accompany these acts) to allow deeper study of the connections among these sexually coercive acts.

The first four chapters explore the nature of specific forms of sexual coercion. In chapter 1, Patricia A. Harney and Charlene L. Muehlenhard review the vast literature on rape, drawing on studies from law, psychology, and sociology. Next, Dean D. Knudsen critically reviews the research on child sexual coercion, a topic that has received considerable attention in recent years. Chapter 3, by Kathleen McKinney and Nick Maroules, analyzes the literature in the area of sexual harassment, focusing on that occurring within the academe and the workplace. In chapter 4, JoAnn L. Miller looks at the nature of prostitution, arguing that prostitution, in a society such as our own, necessarily constitutes a form of sexual coercion. Each chapter considers such acts as defined by professionals, researchers, and society as a whole: how common these acts are, who the victims and perpetrators are, and what the consequences of sexual coercion are.

The fact that these acts are treated separately is not to suggest that they are distinct phenomena. Indeed, we assume that rape, child sexual abuse, sexual harassment, and prostitution are all different manifestations of the same underlying dynamic; all have in common the use or threat of force, trickery, or pressure to exploit women sexually and keep them controlled through fear and sexual terror.

Clearly rape, child sexual abuse, and sexual harassment are sexually coercive. It is less obvious why prostitution constitutes a form of sexual coercion. Indeed, on an individual basis, prostitution may not involve coercion in the sense of being tricked, pressured, or forced into engaging in sexual acts. But in a wider sense, it becomes more difficult to distinguish prostitution from rape or sexual harassment. As a class, prostitutes are used by men "to act out [their] contempt for the lower and degraded sex" (Barry 1979: 117); laws discriminate against the prostitute, not the patron; and the economic realities for women may force some into prostitution and make it difficult to leave.

The overlap among these acts is underscored in chapters 1–4. McKinney and Maroules and Knudsen suggest that sexual harassment sometimes includes rape, as does child sexual abuse, and Miller points out that prostitutes are often raped and sexually harassed and, moreover, many are themselves victims of child sexual abuse.

Kelly (1988) suggests that these acts can be viewed along a continuum of prevalence, and Leidig (1981) suggests that they may be ordered according to their severity. The notion of a continuum of sexual violence is useful for several reasons. Certainly it reflects more closely women's actual experiences with sexual violence and allows one to see how acts of sexual violence are similar to one another (Kelly 1988). It also can serve as a means to integrate diverse but related areas of study to aid in our efforts to uncover the common causes and methods of prevention.

In part II the causes underlying different forms of sexual coercion are explored. In chapter 5, Wendy E. Stock presents a feminist interpretation of sexual violence, arguing that all forms of sexual coercion stem from the sexual inequality in society and serve to control women's lives. From Barry Burkhart and Mary Ellen Fromuth's exploration of the individual and social psychological correlates of sexual violence in chapter 6 emerge several underlying traits and patterns. In chapter 7, Randy Thornhill and Nancy Wilmsen Thornhill suggest a biological or evolutionary root to sexual coercion and examine evidence suggesting a psychological adaptation to rape and sexual violence.

Too often studies focus on the nature and causes of sexual coercion and make only superficial and passing reference to possible solutions. Part III is devoted to understanding ways to prevent sexual coercion. It presents some innovative suggestions for eliminating acts across the entire continuum of sexual violence.

Physical self-defense often comes to mind when thinking about prevention. In chapter 8, Martha E. Thompson discusses the theory and practice of self-defense, which represents an individualized method of sexual coercion prevention. Preventive strategies, however, must go beyond individual solutions and address underlying social problems. We must consider how social institutions can be restructured in order to promote greater mutuality. Thus, in chapter 9, Andrea Parrot calls for a resocialization of children and suggests alternative ways parents can interact with their children to help prevent their becoming victims and offenders. Elizabeth Rice Allgeier and Betty J. Turner Royster propose in chapter 10 a straightforward method, based on the notion of informed consent, that dating couples can use to reduce misunderstandings about sexuality and to deepen their romantic and sexual relationships.

The authors in chapters 11–13 consider how the educational, legal, and economic systems contribute to sexual violence against women and suggest ways to alter institutional structures, norms, and practices to help prevent such violence. Janet Lynne Enke and Lori K. Sudderth focus on the educational system in chapter 11 and argue for a comprehensive, direct approach to teaching sexuality in the schools, beginning in preschools and continuing through college. In chapter 12, Jo Dixon reviews changes that have occurred in the legal system concerning rape and sexual harassment and discusses possible future legal reforms. Heidi Gottfried discusses in chapter 13 the changes needed within the economic institution before sexual inequality and sexual violence can be ended.

The last chapter, by Elizabeth Grauerholz and Mary A. Koralewski, looks at what is known—and not known—about sexual coercion. Although we still have much to learn about this problem, it is clear from the chapters in this book that our understanding of sexual coercion has improved significantly over the past two decades.

Together these chapters provide a comprehensive review of the literature on rape, child sexual abuse, sexual harassment, and prostitution and insight into how this knowledge can be translated into action to promote social change. We intend this book to be a sourcebook for researchers and practitioners in the area of sexual coercion and to provide students with the necessary background to understand this complex social problem.

I
The Nature
of Sexual Coercion

1

Rape

Patricia A. Harney
Charlene L. Muehlenhard

Definitions of Rape

Legal Definitions

In recent decades, legal and traditional definitions of rape have undergone many revisions. According to traditional common law definitions, rape was regarded as an act committed by a man "who engages in intercourse with a woman, not his wife, by force or threat of force, against her will, and without her consent" (Estrich 1987: 8). The Federal Bureau of Investigation (FBI) has defined it as "the carnal knowledge of a female forcibly and against her will" (Estrich 1987: 10). But reforms in rape laws instituted by various states in the 1980s no longer require the victim to prove her nonconsent and also now legally recognize that some men rape the women to whom they are married (Estrich 1987). The Model Penal code is one such example; rape there is defined as "sexual intercourse where the man 'compels [a woman] to submit by force or by threat of imminent death, serious bodily injury, extreme pain or kidnapping, to be inflicted on anyone'" (Estrich 1987: 58–59). Many states now legally define rape in gender-neutral language, as Ohio does: "vaginal intercourse between male and female, and anal intercourse, fellatio, and cunnilingus between persons regardless of sex . . . when . . .(1) the offender purposely compels the other person to submit by force or threat of force, (2) for the purpose of preventing resistance the offender substantially impairs the other person's judgment or control by administering any drug or intoxicant to the other person" (Ohio Revised Code, 1980, cited by Koss, Gidcyz, and Wisniewski 1987: 166). Thus, several types of rape—marital rape, acquaintance rape, male-male rape, female-perpetrated rape of males, female-perpetrated rape of females—are recognized by the legal system.

The recently revised rape laws appear clear-cut in definition, but the interpretations of force and consent are not. Force is easily identifiable in cases that involve extrinsic violence, such as guns, knives, or beatings, but less easily understood in cases where the man uses some other kind of force (such as the weight of his own body) (Estrich 1987). Rape laws generally do not differentiate between aggravated rape, which involves extrinsic violence, multiple assailants, or no prior relationship between the victim and the defendant, and simple rape, which involves "a single defendant who knew his victim and neither beat her nor threatened her with a weapon" (Estrich 1987: 4). Interpretations of rape laws, however, are clearly biased toward regarding only aggravated rape as "real rape" (Estrich 1987).

Estrich (1987) cites *State v. Rusk* as a classic example of problematic interpretation in cases in which force is not obtained by the wielding of a weapon. Rusk, the defendant, met the woman, Pat, at a bar. At the end of the evening, Rusk asked Pat for a ride home. When they got to his house, Rusk invited Pat in. She declined; he asked a second time. When Pat declined again, Rusk took her car keys and entered his home. Pat followed him into the house. He ordered her to take off her clothes. She reported that she felt afraid because of "the look in his eyes" and because he began "lightly choking" her neck. Pat reported that she did not resist further because she feared Rusk would apply greater force. Rusk claimed that he had engaged in heavy caressing of her neck, not light choking. His conviction was overturned, eight to five, by the Maryland Court of Special Appeals but later reinstated, four to three, by Maryland's highest court, the court of appeals. The three court of appeals judges who voted against reinstating Rusk's conviction wrote that, under the circumstances, Pat did not have a reason to fear that if she resisted further, Rusk would harm her. They wrote that Pat did not "follow the natural instinct of every proud female to resist, by more than mere words, the violation of her person" (Estrich 1987: 65). Thus, in simple rapes, force is sometimes judged according to the level of the victim's resistance. Although many legal definitions have done away with the explicit requirement that rape involve "reasonable resistance" by the victim, the *State v. Rusk* decision illustrates that victim resistance is sometimes implicitly required to prove force.

The details of this case also illustrate that men and women sometimes perceive force very differently. What Pat considered "light choking" Rusk thought was "heavy caressing." A man's or woman's interpretation of force may vary according to the degree of force necessary to overcome them. In general, women have less physical strength than men, are less likely to fight back than are men, and are socialized in ways to make them more likely to fear men's strength than men are to fear women's strength. Thus, less physical force is required to overcome a woman than the physical force required to overcome a man. Additionally, women are less likely to exert the force necessary to overcome a man than men are to exert the force necessary to overcome a woman. For these reasons, Estrich (1987) has argued that gender neutrality in rape laws obscures the differences in the force required to overcome a man or a woman and that legal interpretations of rape laws are biased in favor of traditional male definitions of force.

Consent and nonconsent are also central to many legal definitions of rape. Like force, nonconsent may be easily identifiable in stranger or aggravated rape cases (Estrich 1987). In cases involving acquaintances, however, the interpretation of nonconsent is murky. The marital exemption from rape laws is one example. The marital relationship has been viewed traditionally as generalized consent for the man to have sexual intercourse with the woman whenever he wanted (Finkelhor and Yllo 1985). Although many states have revised rape laws so as to recognize marital rape, only seventeen states have fully repudiated the marital exemption (Laura X, personal communication, February 16, 1990).

Problems in interpretation of consent also exist in cases in which the defendant and the complainant were nonmarried acquaintances. LaFree, Reskin, and Visher (1985) interviewed jurors who had served on rape trials and found that jurors were significantly less likely to find a defendant guilty if some type of relationship existed between the defendant and the complainant prior to the rape. Such a finding is significant, considering, as they (1985: 393) state, "Jury verdicts—in either acquitting the defendant or in finding him guilty and thereby certifying an act as rape—contribute to the ongoing process of defining what society considers to be rape."

Police officers also contribute to the definition of rape in the process of unfounding a case—that is, not forwarding it for possible prosecution. The police may unfound cases because they do not believe the victim, because the rape occurred outside their jurisdiction, or because the victim misses a subsequent appointment (Estrich 1987). Chappell and Singer (1977) found that in New York, police officers deemed 24 percent of rape complaints in nonstranger cases without merit in comparison with less than 5 percent of stranger cases so judged. Inasmuch as the unfounding process influences the cases that are prosecuted eventually and the cases in which convictions are made, police officers shape the definition of rape.

Although the rape reforms of the 1970s and 1980s may have improved the existing laws considerably, Estrich (1987) observed that the problem may not be so much with the specific wording of the legal statutes as with their interpretations. Consequently changing the terms of the laws may not be as important as changing society's attitudes about what constitutes rape (Estrich 1987).

Researcher's Definitions

Given that police officers, jurors, attorneys, and judges, to name a few, rarely regard forced intercourse between acquaintances as rape, it is hardly surprising that women who have been forced by a male acquaintance to have sexual intercourse against their will, and men who have forced female acquaintances to have sexual intercourse against their will, often do not regard these experiences as rape. Consequently researchers investigating the prevalence of rape typically exclude the word *rape* from the data collection process. Koss, Gidycz, and Wisniewski (1987: 165) asked women whether they had engaged in "sexual intercourse when you didn't want to because a man threatened or used some degree of physical force (twisting your arm, holding you down, etc.) to make you?" These researchers thus used a definition based on the legal definition of rape (it included the concepts of physical force or threat of force and sexual intercourse against the woman's will) but deleted the word *rape* so as not to bias participants against reporting nonstranger rape. Results from this and other such studies revealed that rape most commonly occurred between people who knew each other, not between strangers (Koss, Gidycz, and Wisniewski 1987; Russell 1984).

The Incidence and Prevalence of Rape

The incidence of rape refers to the number of rapes that occurred during a given period of time, such as in a year. The prevalence of rape refers to the percentage of women who have ever been raped. Estimates of the incidence and prevalence of rape vary widely according to the methodology and definitions used.

One frequently quoted source of statistics on rape is the FBI's Uniform Crime Reports, official tabulations of crime reported in the United States. According to these reports, in 1988 there were 73 completed or attempted rapes for every 100,000 females in the United States. There are several methodological problems that cast doubt on the accuracy of this statistic. Not all rapes are reported, and some rapes that are reported are considered unfounded by the police and thus subsequently excluded from the Uniform Crime Reports. In 1976, the last year in which the FBI collected such statistics, 19 percent of all rape reports were considered unfounded by the police.

Another source of statistics on the incidence and prevalence of rape is victimization surveys, in which random samples of respondents are surveyed. In general, this is a better source of data about rape than are police reports because information can be gathered about both unreported and reported rapes. Nevertheless, these surveys vary considerably in quality; some are so methodologically unsound that little or no confidence can be placed in their conclusions. Russell (1984) described the National Opinion

Research Center (NORC) Survey, conducted in 1967, and the National Crime Surveys (NCS), instituted in the early 1970s by the U.S. government, both using interviews with members of randomly selected households in the United States. In the NORC survey, one adult per household was interviewed to investigate if anyone in the household had been a crime victim during the previous year. Given that many women tell no one about being raped, it is likely that a respondent would not know if a member of the household had been raped. Furthermore, if a woman had been raped by a member of the household, such as her husband or father, it is unlikely that he would report his behavior to the interviewer in the interest of scientific accuracy. The NCS also have methodological flaws. "The National Crime Surveys [NCS] state repeatedly that 'rape is clearly an infrequent crime'" (Russell 1984: 33). Perhaps this conclusion reflects the fact that the surveys included no questions about rape. There were general questions that could conceivably elicit information about rape, such as, "Did anyone beat you up, attack you or hit you with something, such as a rock or bottle?" and "Did anyone try to attack you in some other way?" If a respondent stated "yes" in response, the interviewer asked follow-up questions about the incident, such as, "What actually happened?" If these general questions did not elicit information about rape, however, the interview ended without any questions about this crime (Russell 1984).

There have been methodologically sound surveys on the prevalence of rape. Russell's (1984) research team conducted interviews with 930 randomly selected adult female residents of San Francisco. All interviewers were female and were carefully trained to ask questions in a sensitive manner. The interviews were held in private, and the interviewer and respondent were matched by race and ethnicity when possible. The interviewers asked the respondents about their experience with rape using the following definition: "*forced intercourse (i.e., penile-vaginal penetration), or intercourse obtained by threat of force, or intercourse completed when the woman was drugged, unconscious, asleep, or otherwise totally helpless and hence unable to consent*" (Russell 1984: 35). This survey, in contrast to the NCS, found that rape was clearly a frequent crime: 24 percent of the women had been raped at least once, and 44 percent had experienced either rape or attempted rape. Only 8 percent—less than one in twelve—of the rapes and attempted rapes had been reported to the police.

Several other surveys support the claim that rape is frequent. Koss (1989) mailed a survey to over 5,000 female members of a work site–based health maintenance plan and received a 50 percent response rate. She found that 21 percent of the women had experienced a completed forcible rape. And, Koss, Gidycz, and Wisniewski (1987) conducted a national survey among over 6,000 higher education students in the United States and found that 15 percent of the women in their sample reported having been raped; an additional 12 percent reported attempted rape.

The relationship between the victim and the rapist also emerges from these surveys. Most police reports lead one to conclude that most rape is stranger rape. In contrast, surveys of probability samples indicate that the majority of rapes occur between acquaintances. Russell (1984) found that only 12 percent of all rapes occurred between strangers; 88 percent occurred between acquaintances. The most frequent category of perpetrator was husbands or ex-husbands: 8 percent of the sample had been raped by husbands or ex-husbands, a figure that represents 12 percent of the women who had ever been married. Russell found that 30 percent of stranger rapes had been reported, in contrast with only 1 percent of the date rapes and none of the marital rapes. These differential rates of reporting explain why rapes reported to the police contain such a higher percentage of stranger rapes.

In their nationwide survey of college women, Koss and her colleagues found that only 11 percent of all rapes occurred between strangers; 89 percent occurred between acquaintances (Koss et al. 1988), most of them (53 percent) date rapes. Contrary to the commonly held belief that date rape occurs only on first dates, more women had been raped by steady dates than by casual dates. Similar to Russell's findings, Koss and coworkers found that 21 percent of the stranger rapes had been reported to the police in contrast with fewer than 1 percent of the date rapes. Of the 147 women who had been raped by a steady date, none had reported the incident to the police. The percentages of women who had contacted rape crisis centers were similar to the percentages of women who went to the police. The difficulties associated with obtaining samples of rape victims from police records or rape crisis centers are clear.

Estimating the prevalence of other patterns of rape victimization is even more difficult. Women are sometimes raped by other women—sometimes women in prison (West 1982) and sometimes in lesbian relationships (Hart 1986; Lobel 1986). To our knowledge, no studies have used probability surveys to assess the prevalence of women's being raped by other women.

About one-tenth of all rape victims are males, most of them raped by other men (Warshaw 1988). Male victims appear to have even more difficulty than female victims in discussing their rapes. An emergency room study found that male rape victims were more seriously injured than female rape victims; presumably male rape victims did not report to emergency rooms unless they had injuries demanding medical attention (Kaufman et al. 1980). Typically they did not mention the rape initially; they sought treatment for their injuries, and it was only during the course of treatment that the rape was revealed.

Although almost all male rapes are committed by other males, some males have been raped by females (Sarrel and Masters 1982; Struckman-Johnson 1988). The concept of females raping males brings up many controversial issues:

1. If a woman forces a male to have penile-vaginal intercourse with her, should this be called rape, or is rape limited to situations in which the victim's body is penetrated? Many legal definitions of rape require penetration of the victim by the offender (Koss 1988).

2. Does physical force have the same meaning for men as it does for women? For example, if a man reports that he had unwanted sexual intercourse while a woman held him down, does this have the same meaning to him as it does to a woman who reports that she had unwanted sexual intercourse while a man held her down? Because of the greater weight and upper body strength of most men relative to most women and because of the stigma associated with men's resisting women's sexual advances, it seems likely that the situation reported by the man involved more psychological and less physical coercion than the situation reported by the woman.

3. How much attention should be given to males' being sexually coerced? For example, in a study on men's reports of unwanted sexual intercourse (Muehlenhard and Cook 1988), 62.7 percent of the men sampled had had unwanted sexual intercourse. Occasionally physical coercion was involved, but most of the incidents resulted from peer pressure, verbal pressure from the woman, or the man's own conceptions about appropriate male sexual behavior. This study has received a tremendous amount of media attention—much more than any of Muehlenhard and coworkers' studies on female rape victims. It is important to keep in mind that rape and the fear of rape have much more of an impact on women's lives than on men's lives (Gordon and Rigor 1989).

Characteristics of Rapists

Conclusions about the characteristics of rapists vary depending on the methodology used. A crucial issue is how the sample of rapists is obtained.

Many conclusions about rapists come from biased samples: studies of incarcerated rapists or descriptions of assailants in police reports (Amir, 1971; Groth, 1979). Because less than 1 percent of all rapes and attempted rapes resulted in arrest and conviction (Russell 1984), rapists who are incarcerated are not a random sample. Moreover, stranger rape is more likely to be reported than acquaintance rape. Even when acquaintance rape is reported, these cases are likely to drop out of the legal system before going to trial (Holmstrom and Burgess 1978). When rape leads to a trial, factors related more to jurors' stereotypes than to the quality of the case affect conviction rates. For example, jurors are less likely to find the defendant guilty if the victim and the defendant know each other, if the victim has had sex outside marriage, if the victim is living independently rather than with her parents or husband, or if the defendant is perceived to be a "loser" (such as being unemployed or lacking a sexual partner) (LaFree 1980; LaFree, Reskin, and Visher 1985). Thus, upper-class men who do not rape other men's daughters or wives—who rape their own wives and girlfriends or who rape women who do not behave according to traditional feminine stereotypes—are unlikely to be involved in the legal system. Studies of incarcerated rapists do not inform us about the characteristics of rapists in general; they inform us about the characteristics of "men who do not rape appropriately" (Reynolds, cited by LaFree 1980: 847).

More representative samples of rapists are available, however. In Russell's (1984) interviews of randomly selected women, rape victims were asked about the characteristics of their attackers. An obvious problem with such an approach is that the type of information available is limited. The women were able to report the rapist's race (most rape was intraracial) and estimated age (rapists tended to be young but slightly older than their victims), but they did not always know the rapist's social class, and the frequency of missing data made it difficult to draw conclusions (except in cases of marital rape). Thus, asking randomly selected women about their rapists cannot provide all kinds of information.

Questioning large numbers of men about their experiences is another avenue for gaining information. The likelihood of honest responding can be increased by making the surveys anonymous, and rather than asking men directly if they have ever committed rape, these studies ask men if they have ever engaged in specific behaviors, for example, "Have you ever . . . had sexual intercourse with a woman when she didn't want to because you used some degree of physical force (twisting her arm, holding her down, etc.)?" (Koss and Oros 1982: 456). This approach has difficulties too. Some men are not honest about their histories of sexual aggression, even on an anonymous questionnaire. In addition, some sexually aggressive men might not so label their behavior. There is evidence, based on anecdotal descriptions by rape victims (Bart and O'Brien 1985; Warshaw 1988) and on differences between women's and men's descriptions of their experiences with sexual aggression (Muehlenhard and Linton 1987; Warshaw 1988), that some rapists do not regard their behavior as rape. In a study of prison inmates convicted of rape, Scully and Marolla (1984) found that some rapists who had used a weapon to force the woman to have sex with them did not regard their behavior as rape. Thus, men who rape but who do not use weapons or cause observable physical injury to their victims may be even less likely to regard their behavior as rape. Another limitation of this source of information is that such studies usually use readily available samples of respondents, such as college students. Such samples are often limited with respect to age, social class, and other important demographic variables.

An innovative method for identifying nonincarcerated rapists has been developed by Richard M. McFall (personal communication, December 4, 1989). He has proposed a peer nomination system in which women provide the names of sexually aggressive men. On anonymous questionnaires, women are asked to name men they know who tend to be high, medium, or low in their use of sexual coercion on dates. For each of these three categories, women are asked to provide the name and living unit, if they know it, of four different men. Men who are nominated repeatedly in a specific category are considered to be representative of that category. Researchers could ask these men to participate in studies or could even ask an entire living unit (such as a fraternity) to participate, perhaps in exchange for some incentive. In a pilot study, McFall found that even with as few as 100 female subjects, several men were nominated repeatedly. This technique has the advantage of identifying rapists who are not incarcerated without relying on the rapists' own self-reports. It has the limitation of being most useful in a relatively closed environment, such as a college campus where female students tend to date a limited pool of men. McFall also has some discomfort with the ethics of this technique, which has prevented him from implementing it.

In her nationwide survey of college students, Koss and her colleagues (1987) found that 4.4 percent of the men sampled admitted to rape and another 3.3 percent admitted to attempted rape. They also have identified several variables that predict a man's degree of sexual aggressiveness (Koss and Dinero 1988). The more sexually aggressive a man was, the more likely he was to have been sexually active at an early age, engaging in both consensual and forced sex. Sexually aggressive men reported more hostility toward women and were more likely to accept violence in interpersonal relationships; moreover, they were more likely to use alcohol frequently, to view violent and degrading pornography, and to have peer groups that reinforced highly sexualized views of women.

Other studies have also identified the characteristics of self-reported sexually aggressive men:

1. They are more likely than other men to condone rape and violence against women (Kanin 1967a; Koss et al. 1985; Malamuth 1987; Muehlenhard and Falcon in press; Rapaport and Burkhart 1984).

2. They are more likely to hold traditional gender role attitudes (Koss et al. 1985; Muehlenhard and Falcon in press).

3. They are more sexually experienced than other men (Koss et al. 1985; Malamuth 1987).

4. They are more likely than other men to be hostile toward women, to have dominance as a motive for engaging in sex, to be sexually aroused by depictions of rape, to be irresponsible and lack a social conscience, and to have peer groups, such as fraternities, that pressure them to be sexual (Kanin 1967a; Rapaport and Burkhart 1984; Malamuth 1987).

Sexual aggressiveness can be predicted better by a social control theory asserting that rape occurs due to rape-supportive beliefs perpetuated by power differences between men and women in society than by a psychopathology theory asserting that rape occurs because of the emotional maladjustment of individual men (Koss et al. 1985). In many ways, rapists are "average guys" in a sexist society. Stopping rape will require change at both the individual and societal levels.

Consequences of Rape

Over the past two decades, clinicians and researchers have documented the deleterious effects of rape on women. Rape survivors have been found to score higher on indexes of anxiety (Ellis, Atkeson, and Calhoun 1981), depression (Atkeson et al. 1982; Ellis, Atkeson, and Calhoun 1981), and psychiatric symptoms (Burnam et al. 1988; Kilpatrick, Veronen, and Resick 1979). Moreover, they report poorer social adjustment (Koss et al. 1988; Resick et al. 1981) and an increased incidence of sexual dysfunctions (Becker et al. 1982; Burgess and Holmstrom 1979). Three perspectives are offered frequently to explain the process by which rape impairs psychological functioning: crisis theory (Burgess and Holmstrom 1974), social learning theory (Kilpatrick, Veronen, and Resick 1982), and cognitive appraisal (Koss and Burkhart 1989).

In their pioneering work, Burgess and Holmstrom (1974) drew upon crisis theory (Caplan 1964) and suggested that rape is "forced sexual aggression which results in a disruption of the individual's physical, emotional, social and sexual equilibrium" (p. 109). Accordingly, they coined the phrase *rape trauma syndrome* to describe the acute disorganization phase and the long-term process of reorganization that women experience following a rape. In its acute phase, rape trauma syndrome consists of somatic complaints (physical trauma, skeletal muscle tension, gastrointestinal irritability) and emotional complaints (fear, humiliation, self-blame). Rape survivors experienced nightmares, specific fears (such as a fear of being alone or a fear of crowds), and sexual fears during the long-term reorganization process (Burgess and Holmstrom 1974; Nadelson et al. 1982). Nadelson et al. (1982) found that rape survivors continued to demonstrate depression, fears of being alone, and sexual dysfunction at one to two years following the rape.

Although the research supporting the constellation of symptoms known as rape trauma syndrome was ground breaking, it has been criticized for the absence of control groups and its reliance of nonstandardized assessment techniques (Kilpatrick, Veronen, and Resick 1982). Moreover, the terms used to describe the syndrome (such as *disorganization*) have not been operationalized and thus are not easily evaluated. Consequently the psychological sequelae of rape have been evaluated empirically in the light of social learning theory.

Kilpatrick, Veronen, and Resick 1979, 1982) provided a classical conditioning explanation for the persistent anxiety and fears rape survivors experience. They argued that the fear experienced during a rape is an unconditioned response to the threats of physical harm or death (the unconditioned stimuli). Other situational cues, such as a man, intercourse, ski masks, or other cues specific to the individual situation, become conditioned stimuli that evoke anxiety. The classical conditioning model provides an explanation of the seemingly idiosyncratic fears manifested by a victim following rape and the specific circumstances surrounding the particular situation in which she was raped. Resick (1983) reviewed the research generated by this model.

Koss and Burkhart (1989) argued that the social learning model of rape reactions, with its time-limited approach and its focus on symptomatic behavior, cannot account adequately for the individual variations in reactions to the stress of rape, the chronicity of the posttraumatic stress profile, and the differences observed in adaptation by rape victims. Moreover, the classical conditioning model offered to explain persistent fear reactions cannot account for the ways in which rape differs from other trauma; specifically, Koss and Burkhart argued that this model ignores the interpersonal processes involved in sexual victimization and the social context within which such victimization occurs. As such, they described a conceptualization of the long-term effects of rape that examines cognitive, affective, and behavioral responses to victimization.

Koss and Burkhart (1989) drew on Lazarus and Folkman's (1984) model of stress and coping to argue that an understanding of a victim's cognitive appraisal of the rape is important in explaining the chronicity of some symptoms. Further, as Janoff-Bulman (1985) described the way in which victimization destroys many basic assumptions an individual holds about the world, Koss and Burkhart (1989) suggested that the loss of these long-held beliefs caused by sexual assault can create severe psychological distress. Repeated sexual victimization may confirm negative beliefs about the self and the world, and these beliefs, in turn, can have profound effects on interpersonal relations.

In describing the resolution process of sexual victimization, Koss and Burkhart (1989) drew on the work of Janoff-Bulman (1985), Pasewark and Albers (1972), and Taylor (1983). They suggested that knowledge must be provided to rape victims to correct learned misperceptions that make resolution difficult (for example, "If a woman gets raped, it's her fault"). Koss and Burkhart argued that although self-blame appears to increase a victim's sense of control, such attributions result in long-term negative consequences on her self-esteem. As such, they argued that victims need to be relieved of their sense of responsibility for their victimization. Moreover, victims are likely to experience increased self-esteem when they are encouraged to exert control over situations in which they are likely to attain mastery; such strategies are likely to aid in the coping and resolution process following victimization.

Some authors have suggested that women who are raped can transform their victimization in ways that bear positive outcomes for themselves. Kelly (1988) argued that the myriad ways in which women resist and survive sexual victimization can result in feelings of strength and determination. Kelly called for feminist theorists and researchers to redress the traditional characterization of victims as passive and to recognize the complexity with which women cope with, resist, and survive sexual assault.

All women who live in a society with a high prevalence of rape are affected by it. Gordon and Rigor (1989) found that women restrict their behavior in order to avoid rape. Ironically, many of the tactics women report focus on avoiding stranger rape, in spite of the fact that their risk of being raped by a man they know is much greater.

Future research regarding the consequences of sexual victimization might do well to consider the following issues. First, most research on the effects of rape on victims has relied on victims' reports of rape to the police or to a rape crisis center. Most rapes, however, occur between acquaintances and go unreported. To our knowledge, only two studies reported thus far have examined the consequences of rape using randomly selected samples (Koss et al. 1988; Burnam et al. 1988). While Koss and associates (1988) found few differences in the psychological impact of acquaintance versus stranger rapes, more such studies are needed to investigate other possible differences between these groups. Additionally, while Groth and Burgess (1980) found that male victims of rape describe reactions that sound similar to the effects experienced by female victims, little is known about the consequences of less common forms of rape, such as male victims of male perpetrators and female victims of female perpetrators. Finally, research regarding the long-term cognitive and emotional effects of sexual victimization is necessary for the development of treatments directed not only at symptom reduction but at cognitive processes and concomitant inter- and intrapersonal effects. Because the trauma of rape affects multiple levels of psychological functioning, treatment must involve multiple levels of intervention (Koss and Burkhart 1989).

Conclusion

The legal, psychological, and social issues regarding rape are complex. Contrary to popular stereotypes, the typical rape occurs between typical men and women, under typical circumstances. In the minds of attorneys, police officers, rapists, the general public, and victims, the least common form of rape—sexual intercourse forced by a stranger with a weapon—is held as the standard against which all other rapes are judged. Definitions of force and consent remain colored by traditional assumptions regarding the nature of male-female relationships. Because definitions of rape vary, statistics regarding the incidence and prevalence of this crime are difficult to interpret. Correspondingly, scientific knowledge regarding the characteristics of rapists and victims has been limited by assumptions about the nature of "real rape," although recent evidence suggests that the characteristics of rapists and victims differ little from the characteristics of the typical man or woman. Because the social-situational factors that contribute to rape appear related to those factors that maintain male dominance at the social-structural level, a comprehensive analysis of rape requires further attention to social as well as psychological processes. Accordingly, changes are required at the societal as well as at the interpersonal levels to decrease the prevalence of rape.

2
Child Sexual Coercion

Dean D. Knudsen

Throughout history, adults have used young boys and girls for sexual pleasure (deMause 1974). It was not until the sixteenth century that laws were passed in England to protect boys from sodomy and girls under the age of 10 from rape. The concept of age of consent, which emerged after the exposure of international prostitution rings, developed only in the nineteenth century and set the age at which a girl could consent to sexual activities at 10, then 12, and finally, in 1885, at 16 (Schultz 1980).

Similar developments in the United States resulted in a gradual increase in the age of consent. In 1886, this age was 10 in most states but ranged from 7 in Delaware to 12 in four states; by 1897 most states had raised the age to 14, but three states had the low age of 10 and five had the age of 18 for girls (Schultz 1980). Most states now have established 14 or 15 as the age of consent, defining children under that age as incapable of giving consent to sexual activities.

Consent statutes illustrate changing conceptions of children and childhood that have occurred over the past two centuries. Awareness of sexual coercion of children has produced concerns about control and protection of children and youth, especially in the past two decades. When sexual abuse became recognized as a problem by parents and professionals, legislation was passed, social services for victims and perpetrators were created and expanded, and prevention programs were developed. These responses, nevertheless, have failed to slow the increase in reports of child sexual abuse. Is this growth in reports a reflection of greater awareness of the problem or an actual increase in sexual victimization of children? What is the actual level of sexual abuse? Are incidents predictable and thus preventable?

These questions are not easily answered. Definitions and measurement issues are closely related to the findings of research studies, and sampling problems often preclude any generalizations about the consistency or changes in patterns of child sexual abuse.

Defining Child Sexual Coercion

The concepts of age and coercion are intrinsic to definitions of child sexual abuse. Coercion may take many forms: force or the threat of force, deception, trickery, or other actions the child cannot resist because of his or her ignorance, immaturity, or mental condition. The two basic conditions for consent—knowledge about the social meanings, acceptability, and consequences or risk associated with the behavior and the right to say yes or no—do not apply to child sexual activities with adults because "children, by their nature, are incapable of truly consenting to sex with adults" (Finkelhor 1979a: 694). Further, child sexual coercion is included in those activities usually identified as sexual crimes in legal codes if force or deception is involved.

Legal efforts proscribing child sexual abuse have taken three different approaches (Bulkley 1985):

1. Sexual offense laws define sexual acts that are illegal when forced on either children or adults: rape, attempted rape, deviant sexual behavior (oral and/or anal sex), fondling, indecent exposure, and exploitation.

2. Incest prohibitions originally identified blood relatives with whom sexual intercourse was prohibited, but such restrictions often have been extended to nonconsanguineous kin (step and adoptive parents) and to other forms of sexual behavior besides intercourse, such as fondling or oral sex (Bixler 1983).

3. Child protection laws include all types of maltreatment and are designed to protect the child from continuing abuse from custodians.

All three approaches assume the necessity of protecting a child from adult coercion to engage in sexual behaviors.

Research definitions of sexual abuse have produced varied approaches and measures. Attitudes measured by vignettes depicting specific incidents of child-adult sexual behavior to which individuals respond have indicated that general agreement exists in the most serious types of sexual coercion (Haugaard and Reppucci 1988). Nevertheless, some groups, such as social workers, nurses, and teachers, see some acts as more serious than other groups, such as physicians, psychiatrists, and attorneys, because various professions and disciplines make different assumptions and define all types of abuse in different ways (Carter 1974). Sexual abuse is no exception; seriousness ratings by 295 pediatric hospital professionals for three sexual abuse vignettes—sexual intercourse between parent and child, a parent suggesting intercourse, and mutual masturbation of parent and child—were significantly higher for nurses and social workers than for physicians and psychiatrists. The same study found no significant differences in seriousness of sexual activities by sex of respondent or prior experience with cases of abuse. There was, however, a significant negative correlation of seriousness and experience among nurses; the greater the years in nursing, the lower was the perceived seriousness of the incident (Snyder and Newberger 1986).

Similar findings noted in other studies (Giovannoni and Becerra 1979; Haugaard and Reppucci 1988) suggest that judgments are being made on the basis of several different standards or criteria. The extent of force used, perceptions of the real or potential harm to the child, the context of the incident, the degree of involvement by the child, the intent of the perpetrator, the interpretation of the act by the child, or perhaps even the organizational context of the respondent may affect the ratings (O'Toole et al. 1987). The lack of consensus among professionals regarding definitions of sexual abuse, its seriousness, or appropriate responses in research using vignettes, however, does not eliminate its reality for children.

Researchers focusing on the actual sexual experiences of children have operationalized the legal concepts in various ways. Early work (Landis et al. 1940) used general terms, such as *sexual aggression*, and depended on adult recall of childhood experiences. Recent research has recognized the multiple ways in which child sexual coercion can be conceptualized, including "touch"-"nontouch" activities, intrafamilial-extrafamilial adult-child relationships, differences in ages between victim and perpetrator, the degree of force employed, and specific types of behavior, such as fondling, oral sex, or rape.

Finkelhor's (1979b) definition included all types of activities (sexual overtures to intercourse) between a child 12 or under and someone five or more years older and activities between adolescents 13 to 16 and persons ten or more years older as sexual abuse. He concluded that 19 percent of female and 9 percent of male college students in New England had had childhood sexual experiences with adults. Fritz, Stoll, and Wagner (1981) studied contact molestation, defined as a sexual encounter before puberty with a postadolescent individual, and found that 8 percent of female and 5 percent of male students at the University of Washington reported such experiences. Such differences appear to be more than regional effects; incidence and prevalence rates vary widely depending on the inclusiveness of definitions, types of samples used, and methods of data collection (Peters, Wyatt, and Finkelhor 1986; Wyatt and Peters 1986; Wyatt 1986).

Incidence and Prevalence: The Research Literature

Incidence refers to the number of cases of sexual abuse that occur among those at risk during a specific time period. Using official reports, it was estimated that there were 132,000 child victims in the United States during 1986, for an incidence rate of 20.89 per 10,000 children under 18 (American Humane Association 1988), the highest rate since the collection of such data began in 1976.

Prevalence is the number of children who are victims of sexual coercive activities during their entire period at risk (from birth to age 18). Estimates of prevalence have ranged from 6 to 62 percent for women and from 3 to 30 percent for men (Peters, Wyatt, and Finkelhor 1986), depending on the characteristics of the sample, how the questions were asked, and the definitions used.

Unfortunately, definitions, samples, and methods of data collection continue to confuse the findings. In a selective university sample of 278 undergraduate females, 14.7 percent reported a history of sexual abuse, defined as all activities from touching through intercourse between a girl under 15 years with someone five or more years older (Briere and Runtz 1987). A recent study with a broader sample of 1,089 university students attempted to assess the effects of various definitions of sexual abuse, response rates, and the ordering of questions regarding sexual activities. When abuse was defined as some type of intrusion (oral, anal, or vaginal intercourse), 1.8 percent of the females and 1.4 percent of the males reported being sexually abused. An inclusive definition (exhibitionism, kissing, fondling, oral sex, or genital intercourse) produced much higher levels: 11.9 percent for women and 5.0 percent for men. The proportion of students responding had inconsistent effects on levels of abuse, but the order of questions was unrelated to level (Haugaard and Emery 1989).

Incidence rates also reflect the impact of definitions and methods. The first National Incidence Study (1981) included intrusion, genital contact, and other forms of fondling or inadequate supervision of child's sexual activities in the definition of sexual abuse but limited the cases to those demonstrating harm and those involving parent or substitute parent perpetrators. The second National Incidence Study (1988) included the same behaviors but assumed harm for intrusion and genital contact and counted all situations involving all adult caretakers. The estimates of children sexually abused during a year increased from 42,900, or 0.7 per 1,000 children for 1980, to 138,000, or 2.2 per 1,000 in 1986, using the original definitions, but the estimate for 1986 with the expanded definition was 155,900, or a rate of 2.5 per 1,000 children. Genital contact was the most common form, followed by intrusion and then other forms of contact (1988). These figures are comparable to numbers of victims and incidence rates derived from state child protective services reports, although the number or percentage of children common to both studies is unknown.

The relationship between incidence rates and prevalence rates is not easily elaborated because of different methods of data collection, repeated victimization resulting in duplicated counts of victims—estimates range from 13 percent to 23 percent (National Incidence Study 1981; Knudsen 1989) of reports involving previously reported children—and varied definitions of sexual abuse. However, a large number of children—at least 150,000 per year—are tricked or coerced into some sexual activity with an adult, and probably 20 to 40 percent of females and 5 to 10 percent of males will have some unwanted sexual experience before they reach adulthood.

The word *unwanted* may be of special significance in understanding and estimating child sexual coercion. Legal codes define all sexual activity with a child below the age of consent as coercion, but unknown numbers of children interpret these behaviors as appropriate or acceptable because a powerful adult is involved, it is pleasurable, or it is embarrassing to reveal. This may be especially true for sibling incest (Cole 1982; DeJong 1989). Would the rates increase dramatically if all incidents excluded on such grounds were counted?

Victims, Perpetrators, and Contexts of Sexual Coercion

Child victims of sexual coercion are more likely to be girls than boys at all age levels. Reports from hospital and clinical samples indicate that female victims outnumber males by a ratio of four to one (DeJong, Emmett, and Hervada 1982; Kendall-Thackett and Simon 1987; Cupoli and Sewell 1988; Dube and Hebert 1988; Mian et al. 1986). Similar figures are found for reports to child protective services (CPS) (Eckenrode et al. 1988; Rosenthal 1988; Knudsen 1988; Russell and Trainor 1984) and by the National Incidence Studies (1981, 1988). However, several studies of male victims indicate that fewer of such cases may be reported officially or defined as abuse by boys or their caretakers.

Based on official reports and various samples, boys appear more likely than girls to be assaulted in public places, to be victimized by nonfamily or strangers, and to experience threats, force, and injuries during the incident (Ellerstein and Canavan 1980; DeJong, Emmett, and Hervada 1982; Finkelhor 1984; Pierce and Pierce 1985; Reinhart 1987). Most of the research on male victims, however, suffers from inadequate definitions, limited reporting, problems with recall, and nonrandom samples (Vander Mey 1988), making any generalizations tenuous.

The available data nevertheless allow some identification of victims of sexual coercion, both male and female. An analysis of official reports from 1976 through 1982 indicated that the average age of both sexes at CPS investigation was 10.5 years, with a decline in age over the seven-year period (Russell and Trainor 1984). The 1988 National Incidence Study found that age was closely related to sexual abuse; the rate for 3 to 5 year olds was 2.0 per 1,000 children at risk compared to 3.2 for those aged 15 to 17, though this difference was not statistically significant. Recent studies of clinical or other populations report various ages at first incident, with means ranging from 6.8 years (Dube and Hebert 1988) to 12 years (DeJong, Emmett, and Hervada 1982) for females and 7.0 years (DeJong, Emmett, and Hervada 1982) to 9.8 years (Risin and Koss 1987) for males. Unfortunately, such summary statistics provide no information regarding the relationship between age and type of sexual coercion used, such as probable higher levels of rape or attempted rape among teenage than younger females or the lower levels of victimization of adolescent than younger males due both to their definitions of sexual experiences and their ability to resist sexual advances.

Most sexual coercion directed toward children appears to be fondling, for both boys and girls at all ages (National Incidence Study 1981, 1988; Finkelhor 1984; Wyatt 1985; Risin and Koss 1987; Haugaard and Emery 1989). However, at least two hospital studies found that most sexually abused children experienced oral, anal, or vaginal penetration (Cupoli and Sewell 1988; Dube and Hebert 1988). Such discrepancies probably reflect sample differences, with severe cases especially where physical trauma occurred more likely to be included in hospital populations.

Most sexually abused children—perhaps two-thirds—are victimized only once (DeJong 1989; Wyatt 1985; Risin and Koss 1987; Fromuth 1986; Dube and Hebert 1988). However, forced sexual intercourse that is perpetrated by family members or friends rather than strangers is more likely to involve multiple contacts over an extended period (Briere and Runtz 1987; Dube and Hebert 1988). Actions over an extended period of time may take the form of a courting process (Frude 1982) during which the victim is groomed for further, and more intrusive, experiences. Thus, the duration of the abuse is associated with the type and perpetrator of sexual coercion.

For female victims of all ages, men are the perpetrators in 95 percent or more of the cases (Fromuth 1986; Kendall-Thackett and Simon 1987; Cupoli and Sewell 1988; Dube and Hebert 1988). When both boy and girl victims are included in the analyses, more women are likely to be involved as perpetrators (Briere and Runtz 1989; Haugaard and Emery 1989; Faller 1989).

When only male victims are considered, however, the source of the data becomes extremely important in establishing the perpetrator. Clinical and hospital studies report that at least 85 percent of sexual offenders are men (Finkelhor 1981; Ellerstein and Canavan 1980), but some recent studies of college students suggest that women may be involved in half or more of male sexual abuse when acts or behavior rather than victim reactions are used to define abuse. Fritz, Stoll, and Wagner (1981) indicated that 60 percent of boys were molested by females, and Seidner and Calhoun (1984) found a rate of over 80 percent. Further, Fromuth and Burkhart (1987) reported over 70 percent of college sample males had sexual experiences at young ages with older female perpetrators, though many of the victims did not consider the events abusive. Clearly the definitional issue—whether to include both wanted and unwanted sexual activities—is important, but it probably does not explain the differences in these studies (Haugaard and Reppucci 1988). Instead, male victims and their parents probably are less willing to define sexual activities as abusive or to report them if males rather than females are the perpetrators.

Young perpetrators—both males and females—have been identified by some recent research. A study of 297 male and 8 female adolescent sexual offenders with an average age of 14.8 found that most of the victims were acquaintances or relatives, with only 1 victim in 6 (16.5 percent) a stranger (Fehrenbach et al. 1986). A study of 28 female adolescent offenders indicated that some penetration of the victim occurred in 53.6 percent of the cases, and 46.4 percent involved indecent liberties (fondling and touching but not penetration). The victims were young (all but one under 12),were both males and females, and were related to or known by the perpetrator (Fehrenbach and Monastersky 1988).

Most adolescent offenders, especially those identified in official reports, are males. Of thirty-seven juvenile abusers identified through the Illinois protective service system, (81 percent) were males, and the average age was 13.1 at last reported offense. Nearly half (46 percent) of the victims were boys, and the average age of all abused children was 9.2 years (Pierce and Pierce 1987). Other studies of Uniform Crime Reports (Davis and Leitenberg 1987) and incestuous assaults reported to a hospital sexual assault center (DeJong 1989) further document the coercive sexual behavior by male adolescents. Even younger child perpetrators have been identified; forty-seven males aged 4 to 13 involved in a variety of coercive sexual activities and/or exhibitionism were identified by Johnson (1989). These data, and those from other studies (Becker, Cunningham-Rathner, and Kaplan 1986; Longo and Groth 1983), suggest that sexual activity among young children is common. Unfortunately, no data are available to assess whether the increased information and awareness of this activity reflect changes in childhood behavior, the application of broader definitions of sexual abuse, greater vigilance by parents concerning their children's sexual activity, or availability of an intervention system for dealing with the issue.

Attempts to identify causes of child sexual coercion have focused on the victim, the perpetrator, the family, or the social context. Several early studies identified high-risk factors, notably parental absence or unavailability, poor relationships with parents, conflict between parents, and stepfather families (Finkelhor and Baron 1986a). Later research has continued to document higher rates of sexual activity between stepfathers and stepdaughters, although stress and family disruption appear to be important factors in increasing victimization (Gruber and Jones 1983; Alexander and Lupfer 1987; Paveza 1988; Gordon 1989). Few analyses have placed these risk factors within the larger structural context that permits and encourages male exploitation of females and adult coercion of young or considered the cultural myths that support these patterns (Wattenberg 1985; Conte 1986). If there is an intergenerational pattern of sexual abuse, as Faller (1989) suggests, what is the role of beliefs, subcultural values, and socialization in this pattern?

Many descriptive characteristics are derived from an examination of individual cases, typically focusing on personality characteristics of perpetrator and victim, their social skills, or socialization. Researchers have noted abnormal responses to Minnesota Multiphasic Personality Inventory (MMPI) scales by molesters (Kirkland and Bauer 1982; McIvor and Duthie 1986; Duffee and Bascuas 1987), lack of normal social skills among perpetrators (Overholzer and Beck 1986; Segal and Marshall 1985; Knight 1989), and inappropriate socialization (Parker and Parker 1986). In addition, perpetrator self-centeredness (Gilgun 1988) and responses to sexually explicit materials (Marshall, Barbaree, and Christophe 1986; Marshall, Barbaree, and Butt 1988) have been identified as factors in child molestation.

Such findings, however, do little to predict actual abuse or to identify abusers, and efforts to explain sexual abuse based on personality factors are not successful. As deYoung notes, despite a shared understanding by some professionals of the concept of role reversal between abused daughters and their mothers in incestuous families and a similar agreement by others on the value of fixation as an explanatory factor, "neither . . . is necessary or sufficient to explain why child abuse occurs" (deYoung 1987: 17). All of these characteristics or circumstances are found among nonabusive families. The lack of adequate explanatory theories emphasizes the importance of further research and theory in understanding sexual coercion of children.

Consequences of Child Sexual Coercion

The effect of molestation on the victim has been a dominant concern in legal and treatment responses to the issue. Causal perspectives, definitions of abuse, and the perceived role of the child are important factors in the identification of consequences; for instance, adolescent boys who have experiences legally defined as abuse may not find them traumatic and may not see themselves as victims, or if responsibility for an incident is attributed to the child by parents or other adults, the victim may have additional guilt and shame.

Since the review of the impacts of child sexual abuse by Browne and Finkelhor (1986), evidence has continued to grow that female victims especially often experience a variety of psychological, behavioral, and sexual problems. Descriptive studies of short-term consequences (Adams-Tucker 1985; Elwell and Ephross 1987; Lindberg and Distad 1985; Mannarino and Cohen 1987) and research involving comparisons with control groups (Briere and Runtz 1987; Conte and Schuerman 1987; Einbender and Friedrich 1989; Friedrich, Beilke, and Urquiza 1987; White et al. 1988) have found traumatic effects for victims of coercive sexual activity. Efforts to document long-term consequences suffer from methodological problems such as those inherent in recall data, lack of adequate control groups, and selective samples (Kilpatrick 1987). However, there is evidence that adults who were child victims often suffer from similar problems (Briere and Runtz 1988; Cunningham, Pearce, and Pearce 1988; Harter, Alexander, and Neimeyer 1988; Murphy et al. 1988). Efforts to apply the diagnosis of posttraumatic stress disorder (PTSD) to these women have been made (McLeer et al. 1988; Deblinger et al. 1989), though Finkelhor (1987) has argued that PTSD fails to account for all symptoms, does not apply to all victims, and is not adequate to explain the source of trauma.

There appear to be some female and male victims who do not experience major psychological trauma or long-term negative consequences (Conte 1986; Conte and Schuerman 1987; Briere and Runtz 1987), and the effects of child sexual victimization often appear to be affected by other family or personal conditions. Family support is an important mediator of the molestation experience (Wyatt and Mickey 1987; Fromuth 1986; Conte and Schuerman 1987), and some family problems, notably alcoholism, often produce symptoms that are similar to or that disguise the impact of sexual abuse (Miller et al. 1987; Carson, Council, and Volk 1988). In addition, there appears to be a similar pattern of consequences for physical and sexual abuse, at least among psychiatric patients (Kilko, Moser, and Weldy 1988; Cavaiola and Schiff 1988; Livingston 1987).

Drawing direct causal linkages from coercive sexual experiences in childhood to adult or adolescent attitudes, behavior, or stress levels is an impossible task, made more difficult by the chaotic character of adolescence for even nonabused children (DiPietro 1987). There are some conditions that appear to have greater negative consequences for child victims. The use of force of coercion and the degree of trust the child had in the perpetrator, whether a family member or not, appear to be important factors (Browne and Finkelhor 1986; Feinauer 1988, 1989; Haugaard and Tilly 1988). Other conditions, such as duration and frequency of abuse, age at onset, age of perpetrator, parental reaction, and type of sexual activity, are not consistently identified as having traumatic impacts.

The degree to which male victims experience comparable negative consequences remains inadequately documented. The expectations associated with male socialization would appear to minimize the effects by female perpetrators unless physical force was involved, though several studies suggest that males also experience trauma (Briere et al. 1988; Dimock 1988; Risin and Koss 1987; Vander Mey 1988). Factors that minimize the consequences of abuse for females also appear to be significant for males; however, attribution of responsibility for the sexual abuse tends to be related to sex and age of the victim, (Waterman and Foss-Goodman 1984), suggesting that male victims may receive less support from family and friends.

Recent concerns about the effects of investigation and prosecution on the child victim, independent of the traumatic impact of the incident, have been expressed. Medical, legal, and social service professionals often have different perspectives of causes and appropriate responses (Newberger 1987; Harshbarger 1987; Hansen 1987; Berliner 1987; Saunders 1988). The criminalization of all forms of family violence has resulted in an emphasis on prosecution, which may require numerous interviews with the child and testimony in court, leading to additional psychological trauma for at least some of the victims (Tedesco and Schnell 1987).

Unfortunately, much of the research on effects—and the subsequent application of "data" to policy decisions—lacks a theoretical basis that would allow an integration of research findings into a comprehensive understanding of the causes and consequences of child sexual abuse. Berliner and Wheeler (1987) note that no studies have demonstrated the efficacy of any treatment of the effect of sexual abuse because of a narrow focus on observed consequences; they suggest that those effects best "can be understood as a combination of classically conditioned responses to traumatic stress and socially learned behavioral and cognitive responses to the abuse experience" (p. 415). Lacking theoretical models that concentrate on the identification of the contextual and conditional factors (Zuravin 1989), research is directed toward characteristics of perpetrators and effects on victims rather than on causal factors.

Research about child sexual abuse has produced much information about perpetrators, victims, circumstances, and consequences. At least one female in three and one male in ten will experience unwanted sexual activities as children. Most of the offenders will be relatives or friends; some of those victimized will have serious immediate or long-term psychological problems, though the difficulty in establishing these effects precludes definitive numbers. Nevertheless, sexual abuse of children is an important concern for parents and child advocates.

Directions for Future Research

Despite the growing research literature in the area of child sexual coercion, several problems and issues remain unresolved. Three interrelated issues have special significance for policy decisions because they focus on the diagnosis and identification of sexual abuse, its prediction and prevention, and the control and rights of citizens and families. Each is frequently stated as a question: Do children lie about sexual coercion? Can sexual abusers be identified before they molest? Can potential child sexual abuse be prevented without endangering the rights of families?

These questions must be considered within the framework of the current legal and child protection systems. Identification and reporting of coercive sexual activities are largely dependent on the ability of the child to recognize exploitation and on her or his willingness to tell someone about it. Most prevention programs explicitly or implicitly recognize this by emphasizing the right to say no or through the use of good-confusing-bad touch concepts. However, empowering children to take control of their bodies in the area of sexual abuse rests on a conception of sexual coercion as uniquely destructive compared to emotional or physical abuse. The child's claim of sexual victimization is viewed as true because a child is assumed to have no knowledge of sexuality unless she or he has experienced it. Anatomically correct dolls often are used to assist in the diagnosis, despite a lack of consensus about interpretations of the child's behavior with them (Boat and Everson 1988). Many courts, however, disallow such evidence and require children to confront their alleged abuser (Wollitzer 1988), creating circumstances that may compel the child to deny earlier statements under questioning.

Numerous researchers have attempted to specify criteria for evaluating a child's claim (deYoung 1988a; Faller 1988; Jones and McGraw 1987; Quinn 1988; Sink 1987; Yates and Musty 1988), but the issue illustrates the inconsistency of the legal and protection systems. The refusal to accept the perception and report of a child regarding her or his victimization is in direct contrast to the responsibility placed on the child to perceive potential abuse and to act to prevent it.

Prevention programs directed toward children have shown some limited effectiveness when measured by the child's awareness of appropriate action to take if confronted by an adult (Berliner 1989; Harvey et al. 1988; Conte 1985; Wurtele et al. 1986). However, because the curricula in most cases do not focus on fathers or relatives as perpetrators—those who abuse in most cases—the applicability of these programs is unknown. Further, the difficulties in measurement and the ethical issues posed by evaluation studies (Leventhal, 1987; Conte 1987; Fryer, Kraizer, and Miyoshi 1987a, 1987b) make interpretations tenuous at best. Perhaps the best outcome of the prevention emphasis may be to engage parents in discussions of sexuality with their children (Binder and McNiel 1987), especially in the light of possible unintended negative consequences of school programs (Trudell and Whatley 1988).

The dilemmas are real. Treatment programs for perpetrators and victims have limited effectiveness (Cohn and Daro 1987). Prevention of abuse through identification of perpetrators and prediction of their actions is not possible. Dependence on the child to recognize potential exploitation, to resist advances, and to protect herself or himself has two problems: the immaturity and ignorance of children and the granting of individual rights to small children unprepared for such decisions and in contradiction to traditional family policies and rights. These problems can be solved, however. Not only can we initiate programs about sexuality at young ages in schools and in the homes, but traditional policies regarding parental and state control must be examined for their appropriateness in the 1990s and beyond. Just as knowledge empowers adults, so information can empower children whose lives and families are vastly different from those of earlier generations. Our future generations may depend on such efforts.

3

Sexual Harassment

Kathleen McKinney
Nick Maroules

Definitions of Sexual Harassment

Definitions of sexual harassment are important because they educate people, stimulate discussion, and encourage judgments of behavior. But no definition of the many that exist is complete or acceptable to everyone (Crocker 1983; Somers 1982).

The American Psychological Association's definition of sexual harassment refers to "deliberate or repeated comments, gestures, or physical contacts of a sexual nature that are unwanted by the recipient." That of the National Advisory Council on Women's Educational Programs defines sexual harassment as "the use of authority to emphasize the sexuality or sexual identity of a student in a manner which prevents or impairs that student's full enjoyment of educational benefits, climate or opportunity." Crocker (1983) notes that the strengths of these definitions are that they cover a wide range of behavior as sexual harassment and include the notion of negative effects on the victim. The definitions, however, use ambiguous terminology and words (for example, *full enjoyment, unwelcome, authority*) that may minimize the seriousness of the behavior. Sexual harassment in the workplace is defined as "deliberate or repeated unsolicited verbal comments, gestures, or physical contact of a sexual nature that is considered to be unwelcome by the recipient" (U.S. Merit Systems Protection Board 1981: 2).

Although the definitions vary, most include one or more of the following characteristics: the behavior is unwanted (as perceived by the victim) and/or repeated and/or deliberate, there is some negative harm or outcome for the victim, a wide range of behaviors is included, and the offender has more power than the victim.

The Law of Sexual Harassment

In the 1980s, sexual harassment became a common basis for employment litigation (Baxter 1985). In fact, the high volume of litigation caused state and (particularly) federal courts to refine the principles of law that govern sexual harassment claims.

Sexual harassment is actionable (that is, remediable by an action at law) under multiple legal theories. The focus here is primarily on principles developed under Title VII of the Civil Rights Act of 1964 because the fundamental feature of most sexual harassment lawsuits (including those arising in the workplace as well as academe) is sex discrimination in violation of Title VII.[1] Claims brought under Title VII make available to claimants the resources and mechanisms of the Equal Employment Opportunity Commission (EEOC); permit monetary compensation for back pay, lost benefits, and damages; allow the possibility of job reinstatement; and provide for attorney's fees. Sexual harassment complaints are also actionable as common law torts, such as assault and battery, intentional and negligent infliction of emotional distress, negligence, and intentional interference with contractual relations. Tort remedies are far more expansive than Title VII remedies, potentially including recovery not only for lost wages but also for consequential damages for other economic harm or loss occasioned by the sexual harassment and damages for pain and suffering; most important, they may lead to an award of punitive damages that may far exceed the compensatory award.

In the early and mid seventies cases alleging sexual harassment in the workplace brought under Title VII were dismissed by federal courts, which consistently held that it did not constitute sexual discrimination within the meaning of the statute. In *Barnes v. Train*, for example, the court held that a supervisor's retaliation against a female employee for her refusal to submit to his advances was "underpinned by the subtleties of an inharmonious personal relationship."[2] Similarly, the court in *Corne v. Bausch and Lomb, Inc.* held that a supervisor's repeated verbal and physical advances toward two female employees who were allegedly forced to quit because of his behavior arose as a result of the supervisor's "personal urge," which was distinct from the company's policies and which would provide a basis for a Title VII claim.[3] The court further reasoned that if it held such conduct to be discrimination, all "amorous or sexually oriented advances" among employees would become actionable, forcing employers to hire "asexual" employees in order to avoid liability.[4]

The first federal court decision to recognize sexual harassment as a Title VII violation was *Williams v. Saxbe*,[5] which involved a supervisor's retaliation against a female employee's refusal of his sexual advances with annoying comments, unfavorable reviews, and unwarranted reprimands. In cases such as *Williams*, which became known as quid pro quo harassment, an employer or his agent explicitly ties the terms, conditions, and privileges of the victim's employment to factors that are arbitrary and unrelated to job performance (Vhay 1988).

Title VII quid pro quo cases expanded harassment actions in at least two additional respects.[6] First, they opened the door for harassment claims under additional discrimination statutes. In *Alexander v. Yale University*, for example, the court ruled that an educational institution's failure to respond to sexual harassment complaints provided grounds for a Title IX (Education Amendments of 1972) action.[7] Similarly, state courts held quid pro quo harassment to be actionable under state discrimination statutes prohibiting housing discrimination (Vhay 1988). Second, courts began to define harassment more broadly. In *Wright v. Methodist Youth Services, Inc.*, for example, the court held the quid pro quo harassment on the part of a male homosexual supervisor to be a violation of Title VII.[8]

The EEOC promulgated guidelines on sexual harassment in the workplace in 1980 for the purpose of explaining what behavior constitutes discrimination under Title VII. The guidelines do not have the force of law, but their importance is substantial because they direct EEOC field offices in their enforcement of Title VII. In general, federal courts have relied quite heavily on the EEOC guidelines in sexual harassment cases (Baxter 1985). The guidelines first codified what the courts had already held: quid pro quo harassment in the workplace violated Title VII. They went further, however, and held that discriminatory harassment could arise not only from a superior's actions but also from the actions of coworkers. This new category of harassment became known as environmental harassment and was defined as behavior that had "the purpose or effect of unreasonably interfering with an individual's work performance or creating an intimidating, hostile, or offensive working environment."[9] Under this definition, employers who knew or should have known of the harassment and failed to take prompt remedial action are held to have created a discriminatory condition in violation of the statute.

The EEOC's definition of environmental harassment was first upheld by a state court in 1980.[10] More significant, the EEOC's approach was upheld in *Meritor Savings Bank v. Vinson*, the first sexual harassment case to be decided by the U.S. Supreme Court.[11] The plaintiff in *Meritor* charged that during her three-year employment at a bank, she was constantly subjected to unwanted sexual advances from her supervisor, felt intimidated enough to have had intercourse with him between forty and fifty times, and claimed he fondled her in front of other employees, followed her into the women's restroom, exposed himself to her, and raped her on several occasions. The Court unanimously ruled that environmental sexual harassment is a form of sex discrimination prohibited by Title VII when the conduct in question, as here, unreasonably interferes with work performance or creates an offensive work environment. A 1985 Title IX case, *Moire v. Temple University School of Medicine*, has allowed an environmental discrimination claim in an educational setting.[12]

It is virtually impossible to pinpoint the nature and severity of conduct that will or will not constitute sexual harassment under Title VII. Apart from two essential elements, the determination will be made by the courts on a case-by-case basis in the light of all the facts and circumstances involved in the case (Baxter 1985; Cohen 1987). The two apparently essential elements are that the alleged conduct be physically, verbally, or visually sexual[13] in nature and that the sexual conduct be unwelcome.[14] The court in *Henson v. City of Dundee* listed the elements required to establish a prima facie claim of sexual harassment[15]:

1. The employee belongs to a protected group (that is, is a man or a woman).
2. The employee was subjected to unwelcome sexual conduct.
3. The conduct was based on the sex of the employee.
4. The harassment affected a term, condition, or privilege of the employment.[16]
5. The conduct was committed by a supervisory employee or, if committed by a coworker, the employer "knew or should have known of the harassment and failed to take prompt remedial action."[17]

The most difficult of these elements to resolve concerns the degree of seriousness the offensive conduct must involve in order to become actionable (Baxter 1985). Sexual language, suggestive or embarrassing remarks directed toward women in an office unit, innuendoes, jokes, and gestures are obvious elements in many environmental harassment cases. It is clear, however, that "not every sexual innuendo or flirtation gives rise to an actionable wrong."[18] According to some commentators, isolated or random remarks or actions are insufficient to support an environmental harassment claim (Cohen 1987). Further, many courts have concluded that in the analysis of an offensive work environment an "objective" approach (rather than the subjective perceptions of the plaintiff) is required.[19]

In summary, it has only been since 1976 that the courts have recognized sexual harassment as sex discrimination. The repugnance of situations in which sexual favors have been made a requirement of employment (quid pro quo harassment), as well as those in which sexual behaviors have created an intimidating, hostile, or offensive work environment (environmental harassment), have finally been made actionable at law. This demonstrates the essential embeddedness and responsiveness of law to the changing structural and cultural circumstances of society. As traditional power differentials between men and women underwent dramatic change in economic, political, and social relations, so too are such changes revealed in society's laws.

Despite this enlightened aspect of the evolving law, some commentators argue that discrimination laws represent an incomplete solution to the problems that sexual harassment poses. Vhay (1988), for example, holds that the bootstraps provided by discrimination laws are too short to remedy the range of harms occasioned by harassment; Title VII exempts small business, private clubs, and religious organizations,[20] as well as the acts of coworkers outside the workplace. In *Grove City College v. Bell*,[21] furthermore, the U.S. Supreme Court held that Title IX prohibits sexual discrimination only in education programs or activities receiving federal funds. In addition, discrimination laws provide insufficient and varying remedies (Harvard Law Review 1984). These and other limitations of the discrimination laws suggest the law could and should go further in recognizing the problems, damages, and remedies associated with sexual harassment in the workplace and academe.

Environmental Factors Contributing to Harassment

Clearly sexual harassment is a complex social phenomenon whose occurrence and recognition are influenced by many factors. Terpstra and Baker (1986) have presented a conceptual framework for the study of sexual harassment in which they specify three levels of factors that contribute to its incidence and frequency:

1. Influencing variables at the macro or environmental level: Socioeconomic inequalities, societal sex role attitudes, societal sex ratios, economic conditions, the nature of the labor market, and legal sanctions.
2. Factors at the organizational level: Status or power differentials in the workplace, organizational climate, type of technology, task design, employee composition, and sex ratios.
3. Factors at the individual level: Intent, motivation, attitudinal and demographic variables, attitudes about harassment, and information processing styles and strategies of the victim and offender.

Research by Fain and Anderton (1987) tested the importance of several of these suggested factors at the organizational and individual levels. Using a heterogeneous sample of female victims from the U.S. Office of Merit Systems Review study, they looked at both the bivariate and multivariate relationships among the experience of sexual harassment and several independent variables, including organizational variables (work group sex composition, size of work group, status of victim) and diffuse status characteristics (victim education, minority status, age and marital status).

All of these variables were related to sexual harassment. More specifically, each of the following factors was associated with higher rates of sexual harassment: equal and predominantly female work groups, smaller work groups, nonsupervisory and lower-status positions, moderate levels of education, minority status, single marital status, and the ages 16 to 35. In considering all the variables at once, however, diffuse status characteristics were the only significant predictors of sexual harassment when all the variables were considered.

Dzeich and Weiner (1984) discuss the environmental factors—organizational, interpersonal, and attitudinal characteristics—associated with sexual harassment of students by faculty. The authors highlight the following characteristics: the ambiguity of the mission and method of academia (that faculty may find it difficult to distinguish the appropriate limits of authority and power over students), professional autonomy (individual power and lack of supervision), diffused institutional authority (ambiguous power structure and diffusion of responsibility), the myth of collegiality (professional bonding and in-group loyalty), tolerance of eccentricity (acceptance of behavior that may not be appropriate), perceptions of students (as subordinate and powerless), the pastoral self-image (the view of college as a safe and protected place), academic conservatism (acceptance of the status quo, slow social change), and inequality and tension between the sexes (the lack of women faculty and administrators and conflict between men and women in academic settings).

Benson (1984) has argued that sexual harassment may also occur if the victim has more formal power (such as academic status) than the offender or has equal power with the offender. She refers to the former behavior as contrapower harassment and the latter as peer harassment. Benson discusses anecdotal evidence of contrapower harassment and points out that anonymous forms of harassment safeguard the offender from retribution from the more powerful victim. Her assumption is that although the female professor has more position power than a male student, she lacks power in terms of her ascribed status of female. In addition, it is argued here that due to this status incongruence (female and college professor), offenders may not view a woman faculty member's achieved status as legitimate or important.

Attitudes toward sexual harassment have also been studied and are seen as contributing to sexual harassment. Research has consistently demonstrated that women hold broader definitions of what constitutes sexual harassment, as well as less tolerant or accepting attitudes about sexual harassment than men do (Adams, Kottke, and Padgitt 1983; Collins and Blodgett 1981; Gutek et al. 1980; Kenig and Ryan 1986; Lott, Reilly, and Howard 1982; McKinney 1990, in press; McKinney and Howard

1986). Such gender differences can contribute to miscommunication and to different perceptions of and reactions to the same behavior.

If there is any common feature to the many factors suggested as variables influencing sexual harassment by researchers in this area, it is the factor of power or status. Whether formal or informal, organizational or diffuse, real or perceived, status differences between victims and offenders are the root of the problem of sexual harassment.

Sexual Harassment in the Academe

Prevalence and Characteristics of Harassment

Many empirical studies have explored sexual harassment in the academe, especially using surveys, primarily self-administered questionnaires. Most often probability samples of students are studied; occasionally faculty or staff are also included. These samples are usually from medium to large public universities. In about half the studies, only women are sampled; the other half survey both women and men. Response rates typically are in the range of 40 to 50 percent, with the response rate higher for women than men. The definitions of sexual harassment used in the surveys vary. Some researchers present a general definition; however, most present a list of specific categories of behavior, including items such as suggestive looks, inappropriate touching, sexist comments, and sexual bribery. In most of the research, only incidents of harassment at that institution are studied.

This research is fairly consistent in the findings on incidence of sexual harassment, although the rates vary based on the sample and the definition of harassment. Research on harassment of undergraduates shows that about 21 percent of males and between 30 percent and 89 percent of females report having been victims of at least one incident of sexual harassment (Benson and Thomas 1982; Mazer and Percival 1989; McKinney and Howard 1986). The 89 percent figure is unusually high and included students' reports of harassment by faculty in and out of class, as well as by staff or other students. Rates for graduate students range from 35 percent to 60 percent for women and around 9 percent for men (McKinney, Olson, and Satterfield 1988; Schneider 1987). In combined samples of undergraduate and graduate students, reported rates are from 7 percent to 27 percent for men and 12 percent to 65 percent for women (Iowa State University 1982; Johnson and Shuman 1983; Metha and Nigg 1983; Reilly, Lott, and Gallogly 1986; Wilson and Kraus 1983).

A few studies have looked at the harassment of groups other than students on the college campus. Metha and Nigg (1983) found 11 percent of staff and 14 percent of faculty report being sexually harassed. Lott, Reilly, and Howard (1982) found that 17 percent of male and 70 percent of female students, staff, and faculty reported suffering from sexual insults. One recent study (Fitzgerald et al. 1988) surveyed male faculty about their involvement with students. Responses from 235 male faculty to a mailed questionnaire at one university were analyzed. Over 26 percent of the respondents reported having had a sexual encounter or relationship with a student; 11 percent reported attempting to stroke, caress, or touch a student. In a study of harassment of women faculty by students (contrapower harassment), Grauerholz (1989) reported that 48 percent claimed to have experienced at least one form of harassment, ranging from sexist comments to sexual assaults. Fitzgerald and coworkers (1988) also looked at male faculty as victims of sexual harassment by students. Fourteen percent of respondents reported students had implied or offered sexual favors for a reward; 17.5 percent attempted to stroke, caress, or touch the faculty member; and 6 percent felt they had been sexually harassed by a student. Finally, in a study of contra and peer harassment, McKinney (1990b) surveyed a probability sample of male and female faculty at a midwestern university. Overall, 14 percent of the faculty reported being sexually harassed by peers, and 20 percent reported sexual harassment by students. In addition, 20 percent of the faculty reported receiving obscene or sexual comments on course evaluations and 29 percent reported receiving obscene telephone calls from someone they suspected was a student.

Several trends are clear from these data. First, women are more likely to report being victims of sexual harassment than are men. Second, data from Iowa State (1982) and research by Johnson and Shuman (1983) indicate that female graduate students report higher rates of harassment than undergraduates. Third, rates of sexual harassment vary depending on the specific forms considered. All of the research indicates that minor to moderate forms of harassment—sexist comments, suggestive looks, touching, and sexual remarks—are most common and affect usually a fourth to two-thirds of the respondents. More serious forms of harassment also occur, but the prevalence is much lower. For example, Schneider (1987) reports that 9 percent of the graduate student women in her study indicated pressure from a male faculty member to date, socialize, or become sexually involved. Similarly, 9 percent of the students in the Johnson and Shuman (1983) study reported being victims of physical harassment or requests for sex. Two percent of the men and women in the Iowa State study (1982) reported experiencing sexual bribery.

A few of these studies asked questions about the offender and found, overall, that sexual harassers are more likely to be male. Almost all harassment of females is by males, and a substantial minority of harassment of males is by males (Grauerholz 1989; Lott, Reilly, and Howard 1982;

Mazer and Percival 1989; McKinney and Howard 1986; Metha and Nigg 1983). Most often the offender has more formal status than the victim (McKinney, Olson, and Satterfield 1988; Metha and Nigg 1983), but, with the exception of the studies by Fitzgerald and coworkers (1988), Grauerholz (1989), and McKinney (1990b), this may reflect the fact that the research has focused exclusively on harassment of students by faculty or harassment of staff and faculty by peers. Grauerholz (1990), however, found that faculty women reported more sexual harassment by superiors and peers than by students with one exception: written sexual comments.

Dzeich and Weiner (1984) distinguish between faculty members who are public or private harassers. The public harasser "engages in observable, flagrant posturing toward women. He is the most likely to intimidate or seek control through sexist remarks and advances that may be offensive but are essentially free from sanctions" (p. 120). The private harasser, on the other hand, "uses his authority to gain private access to the student. . . . He not only seeks but depends on privacy because he requires a domain in which there are no witnesses to his behavior. He is . . . the one who demands sexual favors of students" (p. 121).

In a study of male undergraduates and their likelihood of being sexual harassers, Pryor (1987) found several correlates of the predisposition to harass sexually. He reports that males who scored higher on his scale measuring likelihood of sexually harassing (LSH) are more likely to hold attitudes that emphasize sexual and social male dominance, be authoritarian, and have negative views about sexuality than males who score lower on the LSH.

Finally, the survey research examines the responses and effects of harassment reported by the victims. Studies indicate that most of the victims usually did not report the harassment, and if they did, they reported it to friends rather than to individuals or committees with the power of formal social control (Johnson and Shuman 1983; McKinney, Olson, and Satterfield 1988; Metha and Nigg 1983; Reilly, Lott, and Gallogly 1986). Commonly victims ignored the incident or avoided the offender in response (Benson and Thomas 1982; Grauerholz 1989; Iowa State University 1982; Johnson and Shuman 1983; McKinney, Olson, and Satterfield 1988; Reilly, Lott, and Gallogly 1986; Schneider 1987)—occasionally by changing a major, not taking a particular course, or not having a harassing faculty member on one's thesis committee (Johnson and Shuman 1983).

Benson and Thomas (1982) report that 70 percent of the students in their sample said they attempted to confront the offender and that this effort helped reduce the harassment. These women, however, felt they suffered reprisals by taking this strategy. Women faculty in the Grauerholz (1989) study also reported confronting the student offenders when the harassment was not anonymous and generally found this to be effective in stopping the harassment. Interestingly, almost 10 percent of these faculty women said they did nothing because they too feared reprisals (for example, students might spread rumors or write poor evaluations).

Another effect of sexual harassment is the tendency of the student victim to blame the faculty member or other factors external to the self (McKinney 1990). Victims also report experiencing a wide range of negative effects, including feeling emotions such as fear, anger, and embarrassment (Johnson and Shuman 1983; Schneider 1987). In addition, respondents report negative effects on their feelings of trust, on their other relationships, on their academic standards, and on their professional advancement (Benson and Thomas 1982; Johnson and Shuman 1983; Reilly, Lott, and Gallogly 1986; Schneider 1987).

Experiments on Definitions of Harassment

Several researchers have used experiments or factorial surveys to assess respondents' definitions of the situations and behaviors they believe constitute sexual harassment. They have presented subjects (usually college students or faculty) randomly assigned scenarios or vignettes depicting possible incidents of harassment and asked subjects to indicate to what extent they believe the event is sexual harassment. Aspects of the situation and characteristics and behaviors of the victim or offender can be manipulated.

Two sets of experiments provide some information on perceptions of incidents where students harass faculty (contrapower harassment) and faculty harass students. Pryor (1985) and Pryor and Day (1988) studied college students to assess the relevance of attribution theory to judgments of sexual harassment. In both sets of studies, comments were depicted as having been made by a faculty member and by a student. The subjects considered the faculty member's comments as more harassing than the same comments made by a student. In the first study, the importance of the negative intentions of those involved on the subjects' increased judgments of harassment was demonstrated. In the second study, whether the subject was told to view the incident from the actor or target's point of view (perspective) was shown to affect judgments. Subjects were less likely to see the event as harassment when taking the perspective of the offender and more likely when taking the perspective of the victim.

Reilly and coworkers (1982), Weber-Burdin and Rossi (1982), and Rossi and Weber-Burdin (1983) used a factorial survey (similar to a within-subjects experiment) to assess factors affecting perceptions of situations as sexual harassment. Respondents (several hundred undergraduates in all three studies and a small number of faculty in the latter two studies) each read numerous vignettes describing an interaction between a female student and a male faculty member where other variables (such as status, type of prior relationship, and type of behaviors) were manipulated. Factors associated with higher ratings of the situations as harassment were verbal threats or physical action by the male instructor. Factors associated with lower ratings of the incidents as harassment were suggestive behaviors by the female student. In all three studies, the type of behavior by both student and faculty member was important in affecting judgments of situations as sexual harassment.

In summary, empirical research on sexual harassment in academia has emphasized survey research on the sexual harassment of students and faculty and experiments on factors that affect definitions of situations as harassment. This research shows that about 25 to 30 percent of students report being the victim of at least one incident of sexual harassment in the college setting. A few studies also document the sexual harassment of faculty and staff. Rates vary with the sample studied and the definition of harassment used. The rates of victimization are consistently higher for women, and women have more negative views of sexual harassment than men do. Less serious forms of harassment are more common. Victims report the responses, primarily, of ignoring the harassment or informal reporting, as well as a variety of negative personal and social effects. Finally, the definitions of situations as harassment held by individuals are affected by the intentions and behaviors of both the student and faculty member and the perspective (which person they role play) subjects are asked to take.

Sexual Harassment in the Workplace

Studies of sexual harassment in the workplace use survey, quasi-experimental, and experimental methodologies designed to assess various aspects of sexual harassment: measures of the nature and character of sexual harassment, the conditions and structural factors associated with its incidence, differences in individual perceptions regarding what constitutes sexual harassment, as well as the effects on and responses of its victims.

Earlier studies, which tended to focus on the prevalence and other features of sexual harassment in the workplace environment, indicated that the frequency of sexual harassment is a widespread social problem that particularly affects female as opposed to male employees (Safran 1976; Bularzik 1978; Evans 1978; Farley 1978; United States Merit Systems Protection Board [USMSPB] 1981; Brewer and Berk 1982). Many of these studies found that younger women in lower-level organizational positions were the most likely victims of sexual harassment in the workplace (Brodsky 1976; USMSPB 1981). In the USMSPB study, which included over 23,000 randomly selected federal employees, 42 percent of the women respondents but only 15 percent of men reported having been the victims of sexual harassment during the preceding two years. The majority of males who did report being the target of sexual harassment identified the incident as involving actual or potential homosexual behavior. In a study of women in traditional male professions, such as managers and engineers, Lafontaine and Tredeau (1986) found that 75 percent reported having been sexually harassed.

A long tradition of studies has found support for the view that sexual harassment is more a power relation than a form of sexual behavior (Brodsky 1976; Ginsberg, Koreski, and Galloway 1977; Seymour 1979; MacKinnon 1979). Gutek and others (1980) found that female targets reported that a significant proportion of social-sexual behaviors in the workplace were initiated by their supervisor, particularly in the case of the most problematic behavior types (including requests to socialize or date and requests of sexual activity that would hurt the job situation if refused). Similarly, Loy and Stewart (1984) found that the severity of the type of harassment was related to the organizational position of the harasser. So-called verbal commentary harassment—typically innuendo and off-color jokes—most frequently originated with peers, and the more problematic forms of sexual harassment in their operational typology—verbal propositions, physical handling, and physical assaults—were increasingly committed by superordinates. These results were corroborated by Coles (1986) who examined the universe of sexual harassment cases filed with a state enforcement agency over a five-year period and found that the perpetrators were most likely to be supervisors or business owners who were in positions of dominance regarding the complainants.

A number of studies have explored differences in individuals' perceptions, interpretations, and definitions of sexual harassment. Gutek, Morasch, and Cohen (1983) tested aspects of the ways people interpret ambiguous but potentially sexual interactions between the sexes in a work setting by asking respondents in a quasi-experimental design to evaluate a vignette depicting such an interaction. The sex and status of the initiator, the type of behavior portrayed, and the sex of the respondent were manipulated to examine the respondents' interpretations of the vignettes. They found that men viewed ambiguous but potentially sexual behaviors more positively than women. Further, incidents initiated by a woman were viewed as more appropriate than those initiated by a man but only where the female had status equal to or lower than the target, suggesting to the researchers that the status (achieved and formal) of the initiator is more important than the sex of the initiator (an ascribed or diffuse status) when it comes to evaluating the appropriateness of the incident.

Similarly, Powell (1986) relied on survey data to elaborate on a consistent finding of prior research indicating that women "see" more sexual harassment than men (Collins and Blodgett 1981; Gutek et al. 1980). He found that the sex effect on individuals' definitions of sexual harassment remained strong despite the inclusion of sex role identity, as an alternative explanation, into the research design. Pryor (1985) analyzed the social psychological factors that generally contribute to individuals' understanding of a behavior as sexual harassment. Relying on an experimental design in which subjects reported on their interpretation of written scenarios (vignettes), which were systematically varied, he found support for an attributional model of individuals' understanding of sexual harassment. A behavior was labeled as more potentially harassing the more it was out of role with the ordinary expectations of the actor's social role.

Other studies have begun to assess some of the outcomes of sexual harassment in the workplace, a concept that embraces both personal effects and organizational (work) effects experienced by targets. According to Neugarten and Shafritz (1980), sexual harassment has the potential to affect women's economic status, self-esteem, and ability to perform on the job, as well as their mental and physical health. Silverman (1977) reported that 78 percent of harassed women felt angry, 48 percent were upset, and 23 percent were scared as a result of their harassment (MacKinnon 1982a reports similar findings).

Loy and Stewart (1984) found that 75 percent of the respondents who had been harassed said they had experienced one or more symptoms of emotional or physical distress due to their harassment. Nervousness, irritability, and uncontrolled anger were the most frequently mentioned distress responses to all types of harassment; sleeplessness, weight loss, uncontrolled crying, and stomach problems occurred less often. The more serious the type of harassment was, the greater was the likelihood of personal distress. Loy and Stewart also examined the outcomes for sexually harassed women, which they found to vary according to the response strategies of the women to their harassment. The most typical response strategies for all types of harassment were found to be informal passive and active responses; women tended to ignore (interpersonally, not psychologically) the harassment or respond verbally to the harasser. Going to one's boss or supervisor to complain accounted for only 7.8 percent of the total responses of harassed individuals. Decisions to ask for a transfer or quit accounted for 17 percent, and seeking legal help, 2 percent, of the overall responses. In terms of work effects experienced by harassed respondents, Loy and Stewart found that 62 percent cited negative organizational outcomes from their harassment experience. The most common negative outcomes were ignoring and nonsupport from coworkers, demonstrating a failure of coworkers to lend legitimacy to the problem.

Terpstra and Baker (1988) studied actual complaints to the Illinois Human Rights Office and found that cash settlements for sexual harassment ranged from $100 to $15,000, with a mean of $3,234. In addition to work-related costs to both employees and employers, the USMSPB study indicated that sexual harassment cost taxpayers more than $189 million over a two-year period.

Conclusion

Sexual harassment affects at least a substantial minority of individuals, particularly women, in academia and the workplace. The victims suffer a variety of negative (physical, emotional, and performative) consequences from their experiences with harassment. There is some consensus among the many definitions of sexual harassment, with a focus on unwanted behavior, harm, and abuse of power. Legal remedies for sexual harassment exist under both Title VII and Title IX, yet most victims ignore them or use informal means to deal with sexual harassment rather than evoke formal means such as filing lawsuits.

Definitions of sexual harassment used in academia and the workplace, as well as by social science researchers, usually view harassment from the perception of the victim. Similarly, legal definitions require that the (sexual) conduct be unwelcome—that is, not consensual or encouraged by the victim. All definitions also require that the victim incur some type of harm.

The concept of power emerges as crucial to the understanding of sexual harassment. Authors and researchers in this area, however, have not yet dealt with the complexities of the concept of power. Based on some of the research cited here (Benson 1984; Fain and Anderton 1987; Grauerholz 1989; McKinney, in press), it can no longer be assumed that only formal or position power is relevant to sexual harassment. Different types and sources of power (formal versus informal, position or achieved versus diffuse or ascribed) need to be distinguished, and the role of these different types in the process of sexual harassment must be investigated.

Future research should use longitudinal studies, attempt to apply methods other than survey research and experiments (more interviews and observational and field studies), and include offenders, not just victims, and male respondents in the work.

Notes

1. 42 U.S.C. sec. 2000e et seq. (1982).
2. 13 F.E.P. Cases 123, 124 (D.D.C. 1974), *rev'd* as Barnes v. Costle, 561 F.2d 983 (D.C. Cir. 1977).
3. 390 F. Supp. 161 (D. Ariz. 1975).
4. See also Tomkins v. Public Service Electric and Gas Co., 422 F. Supp. 553 (D. N.J. 1976); Miller v. Bank of America, 418 F. Supp. 233 (N.D. Cal. 1976); and Williams v. Sazbe, 413 F. Supp. 654 (D.D.C. 1976).
5. 413 F. Supp 654 (D.D.C. 1976).
6. See, for example, Barnes v. Costle, 561 F.2d 983 (D.D.C. 1977); Garber v. Saxon Business Products, 552 F.2d 1032 (4th Cir. 1977); Tomkins v. Public Service Electric and Gas Co., 568 F.2d 1044 (3d Cir. 1977).
7. 20 U.S.C. sec. 1681 (1982).
8. 511 F. Supp. 307, 310 (N.D. Ill. 1981). See also Joyner v. AAA Cooper Transportation, 597 F. Supp. 537 (M.D. Ala. 1983).
9. 29 C.F.R. sec. 1604.11(a) (3) (1986).
10. Continental Can Co. v. State of Minnesota, 297 N.W.2d 241 (Minn. 1980).
11. 106 S. Ct. 2399 (1986).
12. 613 F. Supp. 1360 (1985).
13. The EEOC guidelines state that sexual harassment requires "conduct of a sexual nature." See, e.g., 29 C.F.R. sec. 1604.11(a).
14. See, e.g., Gan v. Kepro Circuit Systems, 28 F.E.P. Cases 639 (E.D. Mo. 1982); Reichman v. Bureau of Affirmative Action, 536 F. Supp. 1149 (M.D. Pa. 1982); Ferguson v. E.I. duPont de Nemours and Co., Inc., 560 F. Supp. 1172 (D. Del. 1983).
15. 682 F.2d 897 (11th Cir. 1982).
16. *Henson* held that in quid pro quo harassment cases, any effect on the terms, conditions, or privileges of employment met this element. With regard to environmental harassment cases, however, the harassment had to be "sufficiently severe and persistent to affect seriously the psychological well-being" of the employee. Id. at 904.
17. Id. at 905.
18. Ferguson v. E.I. duPont de Nemours and Co., Inc., 560 F. Supp. 1172, 1197–1198.
19. See Rabidue v. Osceola Refining Co., 584 F. Supp. 419 (E.D. Mich. 1984); Scott v. Sears, Roebuck and Co., 605 F. Supp. 1047 (N.D. Ill. 1985); and Jennings v. D.H.L. Airlines, 34 FEP Cases 1432 (N.D. Ill. 1984).
20. See 42 U.S.C. sec. 2000e(b).
21. 465 U.S. 555 (1984).

Cases Cited

Alexander v. Yale University, 459 F. Supp. 1 (D. Conn. 1977).
Barnes v. Train, 13 F.E.P. Cases 123 (D.D.C. 1974)

Barnes v. Costle, 561 F.2d 983 (D.D. Cir. 1977)

Contimental Can Co. v. State of Minnesota, 297 N.W.2d 241 (Minn. 1980).

Corne v. Bausch and Lomb, Inc., 390 F. Supp. 161 (D. Ariz. 1975).

Ferguson v. E.I. duPont de Nemours and Co., Inc., 560 F. Supp. 1172 (D. Del. 1983).

Gan v. Kepro Circuit Systems, 28 F.E.P. Cases 639 (E.D. Mo. 1982).

Garber v. Saxon Business Products, 552 F.2d 1032 (4th Cir. 1977).

Grove City College v. Bell, 465 U.S. 535 (1984).

Henson v. City of Dundee, 682 F.ed 897 (11th Cir. 1982).

Jennings v. D.H.L. Airlines, 34 F.E.P. Cases 1423 (N.D. Ill. 1984).

Joyner v. AAA Cooper Transp., 597 F. Supp. 537 (M.D. Ala. 1983).

Meritor Savings Bank v. Vinson, 106 S.Ct. 2399 (1986).

Miller v. Bank of America, 600 F2d 211 (9th Cir. 1979).

Moire v. Temple University School of Medicine, 613 F. Supp. 1360 (1985).

Rabidue v. Osceola Refining Co., 584 F. Supp. 419 (E.D. Mich 1984).

Reichman v. Bureau of Affirmative Action, 536 F. Supp. 1149 (M.D. Pa. 1982).

Scott v. Sears, Roebuck and Co., 605 F. Supp. 1047 (N.D. Ill. 1985).

Tomkins v. Public Service Electric and Gas, Co., 422 F. Supp. 553 (D. N.J. 1976).

Williams v. Saxbe, 413 F. Supp. 654 (D.D.C. 1976).

Wright v. Methodist Youth Services, Inc., 511 F. Supp. 307 (N.D. Ill. 1981).

Statutes Cited

29 C.F.R. Section 1604.11(a)(3) (1986).

20 U.S.C. Section 1681 (1982).

42 U.S.C. Sections 2000e et seq. (1982).

4

Prostitution in Contemporary American Society

JoAnn L. Miller

> Purely from the angle of economic return, the hard question is not why so many women become prostitutes, but why so few of them do.
> —K. Davis (1937)

My friend Rita was a marching and protesting feminist throughout the 1970s. She was also a woman deeply wounded by sexual harassment and its aftermath. One evening she announced that she had decided to prostitute; she wanted to get reimbursed financially for what she thought she was doing already for free. She believed that her big problem was figuring out how to get started in the business. I concluded that her biggest problem was failing to get out of an exploitation and coercion trap that had already snuffed out every bit of self-respect she struggled so hard to maintain. Rita's story is a familiar tragedy.

Akers (1985) conservatively estimates that prostitution is the primary source of personal income for at least 1 million women and girls in the United States. Prostitution accounts for more than 100,000 arrests annually (U.S. Department of Justice 1988). Because we know that women arrested on prostitution charges are typically streetwalkers (Tong 1984), engaging in the form of prostitution most visible in urban areas, we must acknowledge that the arrest data grossly underestimate the incidence of prostitution in the United States. We also know that prostitution is the offense for which most women arrested in the United States are adjudicated (Leonard 1982; Feinman 1986).

Bryant defines prostitution as "the contractual barter of sex favors, usually sexual intercourse, for monetary considerations without any emotional attachment between the partners" (1977: 165). His definition intimates a simple business contract between two social actors that poses no problem unless one actor violates the terms of the agreement. I contend that an adequate definition of prostitution must account for the actual or potential coercion and exploitation of the prostitute specifically, and women more generally. As sadism and masochism are associated with images of masculinity and femininity, respectively (Benjamin 1988) so are johns and their prostitutes, the exploiter and the exploited.

This chapter presents a sociolegal-feminist perspective on the problem of prostitution in contemporary American society.[1] I limit my analysis to the current situation in the United States for two major reasons. First, prostitution is a massive problem that affects women and girls in virtually every society, now and in earlier historical periods (Bristow 1983). Second, like Shrage (1989), I argue that to understand the true effects of prostitution, the social context surrounding it—including gender relations in a society—must be explicated. To analyze prostitution in the modern American society is an enormous task. My intention is to commence the task sufficiently to invite other concerned scholars to join the excursion.

Sexual Coercion or Sexual Liberation?

Is prostitution a form of sexual coercion and sexual exploitation of women in the contemporary United States? Savitz and Rosen (1988) believe it is not. They report that women arrested for prostitution-solicitation on Philadelphia streets tend to perceive sexual enjoyment in their work and an even greater level of sexual enjoyment from their private-life partners. These researchers tell us that "a considerable number of prostitutes found relatively high levels of erotic enjoyment with customers, at least for intercourse and getting and giving oral sex. . . . Receiving oral sex was the most enjoyable outlet both with customers and with lovers" (p. 203).

Ostensibly prostitution provides one of our society's higher financial and economic options for some women. Catherine MacKinnon writes that "aside from modeling (with which it has much in common), hooking is the only job for which women as a group are paid more than men" (1987: 24–25) in contemporary American society. Is this news the good news for some women or is that the bad news for all of us? If prostitutes enjoy sex and can take home reasonable sums of money through selling their sexuality, maybe some women should be encouraged to sell sex—perhaps a fair reasoning according to the simple-minded "someone has to do it" type of reasoning. Or maybe, as MacKinnon argues, no one should be situated in society such that she has to do it.

Naively, some individuals might think that women who choose to sell their sexuality are emotionally and financially well situated for a career of prostitution work. Prostitution might be viewed as one of the few situations where women have control over their own sexuality. I maintain that a woman's supposed "willingness" to be dominated and controlled by a man with money is symptomatic of a deep problem in the relations between men and women in the contemporary United States.[2] Whether a woman experiences erotic enjoyment from a specific sexual behavior is irrelevant to any discussion on the harms and supposed advantages of prostitution.

Similar to the contemporary pornography debate in the United States, we see an ambivalence expressed by many authors who debate prostitution.[3] As Tong (1984: 37) reports: "Next to pornography, prostitution is the most difficult sex-related legal issue for feminists to address." Is prostitution the prototype of sexual liberation or the embodiment of sexual oppression? The ambivalence tends to be especially pronounced when authors articulate their moral or valuative positions regarding the relationship between prostitution and the distribution of power in society, the enforcement of discriminatory criminal law, and the essential meaning of liberation for women (Shrage 1989).

I argue that prostitution is a form of sexual exploitation and a form of sexual coercion, as does Shrage:

> Although the commercial availability of sexuality is not in every existing or conceivable society oppressive to women, in our society this practice depends upon the general acceptance of principles which serve to marginalize women socially and politically. Because of the cultural context in which prostitution operates, it epitomizes and perpetuates pernicious patriarchal beliefs and values and, therefore, is both damaging to the women who sell sex and, as an organized social practice, to all women in our society. (1989: 349)

Prostitution involves one gender's taking advantage of its superior social status and manipulating the other gender; it can result in low self-esteem, imprisonment (Reynolds 1986), and suicide (Winick and Kinsie 1971). Because members of the less powerful group are compelled or forced, physically or psychologically, to engage in a sexual act, prostitution is fundamentally coercive and exploitative.

The Substantive and Procedural Issues

Recent sociolegal research literature on prostitution incorporates arguments that center on substantive issues—for example, the rape of a woman who prostitutes—or procedural problems—such as the police procedure for arresting a prostitute but not her john or her pimp.

This distinction—substantive versus procedural type arguments—is common in the research literatures on highly controversial legal topics, such as abortion (Glendon 1987; Steiner 1985) or comparable-worth legislation (Paul 1989; Remick 1984). One legal reviewer explains that a "procedural focus . . . reflects frustration over the notorious intractability of substantive arguments. These arguments often seem doomed to deteriorate into a simple, stark clash of irreconcilable fundamental 'subjective' values" (Dolinko 1986: 547). In this chapter I acknowledge the need to address subjective values as well as the need to incorporate the procedural argument with a substantive argument.

Writers emphasizing the substantive problems of prostitution examine the exploitation and oppression of all women in our industrialized and urbanized society, the domination and abuse of prostitutes by their johns and pimps, the rape of prostitutes, and the recruitment to prostitution of runaway adolescents and persons abused and emotionally scarred by intimates. Writers who emphasize procedural problems in their arguments tend to focus on how existing laws define the crime of prostitution, how prostitution laws are enforced or applied, and whether prostitution should be criminalized, regulated, or legalized.

Substantive Problems

The substantive problems surrounding prostitution range in generality from the exploitation and oppression of women in industrialized and urbanized society to the domination and abuse of a particular woman by her pimp. The substantive problems of prostitution include the personal costs or harms of prostitution and the social effects of tolerating prostitution in modern American society.

Exploitation of Women. Karl Marx used the term *prostitution* as a metaphor of exploitation: "Prostitution is only a specific expression of the general prostitution of the laborer, and since it is a relationship in which falls not the prostitute alone, but also the one who prostitutes—and the latter's abomination is still greater—the capitalist, etc., also comes under this head" (Marx and Engels 1975, vol. 3: 295n).

In her thesis on the oppression of women, Vogel (1983) shows how Marxists advance the notion that prostitution is a natural product of bourgeois society. In contemporary American society, the inferior status of women, relative to men, stems from a political economy in which the family structure and patriarchy makes the women at least twice exploited. A woman prostituting is exploited as a worker and again as a woman. Prostitution is linked to the structural position of women in an industrialized, urbanized society in the twentieth century, just as it was a century earlier.

Some writers (de Beauvoir 1952) challenge the idea that prostitutes are exploited or coerced in modern Western societies by claiming that women make voluntary decisions to sell their sexuality. Others, such as Overall (1987: 117), caution against accepting a "free market" model for prostitution. Overall contends that a woman is not entitled to self-exploit any more than an illicit drug user is: "The mere payment of a . . . fee in no way changes the possibility that she is a victim of exploitation, and the nature of exploitation is not such that an increase in fees or improved working conditions will change it" (Overall 1987: 122).

Do women and girls in a patriarchal society that offers women fewer and lesser financial opportunities than men choose to prostitute for financial reasons alone? In an early analysis, Lemert (1951) concluded that, relative to men, the inferior social position women hold in contemporary U.S. society denies them power and control over the material rewards distributed throughout the general population. To equalize the disparate gender-based statuses in society, some women choose to use prostitution to earn large sums of money. Two decades later Winick and Kinsie (1971) similarly argued that women who perceive, albeit erroneously, that substantial sums of money can be earned through prostitution (James 1976; Mann 1984; Rosenbaum 1982) and who also have a "tendency" toward sexual promiscuity are more likely than others to choose prostitution.

Although prostitutes may gross considerable sums of money, most pimps control their workers financially, providing the women and girls with room, board, clothing, and as little as $5,000 spending money per year (Reynolds 1986). Also the costs are great. They include those necessary to be protected from criminal assault (for example, to purchase firearms or to pay for lookouts) and those necessary to obtain legal services (when arrested), medical services (to treat infections or injuries), psychological services, and clothing.

Recently researchers have documented the factors beyond financial considerations that influence the prostitution choice that is made within a social context characterized by structural disadvantages. Jennifer James's (1976) critically acclaimed study of New York prostitutes concludes that numerous factors lead to the prostitution decision:

1. Unskilled or low-skilled women perceive that there are virtually no other occupations available that offer income comparable to that earned through prostitution.

2. The prostitute's life-style provides adventure and independence that are otherwise unattainable.

3. The traditional female role, like the prostitute's role, emphasizes service, physical appearance, and sexuality.

4. The culturally maintained madonna-whore duality—that image of women that characterizes and labels sexually active women as deviants with low social status—encourages some sexually active women to endorse the prostitute's characterization.

5. The cultural significance of wealth, indicated by material goods, leads some women to desire advantages to which they are not otherwise entitled by their position in the socioeconomic stratification system in U.S. society.

In summary, women in contemporary American society are structurally disadvantaged. Partly in response to a structural position and partly as a consequence of numerous other social circumstances, some women are compelled, or feel compelled, to prostitute for their livelihood. By acknowledging the social context of choice in which some women decide to prostitute, we can understand how prostitution is exploitation and an act of coercion. It cannot be viewed simply as a voluntary decision.

Abuse by Johns and Pimps. Prostitution is a highly stratified occupation. Sophisticated and well-educated young call girls are at the top and streetwalkers are at the bottom of the hierarchy (Bryant 1977; D'Emilio and Freedman 1988). The call girl is generally protected from the physical brutality, the torture, and the humiliation associated with sadomasochism that becomes the normative expectation for the streetwalker. The call girl's personal manager is more likely to protect her from abuse through screening her clients than he or she is to abuse her. The streetwalker's pimp, on the other hand, is likely to assault her for refusing a request for sadomasochistic sex with a client (Tong 1984). The streetwalker, the most common type of prostitute, faces a very high risk of physical abuse at the hands of her john or her pimp (Deegan 1988; D'Emilio and Freedman 1988; Silbert 1982). The criminal justice system, however, is unlikely to arrest the man who beats up a prostitute. Why? "It goes with the territory," they say (Tong 1984; MacKinnon 1987).

Prostitute Rape Victims. Gordon and Riger assert that "the only crime women fear more than murder is rape" (1989: 2). A woman who engages in prostitution for her livelihood fears rape, just as all other women do. She is at high risk of being raped, both by strangers and sometimes by acquaintances. Yet rape of prostitutes has received only a passing reference (if any at all) by researchers, who focus on either the problem of rape or the problem of prostitution.

Silbert (1982, 1988) has conducted the only in-depth and comprehensive study of rape among prostitutes. She interviewed 200 adult and juvenile prostitutes in the San Francisco Bay Area at the Delancey Street Foundation, a facility designed to treat female drug addicts, criminals, and prostitutes. She found that 73 percent of the women and girls who participated in the study had been raped in incidents unrelated to the individual's work as a prostitute (1988). Similar to the statistical patterns we find when examining rapes in the general population, Silbert reports that most rapes occurred between 8:00 P.M. and 2:00 A.M. Nearly half of the incidents involved the use or the threat of the use of a weapon. In most of the cases, the victim believed the offender was drinking alcohol or using an illicit drug at the time of the rape.

Unlike the pattern we find among persons raped in the general population, Silbert reports that "almost every rape involved extreme levels of violence" (1988: 80). She also found, unexpectedly, that victims who told the rapists they were prostitutes experienced an escalation of violence and abuse. Many victims (81 percent) disclosed to the interviewers that they were afraid for their lives. The "majority of victims never talked to anyone about the rape" (Silbert, 1988: 83). This research suggests that the victims are as severely traumatized by rape as women raped in the general population. Yet the prostitute-victims report that they have little opportunity to seek recovery and healing that can be obtained through psychotherapy, social intervention, or disclosure to a trusting friend.

Recruiting. Who prostitutes? Why does a young woman begin prostituting? What is the social context in which individuals recruited to a world of prostitution make their decisions? We have no studies to show, nor do we have any reason to believe, that women and girls who prostitute face the same life chances—the same educational, occupational, and financial prospects—as those who are highly likely to succeed in American society. We do, however, have evidence and reason to believe that women and girls recruited to prostitution, especially in the form of streetwalking, manifest extremely low self-esteem (this may also be a consequence of prostituting) and have a history of sexual abuse and child neglect (Bracey 1979).

Bagley and Young (1987) interviewed ex-prostitutes and a matched sample of women from the community at large to examine the role of sexual abuse in a woman's decision to begin prostitution. They found that 73 percent of the ex-prostitutes interviewed had extensive histories of child sexual abuse—an incidence rate at least three times greater than that estimated for women in the general population. Moreover, they found that the severity of the abuse was a significant contributor to the poor mental health and low self-esteem found among the ex-prostitutes who participated in the study.

The Bagley and Young findings are typical. Researchers find that women who prostitute tend to have had early sexual experiences, often under conditions of physical coercion (Bracey 1979; Seng 1986). They tend to manifest poor self-images, perceptions of stigmatization, and manifestations of depression, anxiety, cynicism, and alienation (Brown

1979; Newman et al. 1985; Gibson-Ainyette et al. 1988; Lowman 1987). Many began prostitution at an extremely young age, and many were or are runaways. A child summarizes the social context in which too many young girls and young women make decisions: "If all I'm worth to the adult world is to be used for sex, I might as well get some money for it" (Seng 1986: 58). Tong explains, "Unless one has the concrete means to transcend the institutions that work to limit one's freedom, chances are that one will submit to their constraints" (1984: 60).

Procedural Problems

Laws Defining Prostitutes, Their Patrons, and the Act of Prostitution. The act of prostitution by an adult woman with an adult man is generally considered a mala prohobitum offense (Bryant 1977), one that is not regarded by law or the citizenry to be inherently dangerous, evil, or wrong.[4] Instead it is an offense that is made unlawful by statute. And it is a consensual offense (Feinberg 1988)—an illegal act in which the parties, according to the law, "willingly" participate in a transaction (Territo, Halsted, and Bromley 1989).[5]

All states have statutory provisions that define prostitution as a crime; however, the laws vary across the states with respect to the behavior prohibited by law and the penalties deemed appropriate for convicted offenders. Nevada law, for example, prohibits prostitution only in counties with a population of over 200 thousand persons (Galliher and Cross 1985). Alabama defines promoting prostitution in the first or second degree a felony punishable with a term of incarceration (U.S. Department of Justice 1987). Indiana defines a third-time conviction for prostitution a felony offense (U.S. Department of Justice 1987). Nevada and Alabama law maintain atypical prostitution laws. Indiana law is typical of law that specifies only repeat prostitution offenses are felonies.

Most states define a first prostitution offense as a misdemeanor, punishable with a monetary fine or a short term of jail time. Many states continue to maintain statutory prohibitions against prostitution long after other "sex crimes," such as cohabitation, fornication, and sodomy, were removed from the state's criminal codes (Nettler 1989).

Hutchins (1986) reports that various styles of language are used by the states in their statutory definitions of prostitution. Florida law specifies "The term 'prostitution' shall be construed to include the giving or receiving of the body for sexual intercourse for hire, and shall also be construed to include the giving or receiving of the body for licentious sexual intercourse without hire."[6] New York uses plain and specific language: "A person is guilty of prostitution when such person engages or agrees or offers to engage in sexual conduct with another person in return for a fee."[7] Colorado, however, uses antiquated language to identify the prostitute: "Any prostitute, courtesan, or lewd woman who, by word, gesture, or action, shall endeavor to ply her vocation upon the streets, or from the door or window of any house or in any public place in any city or town of this state, or who, for such purpose, shall make a bold and meretricious display of herself, shall be deemed guilty of a misdemeanor."[8]

Hutchins summarily contends that although the states vary in their use of words to define prostitute and the act of prostitution, from a systematic overview of statutory and case law emerges the inference that the "activity of engaging in sexual conduct for money is prostitution" (Hutchins 1986: 997). Similarly, definitions of promoting prostitution vary across the states, yet they tend to indicate that the activities "include aiding, facilitating, promoting, supervising, managing, financing, or controlling prostitutes or a prostitution enterprise" (Hutchins 1986: 998).

What varies across the states, in language as well as in the behavior deemed unlawful, is the presence or absence of a patron clause. In 1965, New York legislators introduced a patron clause to their existing prostitution law stipulating the same punishment for the prostitute and her (or his) client.[9] In 1961 Illinois enacted legislation specifying that the penalty for prostitution patrons can be up to $200 and six months in jail (Hagan 1985).

Applying and Enforcing Prostitution Law. Even in states with patron clauses, empirical studies show that such clauses are not enforced to the same extent as other clauses of the state's prostitution laws. Hagan (1985) reports that although patrons are routinely arrested in Illinois, they go unconvicted. Among those arrested for prostitution in New York over a two-year period, less than 1 percent were patrons, and even fewer were pimps, although laws clearly classify the pimp's behavior as illegal (Hagan 1985). Clearly these data show discrimination in favor of men who patronize and organize prostitution and against women who provide patrons with prostitution services.

Prostitution is a behavior that engages at least two persons, and it is criminal in all states, even in Clark County, Nevada. Whereas prostitution is illegal de jure, it is at least tolerated de facto in virtually all the states (D'Emilio and Freedman 1988). In its most typical form, a woman prostitute services the desires or demands of a male client, and any recorded arrest for prostitution is limited to the service provider, leaving the service recipient untouched by the law.

In August 1988, the U.S. attorney general approved a plan to revise the extent, nationwide crime data collection and reporting system, the Uniform

Crime Reports, that the Federal Bureau of Investigation (FBI) has administered since 1930. The revised data system, called the National Incident Based Reporting System, will summarize comprehensive information on criminal incidents, organized into twenty-two categories. The redesigned system provides new offense definitions, supposedly reflecting improvements over the old definitions. The new and improved definition for prostitution is: "To unlawfully engage in or promote sexual activities for profit" (U.S. Department of Justice 1988: 24). Clearly the FBI is exacerbating the discriminatory treatment of women by the criminal justice system. Although there can be no act of prostitution without a sexual partner, the FBI will continue to maintain a crime data collection system that reports only the arrest of the illegal service provider. The service recipient, equally criminal as the service provider, will not even be counted if he is arrested.

Kate Millett (1971), among other contemporary social critics, notes that statutory definitions of prostitution invariably implicate two persons for every act of prostitution, yet only the female partner is arrested and prosecuted on a fairly regular basis. Criminal justice data show that women continue to share a disproportionate legal burden for prostitution and prostitution-related activities. Approximately 30 percent of the daily female U.S. jail population are women originally arrested for prostitution. Nearly 70 percent of all the women imprisoned in state or federal facilities as a consequence of a felony conviction were initially arrested for prostitution (Mann 1984). The proportion of men incarcerated in U.S. jails or state or federal prisons on prostitution convictions is so small that it goes unrecorded.

Procedures for Change: Should Prostitution Be Criminalized, Regulated and Decriminalized, or Legalized?

Substantive arguments against prostitution show how severely women and girls are harmed physically and emotionally by prostitution. Streetwalkers especially tend to have troubled lives. When we dare to look closely enough, we see too many young women who were sexually exploited as adolescents or as children and who currently face few and limited opportunities for success in society's traditional occupations enter the ranks of streetwalkers. Their entrance to prostitution is about as voluntaristic as a young man's decision to join boot camp after he was drafted during wartime. Procedural arguments against prostitution show how the existing law, or its application discriminates against women. It takes two to prostitute, yet only one person, the woman, is likely to be arrested for the unlawful behavior.

In reflecting on procedural changes that would end or ameliorate the prostitution problem, analysts tend to present reasons for criminalizing, regulating, or legalizing prostitution.

Criminalizing prostitution means to make the law more enforceable, to enforce the law more uniformly, or to make the punishments for prostituting and patronizing more severe. The justifications that criminalization proponents provide range from principles concerned with the prostitute herself (such as the harm principle or the legal paternalism principle)[10] to the notion that extant law must be invoked and enforced uniformly in a society that values law as its major source or means of social control (Deegan 1988).

Many who argue in favor of decriminalizing prostitution contend that society cannot and should not legislate morality; therefore existing law prohibiting prostitution should go unenforced. Writers who favor the non-enforcement of the law also tend to favor a licensing or regulating approach to prostitution because of problems associated with Acquired Immune Deficiency Syndrome. Regulating prostitution encompasses the monitoring and control of prostitutes and prostitution for the purpose of protecting patrons only—not prostitutes—from venereal disease or related health problems and the urban environment from unwanted solicitations and associated public displays. The health licensing of prostitutes and the development of zoning ordinances that specify tolerated locations for prostitution are examples of regulation methods.

To legalize prostitution means that existing law prohibiting or controlling prostitution should be abolished. Prostitutes and their clients should not be subject to arrest, criminal prosecution, or control through ordinances specifying locations for brothels or other places and contexts for prostitution.

Two premises for legalizing prostitution are advanced by proponents. One is that prostitution can prevent rape through its cathartic effect on a man's sex drive. Social science empirical findings on the question notwithstanding, Tong states precisely why this premise is immoral: "there is something reprehensible about conceiving of prostitutes as a class of sacrificial victims" (1984: 59). The second premise for legalizing prostitution is based on sociohistorical observations. Nineteenth-century feminists, attempting to aid the "fallen woman," turned prostitutes into social outcasts (Bristow 1983; Deegan 1988). Noble intentions can harm.

Conclusions

The criminalizing, decriminalizing, or legalizing of prostitution has not succeeded in resolving the prostitution problem in the contemporary United

States. Following a century of failed efforts, we have no reason to believe that any renewed effort to ameliorate the problem will work. Ultimately the question of prostitution becomes a moral and ethical one for a society to consider: Why do we tolerate prostitution? Why do we tolerate the sale of sexuality? Shrage maintains that

> there is no practice, such as "sex," which can be morally evaluated apart from a cultural framework. . . . Though we can appreciate that making an occupation by the provision of sex may not have been oppressive to women in medieval France or ancient Babylon, we should nevertheless recognize that in our society it can be extremely damaging to women. . . . . In short, female prostitution oppresses women . . . because its organized practice testifies to and perpetuates socially hegemonic beliefs which oppress all women in many domains of their lives. (1989: 351–352)

In contemporary American society we value romantic love that emphasizes "mutual support and implies self-development," and this can be achieved only within committed relationships (Cancian 1987: 105). Prostitution is the antithesis of this state. It assigns its practitioners and its patrons to a marginal status in this culture, reaffirms the madonna-whore duality in society, places the women in a sexually subservient role, and kills eros (Griffin 1981).

Prostitution in the United States requires no specific remedy per se in the form of criminalization, decriminalization, or legalization. It will be remedied when women and men in this culture can celebrate their sexuality and their unique identities. It will be remedied when Rita, my colleague and my friend, is no longer a slave. It will be remedied when virulent patriarchal beliefs are held no longer. It will be remedied only when women and men are economically and politically the same.

Notes

1. I use the term *feminist* in its general sense: intending to represent a political position expressing an "opposition to the sexism and patriarchy inherent in most societies" (Lindsey, 1990: 10). I use the term *sociolegal* to express the position that "law cannot be understood without regard for the realities of social life" (Vago 1988: 37).

2. My point here should not be misunderstood. I do not condone or accept the idea that any woman should subject herself to domination and control. My position is that all master-slave relationships are immoral. There is, however, an extensive literature that shows the difficulty most women in society face when

attempting to break out of problematic slave-type relationships. Some individuals do not perceive a way out and therefore appear to be willing participants in a degrading relationship. Benjamin (1988) provides a lucid, feminist, and intersubjective explanation of the problem.

3. Some authors—Catherine MacKinnon (1987), Kathleen Barry (1979, 1985), and Andrea Dworkin (1987), for instance—express no ambivalence in their analyses regarding the harmful consequences of prostitution or other forms of sexual exploitation.

4. A mala in se offense is considered by law to be a behavior that is inherently wrong. An example is rape.

5. The law is written to account for the "willing" participation of a woman in prostitution acts. My position, however, is that the prostitute's "choice" is no more of a voluntary choice than the prisoner's "choice" is to participate in a prison psychotherapy program that will reduce the length of incarceration.

6. Florida Statutes Annotated, 1985, sec. 796.07 (1) (a).

7. New York Penal Law, McKinney 1980, sec. 230.00.

8. Colorado Revised Statutes, 1964, sec. 40-9-14.

9. At least half the states in 1989 maintained an explicit or implicit patron clause that is at least somewhat similar to New York's with respect to specifying the unlawful behavior and the appropriate level of punishment.

10. To criminalize a behavior on the basis of the harm principle means that "a person's liberty may be restricted to prevent physical or psychic injury to other specific individuals; likewise, a person's liberty may be restricted to prevent impairment or destruction of institutional practices and regulatory systems that are in the public interest" (Tong 1984: 13–14). To criminalize a behavior on the basis of legal paternalism means that "a person's liberty may be restricted to protect himself or herself from self-inflicted harm, or, in its extreme version, to guide that person, whether he or she likes it or not, toward his or her own good" (Tong 1984: 14).

II
The Causes of
Sexual Coercion

5

Feminist Explanations: Male Power, Hostility, and Sexual Coercion

Wendy E. Stock

A Feminist Approach to Understanding Sexual Coercion

This chapter applies a feminist analysis to explain the ubiquitous presence of sexual coercion in our society. This analysis defines sexual coercion as power motivated, upholding a system of male dominance. The nature of sexual coercion as socially constructed, learned behavior is linked to socialization influences that affect males, particularly pornography. For females, the effects of living under a reign of sexual terrorism are related to the function of sexual coercion as a mechanism of social control of women.

Feminist theory provides a theoretical basis for the understanding of sexual coercion as a means by which male dominance and power is established and maintained. It can explain why sexual aggression occurs systematically in this culture, perpetrated by a relatively more powerful class of males upon a relatively less powerful class, females, and how our culture supports this type of dominance by eroticizing sexual aggression. (Because rape is primarily perpetrated by men, the generic masculine is used to refer to perpetrators of sexual coercion.) A definition of the feminist approach to sexual coercion has three components:

1. Acknowledgment of the gender differential in power (economic resources, legal rights, and political representation between men and women).

2. Acknowledgment of how these disparities in power affect all social interactions between women and men, as well as individual behavior and psychological issues.

3. Acknowledgment of the principle of hegemonic control: that the class in power will use all means available to control the less powerful class—force, coercion, intimidation, propaganda, and institutional and ideological control—to maintain its advantage, without necessarily conscious intent or design. Goode (1971) stated that all social systems depend on force or its threat for their maintenance.

This struggle is apparent in the case of economic class (opposition by big business to the labor movement, at times including strike-breaking and violence), race (violent opposition to equal rights and desegregation), and gender (opposition to the Equal Rights Amendment, wage and job discrimination, sexual harassment in the workplace, prevalence of spouse abuse, marital rape, and ideological control in the form of pornography, eroticizing violence, degradation, and objectification of women as a legitimate form of sexual entertainment).

The feminist approach to sexual coercion is not an unsubstantiated theory or an empty polemic. It is based on an awareness of the data of material reality. The only assumption is that of the primacy of power imbalance in creating a social function for sexual coercion to ensure its maintenance. Power inequality is seen as the root of all forms of discrimination and violence directed at women; it is the result of and represents an attempt to maintain that imbalance. When this approach is applied to rape, for example, it becomes evident that rape is not only the result of uncontrolled lust, exaggerated gender role behavior, miscommunication, or a misguided desire for physical intimacy. These factors do not sufficiently explain why rape occurs when alternative sexual outlets are always available, including masturbation, when aggression could be exhibited by a nonsexual attack, or where direct communication by the woman is often ignored, not misunderstood by the rapist. Rather, rape and other forms of sexual coercion can be viewed as both the expression and confirmation of male power, dominance, and control of women.

Rape as a Power-Motivated Crime

Feminist theory contends that sexual coercion is motivated by power, not lust. In Groth's (1979a) clinical study of 500 identified offenders, one-third of the offenders were married and sexually active with their wives at the time of their assaults; the majority of the nonmarried sample were actively involved in a variety of consensual sexual relations with others at the time of their offenses. Groth developed a typology of three basic patterns of rape:

1. Anger rape: Sexuality expresses hostility. One rapist in Groth's study claimed, "I wanted to knock the woman off her pedestal, and I felt that rape was the worst thing I could do to her" (p. 14).

2. Power rape: Sexuality becomes an expression of conquest and a means of compensating for underlying feelings of inadequacy and expressing mastery, control, and authority. The characteristic masturbatory fantasy

used by power rapists is the rape myth in which the victim initially resists sexual advances of her assailant; he overpowers her and, in spite of herself, the victim becomes sexually aroused and receptive to his embrace. According to Groth, a common misperception of such rapists is that their victims enjoy the rape, a belief that confirms a sense of control and power.

3. Sadistic rape: Anger and power become eroticized; sexuality itself is transformed into an expression of anger and power. According to Groth, this offender finds the intentional maltreatment of his victim intensely gratifying and enjoys her torment, anguish, distress, helplessness, and suffering. The assault frequently involves bondage and torture and may be accompanied by explicitly abusive acts, such as biting, burning the victim with cigarettes, and flagellation. Often sexual areas of the victim's body (her breasts, genitals, and buttocks) become a specific focus of injury and abuse. Interviews with Groth's sadistic rapists illustrate the quality of violence and dehumanization of the victim: "As my victim's attitude of submission increased, my sexual excitement, proportionately, increased. I was aware that this excitement derived from the prospect of having a young, pure, upperclass girl and bringing her down to my level." "It came out in the fantasy, the power to hurt, taking out an awful lot of hate that I am unable to show otherwise. A combination of hostility and sexual tension" (p. 25).

Groth found that power rapes accounted for 55 percent of his sample, approximately 40 percent were anger rapes, and about 5 percent were sadistic rapes. Since the sample consisted of primarily convicted offenders, the anger rapist percentage may be inflated and the power rapists underrepresented. Typically there is a greater probability of conviction in cases of anger rapes because of the greater physical abuse and thus more corroborating evidence of assault.

MacKinnon (1982b) states that rape is not primarily an act of violence but a sexual act in a culture where sexuality itself is a form of power, where oppression takes sexual forms, and where sexuality is the very "linchpin of gender inequality" (p. 533).

Beneke (1982) discusses the cultural confusion of power, violence, and sexuality that results in the view of normal heterosexual intercourse as an act in which power is gained by the man and lost by the woman. Beneke notes that two apparently conflicting statements are often made about rape: that rape is a crime of violence and has little to do with sex and that it is merely an extension of the sex roles and sexual behavior regularly enacted between men and women. It is clear that the experience of being raped for a woman involves violence and terror and has little to do with meeting her sexual needs. MacKinnon (1982b) identifies the underlying similarity of rape, sexual harassment, and "normal" sexual relations for women within the patriarchy: "Few women are in a position to refuse unwanted sexual initiatives. . . . If sex is ordinarily accepted as something men do to women, the better question would be whether consent is a meaningful concept" (p. 532).

Beneke raises questions concerning what is identified as a sexual need, what distinguishes sexual from nonsexual needs, and whether "ordinary men" are trying to meet sexual needs when they seek to have sex with women. By analyzing the way men talk about sex and women, Beneke examined similarities between ordinary men and rapists and found that a theme common to younger men was to focus on sex as an achievement: gaining possession of a valued commodity, a woman. Beneke identified four factors underlying this construct: status, hostility, control, and dominance. Status, gained through achievement, involves performing, triumphing, conquering, and acquiring status relative to other males by acquiring the woman as a sexual possession. Hostility is expressed as regarding sex as war and triumph as theft. Control is established by controlling the woman's behavior and one's own performance. Dominance includes components of all of these factors. Beneke concludes that for many men, sex has more to do with these factors than with relational sensual pleasure or sexual satisfaction.

Male Dominance and Sexual Coercion

The use of rape by men to maintain or establish power over women and even over other men has been documented historically by Brownmiller (1975). Brownmiller documents hundreds of thousands of rapes committed throughout history to the present and interracially. In all cases, the woman victim is a scapegoat for a system operated by men. Brownmiller's thesis extends through the continuum of sexual coercion: rape in wartime, racially motivated rape, stranger rape, marital and date rape, incest, sexual abuse of children, and sexual harassment. Sexual coercion that occurs in a dependent relationship "weakens a victim's resistance, distorts her perspective, and confounds her will" (p. 283). In all cases, women's sexuality is viewed as a commodity to be taken by force, either because the male initially has more power over the victim or in order to establish and maintain that power relationship. Males want to retain their control of economic, political, and social resources.

Kelley's (1957) personal construct theory posits that a person makes social predictions on the basis of personal constructs. Using the Greek myth of Procrustes as a metaphor for this process, individuals try to fit the data of daily experience into their personal constructs. When an individual encounters evidence threatening to invalidate these constructs, the revisions required may be of such magnitude that he chooses instead to "make the people fit the construct bed his system provides" (p. 279). Hostility occurs when the individual has wagered more on his personal constructs than he can afford to lose. For example, in the case of rape, the rapist ignores data indicating that the victim is a human being, an equal, another person like himself, in order to fit the data into his view of social reality, which maintains that women are subordinate, not fully human, and controllable by men. In fact, rapists typically attempt to override any attempt by the victims to represent themselves as individual human beings, becoming angered when they are forced to view their victim as a person rather than as an object representing a hated, subordinate class. Women are seen as a gender class rather than as having individual characteristics. This accounts for the age range seen in female rape victims, extending from infancy to extreme old age.

Any movement toward equal status is threatening and disconfirming for men who feel that females are subordinate to males. Rape also exists in societies in which women are completely oppressed and pose no threat to men's control of social, political, and economic resources. Men rape because they have the power and can use it and because the threat of rape and the fear it instills in women serves to maintain their power. Sexual coercion and violence against women is both a reply by males to the challenge by females of their traditional status and an attempt to confirm and maintain their position of power over women. According to Kelley (1957: 278), a hostile person may "resort to vigorous measures in his frantic attempts to make the data fit" his hypothesis. The rapist may see, in his victim's injury, a long-overdue confirmation of his own outlook, a confirmation that has been denied him in the natural state of affairs.

A recent example provides a chilling illustration of this theory: the murder of fourteen women enrolled in engineering school at University of Montreal in December 1989. The murderer, Mark Lepine, age 25, left a suicide note expressing hatred for women, particularly "fucking feminists." He believed that "feminists kind of spoiled his life," according to senior police investigator Jacques Duchesneau after reading the three-page assassination-suicide statement Lepine had left (*Washington Post*, p. A58). Russell and Caputi noted:

> Lepine's crimes were based in this case not on the victims' race, religion, or ethnicity, but on their gender. Lepine targeted young women who had attempted to enter male territory—the very territory that Lepine himself was unable to enter; he failed to complete his application for the graduate engineering program at Montreal. (1990: 17)

Media descriptions of the massacre emphasized the apparent insanity and senselessness of the crime. *The New York Times*, for example, called it "the act of an absolutely demented man" (December 9, 1989: A3). Dr. Yves Lamontagne, director of the Center for Psychiatric Research at Louis-Hippolyte Lafontaine Hospital, stated that mass murders are "not social phenomena, but rather the individual actions of a sick person" (*La Presse*, December 9, 1989: 1). However, he noted, Lepine was known to have led a "relatively uneventful existence." He did not drink or smoke, was not likely a drug user, and had no psychiatric record (Gagnon and Laroche, *La Presse*, December 8, 1989: 1). As noted in a statement released to a feminist newspaper (*Off Our Backs*, March 1990: 35–36), to reduce the killer to a case of deviant psychological makeup with no evidence is to deny that he is a social being. The authors contend that the mass murder of women is a social phenomenon. Russell and Caputi point out:

> To focus on the psychological characteristics and backgrounds of the men who perpetrate hate murders on women obfuscates the social control function they serve. In a racist and/or sexist society, neurotics, psychotics, as well as so-called normals, often act out the ubiquitous racist and/or misogynist attitudes with which they were reared and which they see legitimized everywhere around them.

Another striking illustration of the relationship of male sexual violence to the social control of women is the case of Lawrence Singleton, who in 1969 picked up 15 year-old hitchhiker Mary Bell Vincent, raped her, and chopped off both of her arms with an axe. Singleton's writings and his testimony in court show that he believed he was under attack by the girl, who had somehow "threatened to emasculate me" (Caputi 1987). In this book, the author enumerates historical and current examples of sexual murder as the "ultimate expression of sexuality as a form of power," not "some inexplicable evil or the domain of monsters" only. Sex murder, coined "recreational murder" by the FBI, is part of a tradition named first by Mary Daly as gynocide (1973), later elaborated as "the systematic crippling, raping, and/or killing of women by men . . . the relentless violence perpetrated by the gender class men on the gender class women. . . . Under patriarchy, gynocide is the ongoing reality of life lived by women" (Dworkin 1976: 16, 19).

Sexual Coercion: The Social Control of Women

Caputi (1989: 439) calls rape a "direct expression of sexual politics, a ritual enactment of male domination, a form of terror that functions to maintain the status quo." Sexual coercion, and rape particularly, may then be seen as a societal and political manifestation of Kelley's construct theory of hostility, an attempt to keep women in a state of fear and powerlessness and to protect male power in a patriarchal society. Acts of sexual coercion terrorize women and make them more dependent on males for protection. Brownmiller (1975: 281) writes, "The rapist performs a myrmidon function for all men by keeping all women in a thrall of anxiety and fear. Rape is to women what lynching was to blacks: the ultimate physical threat by which all men keep all women in a state of psychological intimidation."

Riger and Gordon (1981) examined the contention that rape, as a mechanism of social control of women, keeps women in a state of anxiety and encourages the self-imposition of behavioral restrictions in a quest for safety. They found that women do fear crime more than men and engage in more precautionary behaviors. Among women under 35, rape is feared more than any other offense, including murder, assault, and robbery (Warr 1985). Women's fear of crime, especially rape, results in their use of more precautionary behaviors than men (Riger and Gordon 1981; Rozee-Koker 1987) and is the best predictor of the use of both isolation behaviors (Riger, Gordon, and LeBailly 1982) and assertive behaviors (Rozee-Koker 1987). Rozee-Koker (1988) identified the fear of rape as a developmental process that all women experience to varying degrees. Riger and Gordon (1981) found psychosocial and environmental factors associated with high levels of fear among women, including a sense of physical powerlessness, perception of high risk of victimization, and weak feelings of attachment to the neighborhood. Fear levels were strongly associated with the use of either of two types of safety strategies: isolating oneself from danger by avoiding going outside and risk management by using street-savvy tactics (such as wearing shoes that permit one to run or constantly maintaining vigilance in one's surroundings). They conclude that the indirect effects of fear and restrictions of behaviors appear to be much more severe for women in terms of self-restriction and mobility compared to men. The threat of rape functions against women as a mechanism of social control, affecting them disproportionately compared to men and maintaining a self-concept that includes the role of powerless victim.

Rape, as a mechanism of social control, and the fear of rape may serve to enforce a self-concept of passivity, fear, and helplessness in women. Feminist theory on sexual victimization (Brownmiller 1975; Griffin 1971; Medea and Thompson 1974) notes that virtually all adult women live at some level of consciousness with the fear and threat of sexual assault. Burt and Estep (1981: 512) write, "This fear serves to control their behavior, either keeping them passive, dependent, and restricted or blaming and punishing them if they become victims while violating sex-stereotyped expectations." Their data indicate that females develop a sense of sexual vulnerability that has become common sense for women by the time they reach adulthood. Brownmiller (1975), in her analysis of rape as an instrument of social control, emphasized that rape affects all women regardless of actual victimization. Griffin (1979: 21) describes this fear: "The fear of rape keeps women off the streets at night. Keeps women at home. Keeps women passive and modest for fear that they be thought provocative." Riger and Gordon (1981) note that such fear can induce a continuing state of stress in women and can lead to the adoption of safety precautions that severely restrict women's freedom, such as not going out alone at night or staying out of certain parts of town. Unfortunately, these precautions do not guarantee absolute protection, as many rapes (18–56 percent) occur within women's own homes (Schepple and Bart 1983).

Stock, Krause, and Vaughan (1988) investigated the extent to which living in an ongoing state of siege affected the behavior and fear levels among women, regardless of actual history of sexual victimization. High levels of worry were experienced by over 60 percent of the sample on a list of twenty-five typical situations requiring mobility in the physical environment, such as going to a laundromat at night. The more worry women reported, the more restricted their behavior was in terms of frequency of being in the situation. Women participants reported high rates of anxiety symptoms related specifically to fear of rape on five of eight items selected from the DSM-III-R (1987) posttraumatic stress syndrome and Burgess and Holmstrom's (1974) description of rape trauma syndrome. These items included checking doors and windows repeatedly (65 percent), jumping at noises from outside the house (77 percent), rapidly beating or racing heart (73 percent), nightmares and other sleep disturbance (45 percent), and having "irrational" thoughts and feeling silly for having fears (71 percent). These anxiety symptoms were not related to past history of sexual victimization. This preliminary study demonstrated a generalized fear of rape in women accompanied by clinical symptoms common to traumatized individuals, which documents the social creation of psychopathology in women due to living in a constant state of fear. These behaviors, which appear to be psychopathological by male standards, are adaptative and rational for women who must live with the reality of sexual assault.

The Role of Socialization

Feminist theory contends that sexual coercion is learned. Cross-cultural research provides data that render the assumption of an innate basis of sexual aggression questionable. McConahay and McConahay (1977), in a sample of seventeen cultures, found sex role rigidity to be highly correlated with violence, giving more weight to social learning principles than genetic determinants. the authors conclude that sexual arousal, aggression, and traditional sex roles are highly related. Sanday (1981a) found that rape-prone cultures, representing 18 percent of her sample of 156 societies, tended to be "cultures of violence" in which women are regarded as property. Rape-free societies were characterized by sexual equality, leading again to the conclusion that sexual violence occurs within the cultural context of interpersonal violence and male dominance.

A large body of empirical research on the male sex role indicates the pervasiveness and effectiveness of socialization in instilling the values of male dominance. Mosher (1970) identified sex-calloused attitudes that correlated with beliefs that force was justified in obtaining intercourse. Burt (1980) found that sexual stereotyping, adversarial sexual beliefs, and acceptance of interpersonal violence were positively correlated with acceptance of rape myths, defined as beliefs that justify rape and view the female victim as responsible. Check and Malamuth (1983) found that males high on sex-role-stereotyped beliefs were higher on rape myth acceptance, acceptance of violence against women, adversarial sexual beliefs, arousal-to-rape scenarios, and self-stated likelihood of rape. The items on the sex-role-stereotyping scale are clearly related to male dominance and have more to do with power and control in a relationship than merely acceptance of traditional beliefs. Findings on the normative nature of sexual aggression and the high frequency of rape-supportive beliefs suggest the existence of a strong cultural norm supporting the use of aggression by males in a sexual context.

Pornography: The Cultural Eroticization of Sexual Aggression

In our culture, sex is not openly discussed, and sexual information and education remain inadequate. For adolescent males, pornography serves as a major socializing influence, particularly for young males without access to female partners. Through pornography, males learn to define what is sexually arousing. Pornography provides the social constructs of what is later taken for granted as inherent in male sexuality. Given the high rate of sexual aggression committed by males, pornography bears close scrutiny as a major socialization agent. Feminist writers (Brownmiller 1975; Diamond 1980; Dworkin 1981) have asserted that violent depictions of sex in pornography comprise a hate literature against women that has deleterious effects on attitudes and behavior. Recent research supports the contention that pornography, in fusing violent and erotic portrayals in depictions of rape, legitimizes rape.

The rape myth scenario is prevalent in pornography (Smith 1976; Malamuth and Spinner 1980; Burt 1980). In a content analysis of 428 pornographic paperback books, Smith found that almost one-third of the sex acts depicted contained the use of force (physical, mental, or blackmail), predominantly administered by the male to induce the female to engage in sex. The average number of acts depicting rape in these books doubled from 1968 to 1974. Regardless of the level of aggression used against the women, in 97 percent of the cases, the woman has an orgasm, reinforcing the rape myth that women enjoy male sexual aggression.

Rape myth pornography has been found to stimulate rape fantasies (Malamuth 1981a), increase levels of electric shock administered to a female confederate (Donnerstein 1980), reduce perceptions of rape victim trauma while increasing attributions of victim responsibility, and trivialize views of rape as a punishable crime (Malamuth and Check 1985; Malamuth, Haber, and Feshbach 1980). Other research has shown that sexual arousal to sexually violent pictorials and stories is correlated with callous attitudes toward rape and with self-reported likelihood of committing a rape (Malamuth and Check 1981). Zillmann and Bryant (1984) demonstrated trivialization of rape, increases in sex callousness, and decreased support for the women's movement after exposure to nonviolent, degrading and dehumanizing material. This type of material portrays women as "socially nondiscriminating, hysterically euphoric in response to almost any sexual or pseudosexual stimulation, and as eager to accommodate seemingly any and every sexual request" (Zillman and Bryant 1984: 134). Pornography that portrays women in a degraded position, even with no explicit violence has a dramatic impact on both males' and females' beliefs about rape and the role of women in society.

Russell (1988) proposes a theoretical model of pornography as a cause of rape by predisposing some men to rape and undermining some men's internal and social inhibitions against acting out their rape desires. Russell summarizes a considerable body of research on pornography to build a causal theory supported by experimental and correlational data. As Brownmiller (1974: 444) claims, pornography "promotes a climate in which acts of sexual hostility directed against women are not only tolerated but ideologically encouraged."

What is the social function of pornography? What maintains an oppressive ideology is a theoretical question that has been considered with respect to prejudice in general and has specifically been addressed by feminists on the issue of pornography. Leidholdt (n.d.) has proposed that in addition to eroticizing sexual coercion, pornography serves the purpose of objectification in which the powerful group denies physical similarities to the powerless one and exaggerates the physical differences of the less powerful group, which is often portrayed in a caricatured manner. These exaggerated physical differences are used to designate inferior moral, intellectual, and psychological characteristics. Through objectification, the powerful group designates the subjugated group as "not human" and as "the Other" (de Beauvior, 1952). Dworkin (1981: 66) points out that identification with a member of the less powerful group is an extreme psychological threat: "Anything, including memory or conscience that pulls a man toward women as humans, not as objects and not as monsters, does endanger him." Support for this notion is evident in a statement by a leading pornographer, Larry Flynt: "Men all over the country need Hustler . . . they feel inferior and they are . . . because they're afraid of relating to liberated women" (Klein 1978). Flynt's shrewd analysis of pornography bases its marketing appeal on the fear that men have of relating to women as equals and the social function of pornography in bolstering male fantasies and desires to have power over women.

Leidholdt writes that objectification helps to create a gulf between dominant and subjugated groups, preventing the dominant group from identifying and empathizing. The oppressor group effectively exonerates itself from responsibility for its actions and can maintain control with no crisis of conscience. Institutionalized objectification is the psychological foundation of institutional acts of violence; examples include Hitler's Final Solution, prepared for by a systematic propaganda campaign that caricatured Jews as subhuman, and the Mei Lai massacre, made possible in part by encouragement of American soldiers to view Asians as subhuman ("gooks"). In pornography, sexual objectification reduces women to body parts ("tits and ass," "cunts"), sexualized animals (fillies, foxes, beavers, bitches in heat), or corpses. Sexual objectification of women neutralizes sexual violence since it is impossible to commit violence against an object. Leidholdt contends that the sexual objectification of women is the psychological foundation of sexual violence directed against women. The social function of pornography is to provide cultural justification and tolerance for the continuing domination of women by men and the sexual victimization of women.

Consistent with Leidholdt's analysis, MacKinnon (1986) maintains that pornography constructs the meaning of sex in our culture:

> Men treat women as who they see women as being. . . . In pornography, women desire dispossession and cruelty. Men, permitted to put words (and other things) in women's mouths, create scenes in which women desperately want to be bound, battered, tortured, humiliated, and killed. Or merely taken and used. This is erotic to the male point of view. Subjection itself, with self-determination ecstatically relinquished, is the

content of women's sexual desire and desirability. Women are there to be violated and possessed, men to violate and possess them. . . . In pornography, the violence is the sex. The inequality is sex. . . . If there is no inequality, no violation, no dominance, no force, there is no sexual arousal. (pp. 65, 75)

In this view, normal sexuality has come to include force and domination, echoing Beneke's (1982: 16) observation: "For a man, rape has little to do with sex, we may as well add that sex itself often has little to do with sex, or, if you like, that rape has plenty to do with sex as it is often understood and spoken about by men."

Conclusion: Sexual Coercion as Sexual Terrorism

Sheffield (1984: 6) defined sexual terrorism as a system by which males frighten and, by frightening, control and dominate females. Sexual terrorism had five components: ideology, propaganda, indiscriminate and amoral violence, voluntary compliance, and society's perception of the terrorist and the terrorized. The ideology of patriarchy asserts the superiority of males, the inferiority of females, and males' right to uphold this structure with violence, thus providing the rationale for sexual terrorism. The propaganda of sexual terrorism is most clearly seen in pornography but is present in all expressions of the popular culture—films, television, music, literature, advertising—as well as in science, medicine, and psychology. Indiscriminate and amoral violence, the kingpin of sexual terrorism, renders every female a potential target of violence at any age, time, or place. Sheffield (1984) points to the amorality that pervades sexual violence; child molesters, incestuous fathers, wife beaters, and rapists often do not understand that they have done anything wrong. The fourth component of terrorism, voluntary compliance, is created by female sex role socialization that "in effect, instructs men to be terrorists in the name of masculinity and women to be victims in the name of femininity" (Sheffield 1984). Finally, in sexual terrorism, the victim is blamed, the offender excused. In contrast to political terrorism, in which we sympathize with the victim, women who have been sexually terrorized are frequently seen as being responsible for their victimization and the offender is viewed as "sick" and in need of compassion and treatment or as acting out normal male impulses.

Returning to Kelley's (1957) personal construct theory, it is clear that the dimensions of dominance, power, acceptance of rape, and interpersonal violence toward women, and sex-role-stereotyped beliefs function to structure the worldview and the behavior of males in this society. Male hostility toward women is a socially structured event. Using Kelley's (1957:

278) interpretation, the person who is hostile will make "frantic efforts to make data fit his hypotheses, sometimes resorting to vigorous measures." Sexual coercion by men serves the function of creating a state of sexual terrorism for women, with the intent and effect of maintaining social control of women. Although it may be in the short-term political and economic interests of males to maintain their individual and class domination of women, I hope that males can be reeducated and resocialized so that they no longer define as in their interests the maintenance of a position of control over women, particularly using sexual coercion as a means of enforcement. Historically, however, one class has never voluntarily relinquished power to another without a struggle. For sexual coercion to cease, women must accrue enough power through increased access to concrete resources, expertise, and status to make it less possible for males to continue to maintain constructs and beliefs that stipulate male domination of females. As Chisholm (1970: 45) states, "One guideline for achieving change is the taking of power, as no one is giving it away."

6

Individual Psychological and Social Psychological Understandings of Sexual Coercion

Barry Burkhart
Mary Ellen Fromuth

By its diversity, sexual coercion does not lend itself to any single theoretical or conceptual account. However, across the many different events subsumed under this term, there are several theoretical threads and empirical links common to the variety of behavioral outcomes that constitute the universe of sexual coercion. For example, the most evident fact about perpetrators of sexual coercion is that, with few exceptions, they are male. In rape, both stranger and acquaintance forms, child sexual abuse, both intra- and extrafamilial, and sexual harassment, men are the usual perpetrators. This fact must be a centerpiece in all conceptual accounts and should serve as an empirical link across the different domains of sexual coercion.

A second empirical fact about sexual coercion is that it occurs with extraordinary frequency. Juxtaposed to this extraordinary frequency is a curious corollary: many forms of sexual coercion have been characterized by an extraordinary invisibility (Burkhart and Bohmer in press; Koss 1989). In fact, the "discovery" of sexual coercion is recent. The combined vision and voices of feminist social critics (Brownmiller 1985) and feminist social scientists (Koss 1990; Russell 1984; Burt 1980) led to the recognition of rape as a social problem and contributed to the "rediscovery" of child sexual abuse (Finkelhor 1979b). Most of these same writers interpret this invisibility as part of the social psychological context supportive of the victimization of women and children.

Yet another empirical finding with considerable significance for conceptual accounts of sexual coercion derives from the fact that sexual coercion occurs more typically not in unusual or unique circumstances such as criminal events or wars but within the most central and ordinary roles and activities in the lives of women and children. Victimization does not usually happen in dark alleys or battlefields, with strange or even particularly deviant men. Instead, what is most characteristic of sexual coercion is that "such extraordinary events occur in the most ordinary social contexts" (Mandoki and Burkhart in press). Thus, as Klein (1981) argues in his sociohistorical review, what distinctly defines the victimization of women is that it is embedded in their most central and usual social roles as childbearers, nurturers, workers, and sexual partners. The reality of sexual violence of women is that as a child, an adolescent, and an adult, a woman is most likely to be victimized by her families, her familiars, and her intimate partners (Finkelhor 1979b; Burkhart and Stanton 1988; Finkelhor and Yllo 1985). A similar situation exists with children. Children, both boys and girls, are not typically molested by "dirty old men" or by the proverbial stranger with candy but by those known to them—their parents, friends of the family, and authority figures, including teachers (Faller 1989; Finkelhor 1979b; Finkelhor et al. 1990).

In this chapter, we provide a psychological and social psychological analysis of sexual coercion that will do justice to these three basic empirical findings: (1) sexual coercion is extraordinarily common, (2) it appears to adhere to the central but ordinary social roles of women and children, and (3) the perpetration of it is primarily a male phenomenon.

Several introductory caveats are in order given this task. The sexual coercion literature tends toward descriptive rather than analytic research. With some exceptions such as the very recent work on sexual arousal in rapists (Blader and Marshall 1989), theory-driven manipulative research is rare. Such a state is typical of new research areas and no great cause for alarm as long as the maturation of the field leads to conceptually based research. In addition to the relatively limited methodological procedures, research tends to be event specific, that is, organized by referent to particular types of sexual coercion. There is, however, a yet unknown degree of overlap among the various sex offenses. Additionally, researchers tend not only to be separated by their different disciplinary contexts but also by their research focus on either victim or perpetrator, with relatively few researchers investigating both. A central purpose of this chapter, like the rest of this book, is to draw together the different perspectives in this area.

Maleness and Sexual Coercion: Psychological Dimensions

Theories about sexual coercion and maleness tend to be event specific, that is, organized by referent to a specific form of sexual coercion. For example, the child sexual abuse model described by Araji and Finkelhor (1986) is not expected to account for rape or sexual harassment. Furthermore, even within any specific type of offense, there is great diversity among perpetrators (Howells, 1981; Knight, Rosenberg, and Schneider 1985). None-theless, common denominators or defining features in addition to gender can be abstracted from the different specific models of sexual coercion.

Child Sexual Abuse

Sexual coercion is gender linked: males are predominantly the perpetrators and females predominantly the victims. Although overall this statement applies to child sexual abuse, some important qualifications need to be made. Although they are less often the victims of sexual abuse than are girls, boys are also molested in substantial numbers (Finkelhor 1979b; Fromuth and Burkhart 1987) and must be considered in any comprehensive theory. Further, although studies with clinical samples of abused boys suggest that males are overwhelmingly the perpetrators (Adams-Tucker 1984, DeJong, Emmett, and Hervada 1982; Faller 1989), the data are not as clear with nonclinical samples of men. Not only do retrospective studies with nonclinical samples of men consistently find a higher rate of female perpetration than found with nonclinical samples of women (Finkelhor 1979b; Finkelhor et al. 1990), but in some nonclinical samples of men, the majority of perpetrators were female (Fritz, Stoll, and Wagner 1981; Fromuth and Burkhart 1987). Although the data in this area are very inconsistent, these findings highlight the need to consider females as possible perpetrators in some contexts. Unfortunately, because of cultural biases as well as their lower frequency, little research has been done with either male victims or with female perpetrators, and most theories have focused exclusively on the male perpetrator. With this caveat in mind, we now review explanations of sexual molestation.

In recognizing the prevalence of child sexual abuse in this society and the preponderance of male perpetrators, Finkelhor and Lewis (1988) describe a number of features in the male socialization process that may contribute toward their propensity for sexual abuse. First, they describe the "oversexualization of needs" in males in which sex becomes a method to meet emotional needs such as for intimacy and closeness. A second feature in the male socialization process that they speculate might contribute toward child sexual abuse is what they term the "sexualization of subordination": males are socialized to prefer sex partners who are smaller, youthful, more vulnerable, more inexperienced, and more dependent—requirements that children fit more so than adult women do. Finally, they suggest that the socialization process might lead males to develop an "empathy-with-children deficiency." Unlike females, males are not socialized into roles of caretakers and nurturers and hence may not develop the empathy to understand the effects that sexual abuse might have on children. Additionally, as Russell and

Finkelhor (1984) note, men's lower likelihood of being the victims of sexual aggression might also contribute to less empathy for the plight of the sexual abuse victim.

To date, although there has been considerable speculation about how the male socialization process might contribute toward child sexual abuse, the research has not been as forthcoming as it has been with rape. Evidence from the research on attitudes toward child sexual abuse suggests, however, that males indeed may have less empathy for sexual abuse victims than do females. Specifically, compared to women, men tend to blame the incest victim more (Jackson and Ferguson 1983), to view incest as having less serious effects (Eisenberg, Owens, and Dewey 1987), to underestimate the frequency of father-daughter incest (Attias and Goodwin 1985), and to overestimate the frequency of false allegations of child sexual abuse (Attias and Goodwin 1985). These data seem to provide at least indirect support for Finkelhor and Lewis's model.

Over the years, in an effort to begin the process of empirically examining the sexual molestation of children by males, several attempts to classify child molesters have been made (Groth 1982; Knight, Carter, and Prentky 1989). This is an extraordinarily difficult task because of the diversity of events (one incident of fondling versus years of sexual intercourse, the presence or absence of force), the diversity of victims (boys, girls, infants, adolescents), and the diversity of perpetrators (older children, heterosexual pedophiles, homosexual pedophiles, strangers, fathers, situational offenders) involved. The term *child sexual abuse* covers such a wide range of events and behaviors and includes such a wide range of offenders that one can not speak very meaningfully of the typical child molester.

Recognizing the diversity of perpetrators, Araji and Finkelhor (1986) propose a multifactor approach to studying sexual molestation. In their review of the literature, they identify four types of theories that seem to encompass most explanations of child molestation. Araji and Finkelhor view these factors as complementary rather than competing and note that frequently more than one of the factors may be involved in any particular case. They also stress that these factors can be seen from both an individual psychopathology perspective and a sociocultural perspective. The first factor, emotional congruence, encompasses theories that seek to explain why for some men, sexual molestation seems to be fitting an emotional need. The emotional need, they note, may be due to factors such as low self-esteem, arrested psychosexual development, or the need to feel dominant over a sex partner. A second set of theories recognizes that children are a source of sexual arousal for some men. Clearly some molesters have a pattern of sexual arousal toward children (Freund and Blanchard 1989; Marshall, Barbaree, and Christophe 1986). Although the source of this pattern of behavior is uncertain, Araji and Finkelhor suggest that pornography and early sexual history may be implicated in this deviant arousal.

The aspect of early sexual history that has received the most attention to date is the early sexual victimization of the child molester. It is frequently, although clearly too simply, proposed that in response to abuse, females turn their anger inward, while males externalize their anger and may later direct this anger at children in the form of abuse. Studies of child molesters do suggest that a disproportionate number were sexually abused as children (Groth 1979b; Longo 1982; Seghorn, Prentky, and Boucher 1987). As Finkelhor (1986) notes, however, there are methodological limitations in these studies, and direct causal links are impossible to draw. A third set of theories, and one that Araji and Finkelhor conclude has some research support, concerns what they term blockage. This set of theories suggests that some men turn their interest to children because more appropriate sources for emotional and sexual gratification are blocked; for example, they may have difficulty in relating to adult women and repressive sexual attitudes. The final set of theories (disinhibition) attempts to explain why some men are not inhibited by the cultural sanctions against sexual molestation. Araji and Finkelhor speculate senility, mental retardation, and alcohol play a disinhibiting role. Indeed, there is some evidence that alcohol plays a disinhibiting role in some sexual abuse offenses (Araji and Finkelhor 1986).

Sexual Coercion of Adult Females

An examination of the psychological features of male sexual coercion of adult females, despite the differences in types of offenses such as stranger rape and acquaintance rape, uncovered a relatively consistent set of findings descriptive of perpetrators. Further, what is characteristic of these data is that no single variable or single class of variables has been found to be a very powerful predictor. Rather, there is a converging consensus that conceptual and empirical accounts of sexual coercion must be described by complex, multivariate models (Hall 1990; Malamuth 1988).

Such comprehensive, complex models are not yet available. Thus, the focus in the following review will be on examining and evaluating those classes of variables likely to be salient in the development of such models. Examinations of current literature suggest four variable domains relevant to the psychological understanding of adult coercive sexual conduct: misogynist beliefs and attitudes, aggressive patterns and motives, characterological and personality functioning, and sexual motives and arousal patterns.

Misogynist Beliefs and Attitudes. Perhaps one of the earliest and most consistent findings in the empirical literature about sexual coercion is the link of generally misogynist attitudes, specific rape-supportive attitudes, and all forms of sexual coercion (Burt 1980; Burkhart and Stanton 1988; Craig in press; Hall 1990). Drawing on feminist analyses (Brownmiller 1975; Burt 1980; Clark and Lewis 1977; Weis and Borges 1973) conceptually linking sexist cultural contexts and sexual violence, researchers have examined, at the individual level, the connection of such variables as stereotyped views of sexual and gender roles, adversarial sexual beliefs, and rape myth acceptance with the coercive sexual behavior of sexually aggressive males (Hall 1990). Because these processes reflect fundamental cultural values, we discuss these more fully in the section on social-cultural foundations. However, it must be understood that these values have a role in the individual psychologies of offenders. Curiously, however, the mechanisms by which such beliefs and attitudes specifically cause or catalyze the development of sexual coercive behavior have not been investigated. A critical finding, with considerable conceptual implications, is that such beliefs and attitudes are demonstrated early in adolescence. By ages 12 to 14, a relatively high percentage of males (and females) believe that forceful sexual interactions are legitimized by the female's having a bad reputation, being a tease, or using drugs or alcohol (Goodchilds et al. 1988).

Too little attention has been paid to these developmental data. If such values and beliefs function as organizing factors for the learning of later sex role and courtship patterns, then it may be the case that these are, in fact, the foundation for the development of later sexually coercive conduct.

Aggressive Style. Aggressive and/or antisocial conduct also appears to be important in predicting sexual coercion. Several studies (Calhoun et al. 1986; Malamuth 1986; Rapaport and Burkhart 1984) have found that men with histories of sexually coercive conduct were most likely to have conduct disorder symptomology, to be less well socialized and more impulsive, and to be involved in physical violence. Additionally, endorsement of force and acceptance of interpersonal violence (particularly toward women) are characteristic of these men. Finally, in a recent study, Erway (1990) found a relatively high degree of co-morbidity between sexual coercion and interpersonal aggression. Interestingly, the most distinct group were those who were both sexually and physically aggressive, suggesting a synergistic interaction of these two classes of aggressive behavior.

Personality Functioning. Early research addressing the personality functioning of sexually coercive men found that rapists tended to have characteristic personality test profiles (Armentrout and Hauer 1978; Rada 1978; Rader 1977); however, these studies have been criticized for methodological shortcomings, and recent reviews have emphasized the heterogeneity of personality profiles among sex offenders (Hall 1990). When personality functioning is identified as a contributing factor in more complex, multivariate models, however, it is clear that it has a role in defining and describing coercively sexual behavior. For example, Rapaport and Burkhart (1984) found that sexually coercive males could be discriminated from noncoercive males by a complex, multivariate model that included personality variables of low levels of interpersonal responsibility and low levels of socialization.

Consistent with this constellation of personality features, Mosher and his colleagues have proposed that a critical personality variable undergirding sexual coercion is hypermasculinity. Mosher and Tomkins (1987) argued that the socialization of the hypermasculine man results in an overvaluing of a definition of masculinity as being tough, unfeeling, and violent. The consequent personality development produces a need to risk danger for excitement, minimization of empathic responding, and proclivities toward coercive sexual conduct. Sexual aggression, because it contains attributes associated with masculinity, strength, power, forcefulness, domination, and toughness, may be regarded by these men as a properly hypermasculine activity that validates and affirms their masculinity. In a study by Mosher and Anderson (1986), this "macho" personality constellation was found to be correlated with coercion and/or exploitative sexual tactics. Cole (1988) too found that hypermasculinity was one of the strongest correlates of involvement in coercive sexual conduct.

Sexual Styles. Finally, different sexual arousal patterns and a distinctive set of motives for sexual behavior appear to characterize sexually coercion. Early research by Kanin (1967b, 1969) found evidence of a distinctive sexual style displayed by sexually coercive men characterized by some seemingly contradictory features; for example, despite greater sexual experience, sexually coercive men were more dissatisfied with their level of sexual activity and described a pattern of intensely seeking sexual outlets. Initially Kanin (1969) attributed this finding to the pressure from peers for sexual activity. However, recent work suggests that this style may be connected to a more fundamental and distinctive orientation to sexual activity. Burkhart and Stanton (1988) have suggested, similar to Araji and Finkelhor's analysis of child sexual abusers, that the sexual behavior of sexually aggressive males is motivationally overdetermined. That is, for these men, sex comes to serve many motives: power, anger, neediness, as well as purely sexual motives. Cole (1988) found that nonconsensual sexual behavior was best predicted by anger and dominance motives for sex, whereas noncoercive sexual behavior was best predicted by motives of love and hedonism.

The predominance of such nonsexual, compensatory motives in the psychological profiles of incarcerated rapists has led Groth (1979a) to describe rape as a pseudosexual act. Based on his conclusion that power and anger needs are the salient motives for rape, Groth developed a taxonomy of rapists based on the relative primacy of these motives. According to Groth, the three basic rape patterns are anger rape, in which sex serves to express hostility; power rape, in which sex is a tool for domination and conquest; and sadistic rape, in which anger and power are eroticized.

This conceptual tradition has led to the development of research programs guided by a search for the specific components of arousal for rapists and pedophiles (Abel et al. 1977). In a well-reasoned review of this research paradigm, Blader and Marshall (1989) argued that, unlike pedophilia or fetishism, rape of adult women does not appear to be driven by the pull of some deviant stimulus configuration. Thus, unlike pedophiles, who may show a clear erotic preference for children, rapists (except for rare sadistic types) do not demonstrate an erotic preference for the stimulus configuration of an assault. Instead, Blader and Marshall argue, what characterizes rapists is the failure to inhibit arousal in the context of coercive interactions. Consistent with this analysis is the finding that stimuli involving portrayals of sexual arousal by the woman being raped result in the disinhibition of arousal, even by normal men (Malamuth 1986; Malamuth and Check 1983). This finding suggests that the erotic response is such a prepotent stimulus for arousal that in many contexts, particularly if there is any ambiguity about the social meaning of the situation, it can disinhibit arousal even for normal men. However, sexually coercive men, driven by their particular cognitive biases, are disinhibited in contexts that typically inhibit arousal and, in fact, may selectively attend to or misperceive a woman's response (Erway 1990; Rapaport and Burkhart 1987).

Sexual Coercion as a Social Phenomenon: Adult Women

Sexual coercion cannot be defined as an event distinct from and anomalous to its social-cultural context. Indeed, prominent in the literature is the idea that sexual coercion "represents a natural consequence of the firmly embedded cultural tradition of male dominance coupled with an acceptance of interpersonal violence toward women" (Burkhart and Stanton 1988: 55). Thus, to describe fully the conceptual network defining sexually coercive processes, these pathognomic cultural processes and their "natural" consequences must be identified and linked to the sexually coercive behavior. As might be anticipated, this is a difficult task given the complexities of drawing clear, much less causal, connections between behavior and sociocultural contexts, norms, and processes. Given that sexually coercive behavior is typically hidden and cultural processes are, by their nature, the invisible tracks of social movement, mapping these connections is complicated and difficult. Nonetheless, a conceptual network linking sexual coercion to the fabric of social processes has been described eloquently by several theoretical reviews (Brownmiller 1975; Russell 1984; Weis and Borges 1973). Here we provide an outline and review of the salient cultural variables and a specification of the mechanisms by which these cultural processes produce sexually coercive conduct. The variables identified by conceptual and empirical accounts as critical to sexual coercion can be separated into three broad domains:

1. Gender socialization and power differentials.
2. Sexually coercive cognitive schemas and beliefs.
3. Social-sexual interaction scripts.

Although these classes of variables are presented as separate domains, considerable overlap exists among them, and all are dynamically intertwined; thus, these variables interact to enhance and potentiate each other.

Gender socialization is the foundation for sexual coercion. As summarized by Burkhart and Stanton (1988: 55) in a review of acquaintance rape, "differential gender role socialization acts to normalize rape and promote its occurrence through the promulgation of a constellation of rape-supportive beliefs and patterns of interaction between males and females that are conducive to sexual aggression."

This constellation of rape-supportive beliefs belongs to the general domain of sexually coercive biased cognitive schemas, which are those systems of beliefs, attitudes, and information-processing heuristics serving as the catalysts for sexual coercion. Brownmiller (1975) was among the first to define this domain by her description of culturally transmitted belief systems condoning rape. Labeling these "the deadly male myths of rape" (p. 311), she persuasively argues that beliefs such as "all women want to be raped," "no woman can be raped against her will," and "she was asking for it" function as disinhibiting social forces legitimizing and encouraging male sexual violence. Subsequent empirical demonstration that these myths do exist and are endorsed by a substantial proportion of the general public (Burt 1980; Field 1970) supports Brownmiller's thesis. Additional research has demonstrated that these beliefs serve as heuristics in decision making and attributions about coercive sexuality.

A large body of literature has found that men assign greater responsibility for rape outcomes to the victims than do women (Calhoun, Selby, and Warring 1976; Cann, Calhoun, and Selby 1979; Thornton and Ryckman 1983). Similar attributions are made in terms of sexual harassment victims (Jensen and Gutek 1982). These belief structures also appear to affect one's capacity to empathize with victims. In several studies, men tend to identify more with rapists (Krulewitz 1981), while women identify more with victims (Smith et al. 1976). Using the Rape Empathy Scale, which they constructed, Deitz and coworkers (1982) found that females had greater empathy for victims and that such empathy was a better predictor of causal attributions about rape than a traditional measure of attitudes toward women.

Curiously this failure of empathy in mediating attributions is most powerful in nonstranger contexts. The greater the degree of acquaintance is between victim and offender, the less "serious" the event is judged to be (L'Armand and Pepitone 1982) and the less likely the incident is acknowledged to be a rape or sexual harassment (Gutek and Dunwoody-Miller 1986; Klemmack and Klemmack 1976; Skelton and Burkhart 1980).

The interaction of these attributional biases with norms regarding courtship provides a particularly fertile context for coercive sexuality (Weis and Borges 1973). In this culture, males are supposed to pursue sexual contact, and thus all strategies for having sex are stereotypically masculine; women are responsible for limit setting and thus all strategies for avoiding sex are stereotyped as feminine (LaPlante, McCormick and Brannigan 1980; McCormick 1979). Examining the components of these sexual scripts, it is evident how powerfully sexual coercion can be the result of their enactment (Craig in press). For example, Peplau, Rubin, and Hill (1977: 96) found, in a longitudinal study of couples, that "men continue to exert positive control; they play the role of sexual initiator. . . . Women continue to hold negative control, however; they can reject the man's advances or slow the pace of sexual intimacy."

Additionally, these expectations from the sexual script can potentiate sexual coercion when linked to differential gender-mediated expectations. Knox and Wilson (1981), for example, found that males and females had large discrepancies regarding the norms for timing of sexual interaction in a dating situation. Half of the males but only one-quarter of females surveyed believed that intercourse was appropriate by the fifth date.

Such normative misunderstandings are often linked to communication problems. Brodyaga and associates (1975) describe males' belief that females' resistance to sexual overtures constitutes a pseudo-resistance displayed only as ego-saving exercises. Further, what constitutes sexual behavior itself is often not clear. In a series of studies, Abbey (1982, 1987; Abbey and Melby 1986) has demonstrated that men "sexualize" behavior to a greater extent than females, attributing much greater sexual intent than females to various behaviors. The implication is that men define situations as sexual, whereas women do not; thus women may be ill prepared to deal with sexual overtures. Muehlenhard (1988a, 1988b) has also demonstrated how this normative and interactional misunderstanding increases the risk of coercive sexual outcomes. Adding alcohol to this cauldron of miscommunication, misunderstanding, and misbehavior increases the volatility of the mix (George and Marlatt 1986; Kanin 1984), particularly given that alcohol is used by men to compromise women's ability to resist and is also a disinhibiting cue for males' aggressive conduct (Craig, Kalichman, and Follingstad 1989; Kanin 1984; Muehlenhard and Linton 1987).

In summary, the norms and expectations of heterosexual interactions, particularly in a courtship context, are likely to mediate sexually coercive outcomes. Juxtaposed with sexually coercive males' patterns of irresponsibility, poor socialization and empathy, and overdetermined and even predatory sexual patterns, the high rates of sexual coercion are not so surprising.

Children, Coercion, and Context

Beyond its sheer magnitude, one of the more startling findings of epidemiological research on child sexual abuse is how embedded the sexual abuse of children is in the basic fabric of the abused child's life. One of the consistently documented findings in the field is the fairly low rate of abuse by strangers (Finkelhor 1979b) and the high rate by known and frequently trusted adults. To understand the sexual coercion of children, it is necessary to examine not anomalous social contexts but the ordinary settings of a child's life.

The initial approach by the molester may first occur in the context of what appears to be a normal or even supportive relationship. Indeed, referring to sexual abuse prevention strategies for children, Conte, Wolf, and Smith (1989: 330) conclude that "teaching children about the relationship warning signs so that they can identify risk situations seems virtually impossible, since so many of the relationship risk factors are normal, and often positive aspects (e.g., an adult paying attention to a child) of adult-child relationships." Consistent with this, studies with offenders (Budin and Johnson 1989; Conte, Wolf, and Smith, 1989) indicate that the majority of perpetrators describe engaging a child in a relationship, such as by trying to be their friend, before abusing them. In line with Sgroi, Blick, and Porter's (1982) description of the progressively sexually intrusive nature of these relationships, Berliner and Conte (1990: 37), in a study detailing the victimization process from the victim's perspective, found that the sexualization of the relationship typically occurs gradually and "may begin with normal affectional contact or in the context of ordinary activities." It is this ordinariness of the abuse that may first entice the child into the activity and then make it difficult for the child to extricate himself or herself from the situation. The perpetrator may use the child's initial compliance to coerce the child's continued participation and/or silence. The child, having initially complied, also may feel trapped in the relationship and may subsequently feel he or she also bears the responsibility.

This process of "grooming" children preparatory to abusing them is a characteristic modus operandi of the child molester's repertoire of engagement with children. Much of this behavior is almost indistinguishable, in its early stages, from the ordinary nonabusive social affection and attention commonly directed toward children. Thus, the molester can insinuate himself into the child's world without alarming the child or the child's guardian. Furthermore, part of the internal rationalization of the child molester is that his grooming the child is good for the child. This perception may be reinforced by guardians who reinforce the molester's grooming by describing how nice he is and how well he works with children.

Once involved in such a relationship, in order to survive psychologically the child may accommodate to the situation (Summit 1983). As others (Briere 1989; Courtois 1988; Summit 1983) have detailed, a child's perception may change to fit the reality of the abuse until eventually the child becomes isolated in a reality defined by the molester and his abusive interactions and may view the abuse as inevitable.

As with women, children are typically abused in the context of engaging in their social role. Child sexual abuse is best conceptualized as an abuse of power. An older child, an adolescent, or an adult misuses his/her greater strength, greater knowledge, or position of authority to molest. The inherent subordinate role of children then places them at risk for sexual molestation. Children are raised to obey adults, and even adolescents, in positions of authority. As Summit (1983) notes, although we give permission to our children to avoid strangers, we do expect them to obey and be affectionate toward caretakers. Additionally, children are socialized to depend on adults for support and for guidance. It is this trust and dependency that the molester exploits.

Some children may be more at risk for sexual abuse because of their greater emotional neediness, which is evident to and exploited by molesters. Self-report studies with convicted abusers (Budin and Johnson 1989; Conte, Wolf, and Smith 1989) indicate that some molesters specifically target vulnerable children for abuse. Although methodological issues with correlational studies preclude any firm conclusions, studies with victims also suggest that some children are more at risk for abuse than others (Finkelhor and Baron 1986b; Finkelhor et al. 1990). Finkelhor and Baron (1986b) conclude that, in general, the background variables that have the strongest connection to the sexual abuse of females are those dealing with family factors, including parental absences, marital conflict, poor relationship with parents, and the presence of a stepfather. In a recent retrospective study with a national nonclinical sample, Finkelhor and associates (1990) found that the single most powerful predictor of abuse in both sexes was an unhappy family life growing up. This factor continued to be a strong predictor of sexual abuse even when only extrafamilial cases were considered, suggesting it is indeed a risk factor rather than a consequence of abuse.

In attempting to explain the relationship between these background factors and being at risk for sexual abuse, Finkelhor and Baron (1986b) propose that these factors may lead to less supervision of the child and/or greater emotional neediness, both of which may make the child a target for abuse. They note that such a child "may be more amenable to the offers of friendship, appreciation, and the material rewards that the offender makes, and she may be less able to stand up for herself" (p. 77). This description is chillingly similar to the type of child some offenders report targeting. For example, in interviewing offenders about how they selected children, Conte, Wolf, and Smith (1989: 296) received responses that included "quieter, easier to manipulate, less likely to object or put up a fight, goes along with things" and "I would probably pick the one who appeared more needy, the child hanging back from others or feeling picked on by brothers and sisters. The one who likes to sit in my lap. The one who likes the attention and stroking." It should be stressed, however, that although some children may be more vulnerable and at higher risk for abuse, many children are going to be abused regardless of their own characteristics or their own behavior.

The status of children in this society adds to the vulnerability of all children. As Summit so eloquently described, children are powerless and lacking in credibility. When approached by an abuser or involved in an abusive relationship, children may not object to or report the abuse for fear that no one will believe or support them.

What happens if they do disclose the secret also illustrates the powerlessness of children and their lack of credibility. Not only may they not be believed by family members, but the children may not be believed by professionals. Everson and Boat (1989), in a study of false allegations of child sexual abuse, found a subset of child protective workers who appeared to be predisposed to question the credibility of a child. Other studies examining attitudes and reporting trends have found that some health (Eisenberg, Owens, and Dewey 1987) and mental health professionals (Kalichman, Craig, and Follingstad 1988) still hold incest victims at least partially responsible for their own victimization. In the light of this and the other pressures children who report receive, children's false retractions of allegations of abuse are understandable.

There are curious parallels to this particular social context of child sexual abuse in the process of rape, particularly acquaintance rape. Perhaps the most striking is the manner by which perpetrators of both child sexual abuse and acquaintance rape rationalize their behavior. Both child molesters and rapists deny the existence of any misconduct by reference to either social myths or their own idiosyncratic rationalization. The net effect of this process is to deny the status of victimization to the victim. Thus, both child sexual abuse and acquaintance rape survivors do not define this victimization as real or consequential and, in fact, often assume responsibility for their own victimization. The child abuse victim's accommodation to his or her victimization may result in a refutation of the actuality of the event. And in acquaintance rape, Sommerfeldt, Burkhart, and Mandoki (1989) found that almost half of victims engaged in some form of self-blame for their victimization. Thus, it is not surprising that themes of guilt and shame have been found to be common themes in the recovery of child sexual abuse survivors (Courtois 1988) and in acquaintance rape survivors (Mandoki and Burkhart 1989; Sommerfeldt, Burkhart, and Mandoki 1989), as well as in sexual harassment survivors (Jenson and Gutek 1982).

Conceptually and empirically, the links between women and children's powerlessness and sexist, rape-supportive beliefs and the sexual exploitation of children and women are evident. Sexual coercion does not occur in a cultural vacuum; it is best understood as an epiphenomenon of a society that establishes and perpetuates the cultural role of women and children as legitimate objects of victimization.

Summary and Conclusions

Accounting for the ordinary is often the most difficult of tasks, particularly when the ordinary is not at all obvious. Were sexual coercion an infrequent event occurring in anomalous contexts and entirely predictable based on the psychological analysis of a few aberrant men, then the focus of this chapter would have been much narrower, and, as a consequence, probably much clearer. However, sexual coercion is woven into the fabric of our cultural, social, and personal psychologies and is not easily defined or disentangled from this context. Thus, although so common as to be ordinary, it is not at all obvious how sexual coercion should be understood. Our hope is that this chapter will have practical utility to the understanding of sexual coercion.

We conclude by drawing out several implications of our analysis. First, echoing many reviewers and researchers (Brownmiller 1975; Burt 1980), it is important to acknowledge the embeddedness of sexual coercion in the structure and processes of our culture. Failing to do so leaves researchers and policymakers blind to the reality of social power and powerlessness as mediators of sexual violence and can lead to the kinds of restrictive and wrong attributions seen in "blaming the victim" rape myths. The recent case in Florida where a jury found a perpetrator not guilty of rape because the victim was not wearing panties and thus "got what she deserved" is but a concrete illustration of a still powerful social current holding women and children responsible for their own victimization. Only until we acknowledge, in Pogo's words, "I have seen the enemy and they are us," can we begin the necessary task of "revamping a significant proportion of our social values" (Brownmiller 1975: 229).

Further, although we must understand this social context, our analysis is not complete until we attend to the psychological functioning of men. Clearly not all men are equally vulnerable to the cultural diathesis of violence and sexual aggression, so we must continue to uncover and identify those individual difference variables that make a difference in men's propensity toward sexual coercion. In this view, we also call for research addressed to those factors that buffer males from these cultural diatheses. Too little attention has been paid to variables that have the potential to be useful in developing programs of prevention and intervention, a task of pressing significance.

7

Coercive Sexuality of Men: Is There Psychological Adaptation to Rape?

Randy Thornhill
Nancy Wilmsen Thornhill

This chapter outlines a hypothesis about coercive sexuality derived from theoretical (evolutionary) biology: that men's coercive sexuality reflects sex-specific psychological adaptation to rape, that is, psychological features of men designed by a history of evolution by selection in the context of coercive sex and having the evolutionary function of motivating and regulating men's coercive sexuality. If this hypothesis is true, there must exist design for rape itself in the psychology of men's sexual motivation and action. Rape stems from psychological adaptation. However, it has not been determined if rape is an incidental effect of psychological adaptation to circumstances other than rape or is due to psychological adaptation to rape itself. We discuss the natural history of men's coercive sexuality, laboratory studies of men's sexual arousal, and other information on men's sexuality in the light of the hypothesis that the sexual psychology of men contains psychological design for the purpose of rape. Current knowledge of the coercive sexuality of men is consistent with this hypothesis but cannot demonstrate adaptation to rape. Whether or not there is adaptation to rape in the psychology of men, research on the evolved design of men's sexual psychology could lead to a much better understanding of rape because such research can identify the specific environmental information that the sexual psychology of men processes and therefore the circumstances that determine the use of coercive sex by men. In this chapter, we focus on rape, although we briefly look at other types of sexual coercion, such as sexual harassment and incest.

For useful discussion and/or correspondence about material in this chapter, we thank Laura Betzig, David Buss, Leda Cosmides, Astrid Kodric-Brown, Pete Stacey, Patrick Thornhill, John Tooby, Margo Wilson, and especially Martin Daly and Don Symons. Aubri, Margo, and Patrick Thornhill were inspirational. Steve Andrews's help with library work is greatly appreciated. E. Grauerholz, M. Koralewski, and an anonymous reviewer provided helpful suggestions for improving the manuscript. We thank Irene Farmer for professionally typing the manuscript. We acknowledge the financial support of the Harry Frank Guggenheim Foundation, and R.T. acknowledges the financial support of Paul Risser, vice-president for research at the University of New Mexico, and of the Alexander von Humboldt Foundation.

Background Information

Before we discuss men's sexual coercion and how it bears on the hypothesis of psychological adaptation to rape, we discuss briefly some background information that may be useful for understanding the adaptationist approach.

Adaptation refers to the complexly organized, goal-directed or purposeful phenotypic features of individual organisms [see R. Thornhill (in press), for review]. Adaptations are properties of individuals and not of families, populations, or other groups (Williams 1966). Adaptations are the long-term products of evolution by selection. Although there are several agents of evolution—that is, natural processes that are known to cause evolution or changes in gene frequencies of populations—only selection can make phenotypic design or adaptation.

Selection is nonrandom differential reproduction of individuals. When it acts in a directional cumulative manner over long periods of geological time, it creates complex phenotypic design out of the simple, random genetic variation generated by stochastic evolutionary agents (such as drift and mutation). Selection acts on differences among individuals in fit to their environments, thereby accumulating genes that (through ontogeny) lead to traits that fit individuals to their environments. An adaptation, then, is a phenotypic solution to a past environmental problem that persistently impinged on individuals for long periods of evolutionary time and thereby caused cumulative directional selection, which in turn caused cumulative directional change in the gene pool. Evolution by selection is not a purposive process but incorporates purpose into its products by gradual, persistent effects.

Adaptation is identified by a phenotypic feature that is so complexly organized for some apparent purpose that chance cannot be the explanation for the feature's existence. Thus the feature cannot merely be the chance by-product or incidental effect of an adaptation or the product of random genetic drift. The feature has to be the product of long-term evolution by directional selection. Once a true adaptation is recognized and its apparent purpose perceived, the next step is to examine in detail and fully characterize the functional design of the adaptation to determine the adaptation's actual evolutionary purpose. An adaptation's evolutionary purpose means specifically how the adaptation contributed to reproduction of individuals during its evolution or, put differently, the precise relationship between a phenotypic trait and selection during the trait's evolution into an adaptation (for full discussion of the study of adaptation see R. Thornhill, in press).

Evolutionary Psychology and Rape

Psychological adaptation must causally underlie all human feelings, emotion, learning, and behavior (Cosmides and Tooby 1987; Symons 1987a). Psychological change and behavior are the products of the processing of environmental information by psychological mechanisms. In turn, psychological mechanisms reflect psychological structure and design. Thus, rape must reflect psychological adaptation. An empirical challenge in understanding rape is determining if the psyche of men includes psychological adaptation to the circumstance of coercive sex itself or if rape is an incidental effect of the combination of coercive psychological adaptation to the nonsexual domain of human life and noncoercive sexual psychological adaptation of men.

The hypothesis of psychological adaptation to rape contends that there are psychological mechanisms that function specifically for the purpose of rape because they were designed by selection acting on males in the context of coercive sexuality. More specifically, the selection assumed by the hypothesis is as follows: During human evolutionary history, nonrandom differential offspring production by adult males occurred in the context of sexual access to reproductive-age females who were unwilling to mate. By implication, males whose psychological machinery sexually motivated them to be sexually aroused by, to pursue, and to mate with unwilling females are our evolutionary male ancestors.

Whether or not there is psychological adaptation to rape, rape cannot be fully understood by ideas that are not explicit about the psychological adaptations that control men's sexual motivation and action. Psychological adaptations are information-processing mechanisms that provided solutions to information-processing problems that influenced reproductive fitness during human evolution. As a result of selection during long-term human evolution, human psychological adaptations are specially engineered for processing nonarbitrary environmental information and thereby guiding behavior toward adaptive ends.[1] This psychological information processing is conducted by psychological adaptations of perception, memory storage and retrieval, cognitive analysis, and so forth. Psychological adaptation and design is characterized in evolutionarily functional terms by the kind of information processed and not by neurophysiology or neuroanatomy (Cosmides and Tooby 1987; Tooby and Cosmides 1989); this means that the precise environmental conditions that affect men's coercive (and noncoercive) sexuality will be elucidated only by the kind of information that discovery of the sexual psychology of men is designed by selection to process.

Sex-specific Psychological Adaptation

Implicit in our use of the term *sexual psychology* of men is the assumption that the sexes differ in psychological design in the domain of sexual matters. It is often assumed in the social and behavioral sciences that human psychology is entirely sexually monomorphic in design and is composed of only a few general-purpose learning adaptations (Symons 1987a, 1987b). Given current knowledge of the functional specificity of the vast numbers of adaptations whose functional design is understood (the human heart, for example, is specially designed to pump blood in the human body), as well as theoretical advances in understanding how selection works in molding adaptations as specific solutions to specific environmental problems, it is most likely that the aspect of the human psyche involved with sexual matters is sexually dimorphic. The human psyche is undoubtedly composed of many highly specialized adaptations. Some of them are designed to process information (some of it through learning) that is specific to the very different sexual problems males and females have faced in human evolutionary history (Symons 1987b).

This sexual dimorphism stems from the fact that in humans there is a large sexual asymmetry in the minimal reproductive effort required for the production of offspring. The minimum for a man is a few minutes of time and an energetically cheap ejaculate; the minimum for a woman is nine months of pregnancy and a long period of lactation. This sexual asymmetry during human evolution resulted in males who could gain sexual access to multiple females, outreproducing males who could not. The strong selection on males in the context of competition for sexual access to many females led to the evolution of men's general behavior during interactions with potential mates, and because females were evolving under a different type of selection in the context of competition for mates and under selection to be choosy about mates, a major human sex difference is observed: compared to women, men are less discriminating about sexual partners—they are more motivated to seek copulation with many partners and more eager to include copulation as part of an interaction with the opposite sex. Selection acting on females in the context of competition for mates in human evolutionary history favored females who could gain access to males whose resources and genetic endowment promoted offspring survival. The selection on females associated with competition for multiple mates was weak relative to the same selection on males because sexual access to multiple females by males results in more offspring than access to multiple males by females. Women are more discriminating of mates than men because in human evolutionary history females made a larger minimal investment in offspring (thus losing more reproductive potential than males from a poor mate choice), which resulted in stronger selection on females than on males for mate choice. Furthermore, in humans, females are the objects of more sexual competition than males (and must have been in human evolutionary history as well, given evolved male sexuality); thus females have a greater opportunity than males to choose. (For orientation to the literature on the evolution of human sex differences, see Symons 1979, 1987b; Smith 1984; Buss 1987, 1989; Townsend 1987, 1989.)

Because of the different ways that selection in the context of sexual matters acted on males compared to females during human evolutionary history, evolutionary psychologists believe that the human psyche contains a great deal of sexually dimorphic structure: sex-specific psychological adaptations specialized to deal with the sex-specific sexual environment.

Is Rape Learned? Is It Heritable?

Learning is often used in the social science literature on rape as if a useful or complete explanation is provided by labeling men's and women's sexual behavior as "learned" (for reviews see Russell 1982, 1984; Ellis 1989). Such a view goes against scientific knowledge of ontogeny in two ways: it trivializes the reality of the causal gene-environment interactions during the ontogeny of the behaviors that are subject to the label "learned," and it ignores the vast number of necessary experiences during the ontogeny of any behavior typically referred to as "learned," only a very small number of which would be candidates for the label "learned." The term *learned* is too simplistic by itself to warrant its use as the only or most important causal explanation of any human behavior. Sexual behavior of an individual human develops as the product of the intimate and inseparable interaction of both genes and environment. Social learning is only one of a very large number of necessary environmental influences during the development of the sexuality of a woman or a man. (An excellent overview of the current understanding of ontogeny as it applies to human sexual development is provided by Daly and Wilson [1983: chap. 10].)

We emphasize that the view of men's sexual psychology proposed by the hypothesis of adaptation to rape does not imply the absence of learning. Social and cultural learning experiences during the ontogeny of men's sexuality are central to this perspective; however, the learning process involved is not arbitrary but instead is guided by evolved sexual psychological adaptations that bring about selective perception, cognition, memory, and information evaluation specific to rape.

There is significant interest in the literature of human rape in the issue of the heritability of rape (see Ellis 1989 for review, especially pp. 86–88). *Heritability* is a term that describes the extent to which the variation among individuals in a phenotypic trait is caused by genetic, as opposed to environmental, variation among individuals. (Note that the term *heritability* does not apply to the traits of an individual. The dichotomy between genetics and environment cannot be applied to the features of an individual.) We emphasize that the hypothesis of adaptation to rape does not imply that rape is heritable. That is, the hypothesis does not imply that variation among men in inclination to rape reflects genetic differences. Rather, there is adaptation to rape, and adaptations are species-typical features whose genetic under-pinnings involve genes that are virtually fixed or invariant in the human gene pool. Thus the hypothesis of psychological adaptation to rape predicts that the heritability of the psychological design for rape will be near or at zero. This is not to say that male personality features that may contribute to rape (such as aggression) are not heritable; some may be (Ellis 1989: 86–97), but the heritability of personality features is not relevant to the issue of whether there exists adaptation to rape.

The hypothesis of adaptation to rape proposes that the psychological rape adaptation regulates men's use of coercive sexuality in a facultative way, which is dependent on environmental conditions. During human evolution the causal conditions were associated with adaptive use of rape by human males. The salient variation, then, in men's use of coercive sexuality is predicted to be dependent on variation in the environments experienced by men.

Mating Strategy of Men

According to the hypothesis of adaptation to rape, rape is a sex-specific, species-wide aspect of the evolved mating strategy of men (Shields and Shields 1983; Thornhill and Thornhill 1983). Men's mating strategy consists of three tactics: honest advertisement and courtship, deceptive advertisement and courtship, and coercion. Coerced matings are those achieved by physical force or by explicit or implicit threat of physical or social malice.

The general sex difference in mating strategy can lead to disparity in the evolved self-interests of men and women about whether mating should occur and its timing and frequency of occurrence. Because women are more selective of mates and more interested in evaluating mates and delaying copulation than men, in order to achieve sexual access men often must break through feminine barriers of sexual hesitation, equivocation, and resistance (see Kirkendall 1961 for a review of human heterosexual sexual interactions). Men get women to comply with their wishes to copulate by using all three tactics of their mating strategy. These tactics can be used singly in pursuit of single matings or together in pursuit of single matings.

Coercive Sexual Behavior of Men

It is clear that men frequently include the pursuit of sexual access by coercion in their repertoire of sexual behavior. There is no question that many men's sexual repertoire is a mix of noncoercive and coercive, including physically coercive, approaches.

In addition, men often pursue single matings by using a mix of tactics. It is erroneous in general to dichotomize copulations into those resulting from honest versus deceptive courtship or from force versus nonforce. Courtship and the interactions associated with maintenance of pair-bonds include explicit and implicit promises about commitment that are not always realized, in part because of lack of positive intention (Kirkendall 1961). We suggest that a forced versus unforced dichotomy may apply only to a small subset of human copulations—for example, when a man without any sexual negotiation or honest or deceptive courtship uses physical force or the threat of physical harm to capture and copulate with a woman against her will. The legal system in modern societies is concerned with whether an alleged forced copulation was or was not legally forced, because the answer determines if the crime of rape was committed. The difficulty that the legal system has in distinguishing forced from unforced sexual intercourse illustrates the problem with the concept of rape that results from the use of the combination of the three mating tactics by men to secure single matings.

Not only are the three mating tactics used in combination to obtain single copulations, making the distinct dichotomies of honest versus deceptive courtship and forced versus unforced copulation typically unrealistic, the three tactics grade into each other to the extent that there are only arbitrary boundaries between them. Viewing the three tactics as objective and distinct categories that lead to copulation does not accurately describe the sexual behavior of humans. Sexual coercion or noncoercion is a continuum. The literature dealing with rape by husbands, boyfriends, and dates (Kirkendall 1961; Russell 1982; Pirog-Good and Stets 1989; see review in R. Thornhill and N.W. Thornhill 1990) clearly demonstrates that there is often no distinct objective boundary between coerced and noncoerced matings and that sexual coercion of one form or another is often characteristic of men's pursuit of sexual access. In humans, courtship and the interactions of pair-bonded mates surrounding copulation may include male violence toward a mate or her offspring, or explicit or implicit threats of male violence, that grade into displays and vows of emotional commitment by a man. Most commonly, however, explicit or implicit threats of unpleasant nonviolent consequences (such as a man's withdrawal of financial support or emotional involvement), rather than actual or implicit male violence, grade into noncoercive male activity during male-female interactions leading to copulation.

The occurrence of only an arbitrary line between forced and unforced matings by men suggests that actual or threatened coercion probably is a significant factor in the events leading to a large percentage of human copulations. We suggest that it is the continuum between forced and unforced copulations, even more than the combination of sexually coercive and noncoercive tactics during pursuit of single copulations, that creates the great difficulty in all endeavors to deal with the concept of rape, whether in the legal context or everyday life.

Behavior provides a window to psychological adaptive design because it is a manifestation of psychological adaptations. The general mating strategy of men often includes sexual coercion, and sexual coercion of one form or another may be involved in most matings in humans. Thus it would seem that obtaining sexual intercourse by coercion is as much a part of men's sexual behavior as men's use of noncoercive sexual approaches. In sum, the sexual behavior of men is consistent with the existence of psychological adaptation for the purpose of rape. However, current knowledge of men's sexual behavior does not provide evidence of psychological adaptation to rape itself. It is conceivable that the widespread use of coercive sexual behavior by men is an incidental effect of species-typical adaptation to coerce desired rewards and sex-specific adaptation to copulation.

Conditions Influencing Rape Motivation

The evolutionary theory of individual "interests" is based on evolved self-interests (Alexander 1987; Daly and Wilson 1988). In general, the evolutionary theory of individual self-interests leads to the expectation that men will be motivated to force or otherwise coerce copulation when their evolved individual interests are served; a woman's evolved interests surrounding mating should be considered by a man only when in so doing his own interests are served. There is a continuum of overlap of evolved self-interests—from no overlap to considerable overlap—between men and women who socially interact. It is this continuum that the hypothesis of adaptation to rape predicts will conditionally influence a man's sexual motivation to pursue coercive sexual behavior with individual women. As the symmetry of evolved self-interests of heterosexual interactants declines, the probability of sexual coercion by men is expected to increase. This prediction, if met, would imply precise psychological regulation of men's motivation to use sexual coercion and thus a sexual psychology that includes features designed for rape.

Consider asymmetry and congruence in the evolved self-interests of pair-bond mates. Two important factors that promote similarity of interests between men and women in mateships are offspring of genetic parentage shared by the male and female of a mateship and the woman's sexual fidelity; these two factors are interrelated. Men must provide resources and other benefits in order to achieve sexual intercourse with consenting mates because women's sexual attraction to men is strongly tied to men's status and resources (Symons 1979). When a man provides abundant resources to a mate and her offspring, the woman's evolved interests are served, and it is expected that this will reduce or eliminate the woman's motivation to seek alternative mates. Under such conditions, conflicts of interest (thus coercion of one party by the other) should be minimal. Infidelity by a pair-bonded woman leads to uncertain paternity for her mate and thereby causes a divergence of evolved interests of pair-bond mates. When women perceive that their evolved self-interests are not served by a pair-bond mate, they are expected to pursue alternative mates, to show a decline in emotional commitment to the pair-bond mate, and to exhibit less sexual interest in and less sexual arousal with the pair-bond mate. It follows from this reasoning that pair-bonded men are expected to have evolved to view a reduction in, or absence of, sexual interest (inasmuch as this interest reveals commitment and fidelity; see R. Thornhill and N.W. Thornhill 1990) of a mate as circumstantial evidence that she has or may have another mate. Thus the hypothesis of adaptation to rape predicts that pair-bonded men will be motivated to coerce sexual intercourse with mates when men suspect or discover infidelity. There is evidence in the literature on marital rape supporting this prediction (Russell 1982; R. Thornhill and N.W. Thornhill 1990).

Besides variation in conflicts of interest over sexual matters between men and women, the hypothesis of adaptation to rape predicts several other environmental conditions that should impinge on men's willingness (or unwillingness) to engage in overtly coercive sexual interactions (R. Thornhill and N.W. Thornhill 1990), among them age and social status of men. Young men (mid-teens to early twenties) are those who are in the age range of most intense mate competition and highest risk taking and mortality because they are attempting to enter the breeding population (Alexander, 1979; Thornhill and Thornhill 1983; Wilson and Daly 1985; Trivers 1985). Because sexual competition is greater and mortality more likely in young than in older men (leading to the perception by young men that risky behavior is of low cost), the use of coercive sex is expected to be more consistent with the evolutionary self-interests of young compared to older men; thus young men are predicted to feel that coercive sex is justifiable for themselves and to exhibit more motivation to use coercive sex.

The hypothesis also leads to the expectation that men's motivation to pursue coercive sexual intercourse will be related to men's social class. Women prefer men of high social and economic status as mates (Symons 1979; Buss 1987, 1989; Townsend 1989). Sexual access to preferred mates (young and attractive) is thus positively correlated with the status, resource holdings, and prestige of a man. This correlation has been demonstrated repeatedly in industrial societies (Buss 1987, 1989), in traditional societies (Betzig 1985; Betzig, Mulder, and Turke 1988), and in the historical record (Betzig 1985). Because of the correlation between male status and access to preferred mates, it is predicted that low socioeconomic status men will have a more permissive and motivational attitude toward their own use of rape.

This discussion highlights our view that the hypothetical rape adaptation regulates men's motivation to use coercive sex in a conditional manner. Men's sexual psychology is designed by selection to process environmental information pertaining to sexual matters. The conditions discussed indicate the complexity and specificity of some of the information that the hypothesis of adaptation to rape predicts should be important in motivating coercive sex of men (R. Thornhill and N.W. Thornhill 1990). Thus the hypothesis predicts the existence of psychological mechanisms designed specifically to control men's coercive sexual pursuits.

Men's Sexual Motivation

The view that men's sexual psyche contains adaptation to coercive sexual access predicts that their use of noncoercive and coercive mating tactics will be associated with high levels of sexual arousal and competence. However, if men are sexually aroused only or primarily when they perceive that a potential mate is interested in coitus or if significant sexual arousal in men requires perception of nonresistance in a potential mate, the psychology of sexual motivation is not designed by selection to achieve copulations with women who are sexually uninterested or actively resistant; that is, the idea that men have psychological adaptation to rape is false.

There is an extensive literature on men's sexual arousal to audio and visual sexual stimuli in the laboratory setting (R. Thornhill and N.W. Thornhill 1990; Malamuth 1981b, 1984). The studies generally take one of two forms. Either the research design includes men incarcerated for sex crimes (typically rape) and compares their sexual responses with those of male volunteers from the general population in an effort to determine rapists' sexual arousal patterns (or compares rapists' sexual arousal to rape versus nonrape scenarios), or the studies utilize male student populations and measure their sexual responses to coercive and noncoercive sexual scenarios in an effort to measure propensity to rape. Sexual response in the studies is measured by self-reported arousal, by a phallometric device, or by both. The studies manipulate not only sexual coerciveness and noncoerciveness apparent in the video or audio stimuli but, in various combinations, violence, depicted female sexual arousal, and sex of the person reading the stimulus story (in the case of audiotapes). Other factors are manipulated as well, depending on the study, including the type of instructions given to participants (for example, the instructions might include a statement indicating that response to unusual sexual stimuli is normal) and alcohol consumption or belief of alcohol consumption by participants.

We reviewed over fifteen lab studies encompassing some aspects of the described experimental designs. The studies that compare rape offenders' responses to coercive and noncoercive sexual stimuli show that rapists are equally aroused by both coercive and noncoercive sex. Moreover, these results are generally comparable for nonrape offenders. The studies collectively imply that young men in general are as sexually motivated, as measured by sexual arousal in the laboratory setting, by explicitly sexual stimuli depicting mutually consensual heterosexual sex as they are by sexual stimuli depicting coerced sexual interactions, including physically forced sexual assault. Some young men in the studies show some initial inhibition in sexual response to rape depictions; however, in general these inhibitions can be removed easily by each one of the following: (1) sexual arousal of the depicted rape victim, (2) alcohol consumption or mere belief of alcohol consumption, (3) instructions that sexual response to unusual stimuli is normal, (4) rape depiction being narrated by a woman rather than a man, and (5) not requiring men to self-report their sexual arousal while their arousal is simultaneously being assessed by phallometry. In other words, even when young men initially have a restrictive rape ideology and view coerced sex as unacceptable, the specific conditions surrounding sexual coercion can disinhibit the restrictions, allowing a more permissive and motivational rape psychology to emerge. Sexual arousal of women in rape depictions is only one of several conditions that disinhibits men's sexual arousal to rape depictions; moreover, the victim's arousal in rape depictions is not necessary for men's sexual arousal to the depictions.

Often laboratory studies are contrived and may not be relevant outside the laboratory. There is some evidence that men's sexual response to the laboratory portrayals may be related to actual sexual behavior of men, including coercive sexual behavior. First, research reviewed in R. Thornhill and N.W. Thornhill (1990) shows that sexual arousal of male undergraduate college men (both for penile tumescence and self-report) to rape depictions in the laboratory is consistently and significantly positively correlated with reported personal use of force against women in sexual relations and reported likelihood of committing forced sexual behavior in the future. Second, penile tumescence reaction to audio and video stimuli is in general felt to be the best method of identifying the sexual preferences of men with preferences such as homosexuality, bisexuality, or pedophilia who seek psychiatric assistance to help them with their sexual interests and behavior (Greer and Stuart 1983; Langevin 1983). Third, the sexual arousal of men with homosexual, bisexual, or pedophilic sexual preferences to laboratory depictions seems to be correlated with their history of actual sexual behavior (Langevin 1983). Finally, the typical mate preference of heterosexual men is young women (Symons 1979; Thornhill and Thornhill 1983; Buss 1987, 1989; Townsend 1987. 1989). Laboratory studies of sexual arousal reveal that heterosexual men show the greatest penile response to women, who are typically portrayed as 18 to 25 years old in the studies, and significantly less response to pubescent or prepubescent girls (Langevin 1983).

The information on men's sexual responses in the laboratory to coercive and noncoercive sexually explicit scenarios is intriguing and indicates a male sexual psychology that does not require female consent for arousal. Such a male sexual psychology is exactly that expected to exist if men possess psychological adaptation to rape.

These studies deal only with the dimension of sexual motivation pertaining to penile erection and not the aspects of sexual motivation pertaining to the actual initiation and performance of sexual coercion. There are no reliable data on the comparative sexual competence of men in coerced and noncoerced sexual settings. We have evaluated critically the literature on sexual dysfunction of rapists elsewhere (Thornhill and Thornhill 1983) and will not reevaluate this literature here except to point out that the literature on "premature" ejaculation and sexual impotence during rape is based on alleged or convicted rapists and is therefore biased and cannot be used for evaluating the sexual performance of men in general during coercive sexual interactions. The most relevant point pertaining to the sexual competence of men under conditions of sexual coercion is that many men achieve sexual intercourse by coercion, including physically forced sexual access, according to the literature on acquaintance rape, rape by boyfriends and husbands, rape of children, and homosexual rape in prisons. Indeed, men's widespread use of coercion to achieve sexual intercourse suggests widespread general sexual competence of men in the context of forced sex.

The laboratory studies and the widespread sexual competence of men during sexual coercion, however, do not demonstrate adaptation to rape. To demonstrate adaptation to rape, it must be shown that there is design specifically for the purpose of rape. It is phenotypic design for a specific purpose that eliminates alternative hypotheses of incidental effect.

Earlier we outlined some conditions that we expect to influence male motivation to engage in coercive sexual interactions. Studies of the integration between the sexual motivation of men and their other motivational states that eliminate or strengthen their coercive sexual motivation can be used to determine if there is predictable psychological regulation of men's coercive sexuality. Sophisticated regulatory machinery to achieve a specific purpose is the hallmark of special-purpose adaptation.

Rape: Multiple Motives

The hypothesis of psychological adaptation to rape may seem questionable on the basis of certain current opinion about the motivation behind rape. The question of whether rape is a sexual act, a violent act, or an act of male domination of a woman is a central theme in a large literature that has grown out of the important place of rape in the feminist movement (Shields and Shields 1983; Thornhill and Thornhill 1983). The major error in this debate is that the motive behind rape is viewed as either sexual or violence and domination.

Like any other human behavior, motivations for rape are numerous. The motivation that leads men to rape, whether by physical force, threat of physical force, or other forms of coercion usually includes the desire to copulate or otherwise have a sexual experience. In the data set of McCahill, Meyer, and Fishman (1979) involving 1,401 victims of heterosexual rape in Philadelphia, 83 percent reported penile-vaginal intercourse. Repeated intercourse by the same offender occurred in about 25 percent of the cases. Cunnilingus, rectal intercourse, and acts of penile-labial contact without vaginal penetration were rare (6 percent, 5 percent, and 6 percent, respectively). Rape victims are unlikely to view the rape as a positive sexual experience (Finklehor and Yllo 1985), but this is not the key factor here. The issue is whether men in part are sexually motivated to rape. The answer is that they usually behave as if they are motivated to rape by the desire to have a sexual experience, which typically includes copulation.

Furthermore, the vast majority of heterosexual rapes involve young women. This is the case for reported (Thornhill and Thornhill 1983) as well as unreported heterosexual rapes (McDermott 1979; Russell 1984; Belknap 1989). In addition, our own analysis of the McCahill, Meyer, and Fishman data reveals that penile-vaginal intercourse during sexual assaults almost always occurs when victims are of reproductive ages (12 to 44 years old), but penile-vaginal intercourse is relatively uncommon when sexual assault victims are of prereproductive or postreproductive ages (N.W. Thornhill and R. Thornhill 1990). The sexual interest of heterosexual men is focused on young women. That rapists primarily rape young women is congruent with the idea that sexual attractiveness is a contributing factor underlying rape behavior. Even in the case of sexual assault of postreproductive women, children, and men, a sexual motive cannot be excluded automatically. Some men copulate with domestic livestock, artificial vaginas, and plastic dolls; some masturbate with vacuum cleaners. Surely desire to have a sexual experience is a component of all sexual behavior and interest of men.

Rape also frequently occurs in a motivational setting of male violence. For example, McCahill, Meyer, and Fishman (1979) found that a majority of victims (64 percent) reported being pushed or held during the incident; victims are often slapped (17 percent), beaten (22 percent), and/or choked (20 percent); and 84 percent of victims experienced some kind of nonphysical force during the incident (such as threat of bodily harm). Chappell and James (1976) reported that 78 percent (of 100) incarcerated rapists who had used violence during the sexual assault said they desired the victim to "give up and do anything," indicating that violence allows the rapist to achieve a sexual experience that can be achieved in no other way. It is remarkable that the incidence of rape-murder is not higher than it is (see Thornhill and Thornhill 1983) given that physical violence is a frequent mechanism by which forced sexual access is achieved, at least for incarcerated rapists.

We hypothesize that the sexual motivation of men and their motivation to dominate and control the sexuality of mates are functionally integrated in the sexual psychology of men as a result of evolution by selection. This psychological integration is a sex-specific and species-wide adaptation. We interpret men's striving to dominate and sexually please mates as aspects of their general striving to control the sexuality of women in order to increase the probability of paternity. (See Dickemann 1981; Daly, Wilson, and Weghorst, 1982; Smith 1984; Daly and Wilson 1988; and Flinn 1988 for discussion and evidence of the importance of mate control by men and of selection in the context of paternity confidence in human evolution.) We contend that the evolutionary function of the integration of the psychological mechanisms of sexual motivation and control of mate's sexuality is the promotion of discriminative investment in mates by men, with increased investment by a man in a mate whose sexuality is controlled and thus more likely to produce that man's offspring and not another's. Note that we are not arguing that men's sexual arousal requires domination and sexual control of a mate. Instead we are arguing that domination and sexual control of a mate will facilitate the sexual arousal of men in both coercive and noncoercive situations.

We suggest that violence per se will not be sexually stimulating for most men but that men will find aggressive as well as nonaggressive control of a mate's sexuality to be sexually facilitating. We have reviewed the relevant aspects of the literature on the relationship between sexual motivation of men and nonsexual and sexual violence. Men (rapists and nonrapists) are not sexually aroused in the laboratory by depictions of violence that lack sexual content. However, there is evidence that heterosexual men are sexually aroused by stimuli in the laboratory setting that portray aggression toward and domination of a woman by a man in the sexual context (R. Thornhill and N.W. Thornhill 1990).

The prediction that men will find stimuli of aggressive—including violent—control of women's sexuality to be sexually facilitating is also supported by the common inclusion in best-selling erotic magazines (Malamuth and Spinner 1980) and in hard-core erotica (Dietz and Evans 1982) of sexual violence with women as victims and men as perpetrators. According to the President's Commission on Obscenity and Pornography (1970), the pornographic magazine and movie business caters to the average man and not just to men with anomalous sexual preferences. This implies that many men are sexually motivated by vicariously assuming physical control over their sexual partners while fantasizing with pornographic material.

The prediction is supported also by the frequent observation that rapists (including pedophilic rapists) commonly report that their domination of the victim and the associated feeling of power that they have over the victim is sexually stimulating (see R. Thornhill and N.W. Thornhill 1990).

Earlier we mentioned that men's sexual arousal to audio and video depictions of rape in the laboratory is strengthened by sexual arousal of the rape victim. The female victim's arousal is a common theme in pornography portraying rape (Malamuth and Spinner 1980; Dietz and Evans 1982). This suggests also that women's sexual responses are facilitators of the sexual motivation of men when viewing forced-copulation depictions. We suggest that the sexual response of victims in rape depictions is sexually stimulating to men because it implies control of the woman's sexuality. We feel that this interpretation will apply to the sexual arousal of men in both forced and unforced sexual settings.

Our view of the functional integration of the sexual motivation of men and their motivation to dominate and control mates implies that desire to control the victim may be as common a motive behind rape as is the desire to have a sexual experience. We would be very surprised if men are not frequently elated and sexually stimulated by their control of and dominance over sexual partners to whom they can gain access only by coercion. We would be equally surprised if this were not also the case in mutually consensual sexual interactions.

The motivations behind rape, just like any other human behavior, are complex, multifaceted, and intertwined. In part, the psychological drive that leads to rape is sexual; the rapist seeks an experience of sexual gratification. The other motivational states of rapists—violence and domination and control of victims—are expected to be, from the evolutionary approach we have proposed, components of the overall motivation of forced copulation.

Humans have evolved to seek proximate rewards and avoid proximate punishments that correlated with individual reproductive fitness in evolutionary history. The motives of sex, violence, and domination are exactly the proximate motives expected to be associated with rape if selection has produced in men psychological adaptation to rape.

Conclusions

In order to qualify as an evolutionary adaptation, a feature of an organism must meet the criterion of design for a specific purpose and not be explicable by chance. Thus, if men have adaptation to the circumstance of rape, there should be evidence of design for rape. In men's psychology of sexual motivation and action, there are features that suggest design for coercive sexuality: the complex of emotional-motivational-cognitive physiological mechanisms that cause and regulate men's sexual arousal and action in the context of dealing with sexually unwilling and resistant partners.

The hypothesis that men's sexual psyche includes adaptation to rape is consistent with, and is not falsified by, the natural history of men's sexual behavior. The common use of coercion by men to achieve sexual access suggests that men's sexual psychology is adapted to motivate reproductively competent sexual performance regardless of whether mating is achieved by force or nonforce. This sort of sexual psychology of men is indicated also by laboratory studies showing similar or equal sexual arousal of men when exposed to audio or video depictions of rape versus mutually consenting matings.

Evidence for the existence of psychological adaptation to rape could derive from detailed information about the conditions that reduce or increase men's motivation to pursue coercive sex. For example, we expect that likelihood of social detection and punishment of rape will reduce the motivation to pursue coercive sex for men (R. Thornhill and N.W. Thornhill 1990). We expect age and social class of men to be important conditions too. Moreover, rape in pair-bond mateships is predicted to be associated with actual or suspected infidelity on the part of the female member of the pair. Laboratory studies and other evidence indicate that heterosexual men's sexual arousal is facilitated by their control of women's sexuality, including violent control. This suggests functional integration in the psyche of men between sexual motivation and the motivation to control mates sexually, a design feature predicted by the view that men's sexual psychology contains adaptation to rape.

Much more information is needed to test the hypothesis that the sexual psychology of men includes adaptation to rape. The key to distinguishing between the incidental effect hypothesis and the hypothesis of adaptation to rape is determining if men's sexual psychology is designed to process rape-specific information. Such a design would demonstrate adaptation to rape. We believe that the experimental procedure that has been used to study the sexual arousal of men to audio and video stimuli in the laboratory (Malamuth 1981b, 1984) may be especially valuable for determining if men have adaptation to rape. Such studies potentially can control confounding variables precisely and therefore illuminate the actual information that men's sexual psychological adaptations are designed to process.

Commonly the behavioral manifestations of men's sexual psyche have antisocial effects. Men produce essentially all the socially unacceptable, illegal, and repugnant sexual behavior in the world (Langevin 1983; Finkelhor 1984), and almost all of this behavior has a coercive element. The usual manifestation of the coercive aspects of men's sexual psychology in men's behavior is in their sexual harassment of and pursuit of coerced matings with young women—stepdaughters, dates and other acquaintances, total strangers, and pair-bond mates—to whom they are not closely related genetically. Less common manifestations of this psychology in men's behavior are forced sexual access to children who are not related to the offender; genetic daughters, typically when they are young women (N. Thornhill, in press); young men, who are preferred by homosexual men with androphilic (rather than pedophilic) orientation; and women of postreproductive ages. The least common manifestations of this psychology in men's behavior are forced sex within nonhuman animals, genital exhibitionism, and frottage (Langevin 1983). The salient feature in all these manifestations of psychology in men's behavior is the sexual arousal and action of men without partner's consent.

Our guess is that the overwhelming preponderance of men as perpetrators of antisocial sexual behavior can be explained in the ultimate or evolutionary sense only by men's, not women's, psychological adaptation to rape. However, regardless of whether rape is caused by psychological design specifically for rape or is a by-product of other psychological adaptation, we believe that many novel findings about coercive sexuality could result from exploration of the empirical implications of the hypothesis that men have psychological adaptation to rape.

Note

1. Ends that promoted fitness in the evolutionary past but there is no assumption or requirement of current adaptiveness.

III
Preventing Sexual Coercion

8

Self-Defense against Sexual Coercion: Theory, Research, and Practice

Martha E. Thompson

I had missed the last bus, had no money for a cab, and had to get back to my dorm at the other end of campus. A heavy rain started to fall when I was halfway across campus, and I had no umbrella with me. When a car pulled over and the driver asked me if I wanted a ride, I gratefully said, "Yes." The back door opened, I climbed in, and the driver sped off while I was still closing the door. There were four young men in the car. Although my heart was pounding and a cold, heavy feeling was seeping throughout my body, I managed to say, "Here's my dorm; you can let me out right here." The driver stopped the car. I jumped out and ran all the way back to my dorm.

For a long time after this incident, I castigated myself for getting into the car and felt fortunate that the driver stopped the car so I could get out. Although I was not attacked, I was haunted long after by my vulnerability. I have since heard other women describe similar episodes and similar feelings of self-blame and helplessness.

Through the sharing of these common experiences and feelings in consciousness-raising groups, the contemporary women's movement identified early on the widespread incidence of rape and the need for self-defense (Bond and Peery 1970; Griffin 1971; Mehrhof and Kearon 1973; Moon, Tanner, and Pascale 1970; Pascale, Moon, and Tanner 1970; WBAI Consciousness Raising 1973). Over the last twenty years, researchers have continued to document women's and children's risks and fears of sexual coercion (Bart and O'Brien 1985; Gordon and Riger 1989; Heath and Davidson 1988; Randolph and Gredler 1985).

In response to the immediate needs of women and children to protect themselves, people from a variety of backgrounds have developed prevention and self-defense programs. Most of these programs have not been evaluated

---

Gail Radford and Susan Stall gave me their inspiration, insight, support, and constructive comments on several versions of this chapter. Elizabeth Grauerholz provided incisive editing. Finally, I thank the women and men I have met through *Model Mugging* for sharing my belief that collectively we can create a society free from violence.

for their effectiveness and the connections among child sexual assault prevention, self-defense against rape, and sexual harassment prevention programs. In this chapter, I examine child sexual assault prevention, self-defense against rape, and sexual harassment prevention research and theory. The differences and similarities in these three bodies of work suggest directions for theory, research, and practice of self-defense against sexual coercion.

The Current State of Self-defense Theory, Research, and Practice

There is no body of work that is readily identifiable as self-defense against sexual coercion, but there are analyses and critiques of child sexual abuse prevention, self-defense training against rape, and sexual harassment prevention programs (Bateman 1986; Conte, Rosen, and Saperstein 1986; Livingston, 1982; Miller-Perrin and Wurtele 1988; Tharinger et al. 1988). A comparison of these critiques and analyses reveals differences in program origins, content, methods, and issues but complementary themes in research findings.

Origins

The origins of self-defense and prevention programs are highly diverse. The varied groups that developed these programs suggest that resistance to sexual coercion is multifaceted, involving the whole self (body, mind, and emotions), as well as social factors, such as the oppression of women and children, the structure of educational institutions, and the law and its enforcement.

Child sexual assault prevention programs have been shaped by psychologists, other health professionals, and educators (Tharinger et al. 1988). Self-defense programs designed for rape prevention have been influenced by feminist analyses of women's oppression in society, the martial arts, and law enforcement (James 1981; Smith 1986; Storaska 1975; Telsey 1981; Tesoro 1988). Sexual harassment prevention programs have been stimulated by the interpretation of Title VII to include sexual harassment as a form of sex discrimination (Livingston 1982).

Programs

Given the differences in origins, not surprisingly, the content and methods of programs in child sexual abuse prevention, self-defense against rape, and sexual harassment in schools and the workplace differ. The range of content and methods indicates that an effective self-defense program uses multiple teaching strategies and is multidimensional, including attention to knowledge, skills, and attitudes.

By and large, child sexual assault prevention programs teach children prevention concepts, such as body ownership (a child has a right to determine who touches her or him), touch continuum (touch can range from good to bad touch), and secrets (adults should not ask children to keep secrets about being touched) (Conte, Rosen, and Saperstein 1986; deYoung 1988b). Children are taught these concepts with a variety of tools (such as puppets, books, and films) emphasizing knowledge of child sexual abuse prevention (Conte, Rosen, and Saperstein 1986; Tharinger et al. 1988).

Self-defense training programs against rape typically focus on teaching women physical defense skills (Telsey 1981; Quinsey et al. 1986). They emphasize the use of the voice and psychological strategies designed to set boundaries and boost self-esteem and prevention concepts, such as body ownership (James 1981; Johnston 1987; Kidder, Boell, and Moyer 1983; Smith 1986; Telsey 1981). These programs are typically designed for teenagers and adult women.

Sexual harassment prevention programs tend to use traditional teaching methods, such as lectures, films, and reading material, to develop an awareness of sexual harassment, strategies for dealing with it, and institutional policies and procedures for challenging it (Livingston 1982). These programs have been developed primarily within higher education and work settings.

The variations in program content and methods suggest that effective self-defense against sexual coercion requires individuals to have relevant knowledge to use multiple psychological and physical skills and to develop attitudes that encourage people to defend themselves. The diversity of teaching methods suggests that both traditional and nontraditional teaching methods may be required in self-defense programs. Finally, the varied groups targeted for self-defense education suggest that diverse age groups in diverse settings need these programs.

Issues

Collectively the debates within each area suggest issues that must be addressed by any self-defense or prevention program. There is debate in the child sexual assault prevention community about whether children could or should be taught to defend themselves against sexual assault. Writers urge caution in teaching children prevention concepts and skills, raising concerns about the degree to which programs reflect adults' issues rather than children's, the ability of children to understand prevention concepts, the tremendous power adults have over children, and the lack of research on the impact these programs have on children's feelings of safety and trust (Conte, Rosen, and Saperstein 1986; Conte 1987; deYoung 1988b; Gilbert,

1988; Gilgun and Gordon 1985; Kraizer 1986; Kraizer, Fryer, and Miller 1988; Swan, Press, and Briggs 1985; Tharinger et al. 1988; Wurtele, Marrs, and Miller-Perrin 1987).

Practitioners of self-defense against rape make different assumptions about women's capabilities for physical self-defense and consequently disagree about the most effective self-defense strategies and women's risk of injury when using these strategies. For instance, practitioners with roots in martial art and/or feminism have emphasized active resistance (Johnston 1987; Smith 1986; Telsey 1981; Tesoro 1988). In contrast, practitioners based in law enforcement have tended to advocate avoidance behaviors (such as home security systems or walking in lighted areas) or the use of traditionally feminine behaviors, such as crying and pleading (Storaska 1975).

Unlike child sexual assault prevention and self-defense programs, sexual harassment programs are typically offered specifically to reduce sexual attacks within the work or educational environment in which the program is offered. There is disagreement about the extent to which these educational programs will actually have an impact on those environments (Livingston 1982).

Research

Ideas about child sexual assault prevention have been tested primarily in experimental evaluations of specific prevention programs and with children ranging in age from 4 to 11 years. Research in this area indicates that children's ability to grasp prevention concepts increases with age (Conte et al. 1985; Tharinger et al. 1988).

The most effective training programs for children, regardless of age, give them the opportunity to learn, observe, and practice concrete skills rather than abstract ideas (Fryer, Kraizer, and Miyoshi 1987a; Harvey et al. 1988; Kraizer, Fryer, and Miller 1988; Poche, Brouwer, and Swearingen 1981; Wurtele, Marrs, and Miller-Perrin 1987). Children with high self-esteem are most likely to demonstrate self-defense behaviors (Fryer, Kraizer, and Miyoshi 1987a).

Experimental evaluations of self-defense against rape programs are limited (Kidder, Boell, and Moyer 1983; Ozer and Bandura 1990). Information about rape resistance has been gathered primarily through in-depth interviews with women who have been attacked or analyses of reports of rape attacks (Bart 1981; Bart and O'Brien 1985; Kelly 1988; Quinsey and Upfold 1985). Collectively, these studies include women of diverse ages (14 to 72), racial and ethnic groups, and social classes.

Research on rape resistance shows that the ways women resist depend on the situation and available resources (Abarbanel 1986; Bart 1981; Bart and O'Brien 1985; Kelly 1988). Women's resistance is not related to the size or ability of the rapist or to subsequent injuries (Bart and O'Brien 1985; Quinsey and Upfold 1985). It includes preventing an attack, interrupting an attack, modifying the direction of an attack, and limiting the psychological or physical impact of an attack (Kelly 1988). Women who have successfully thwarted a rape attack have tended to use a combination of verbal and physical strategies (Bart 1981; Bart and O'Brien 1985).

Research on self-defense against rape programs suggests that an effective program is based on knowledge of actual attacks, promotes women's self-worth and self-esteem, teaches skills based on what women already do, gives women opportunities to practice their skills, and creates an environment of feedback and support (Kidder, Boell, and Moyer 1983; Ozer and Bandura 1990; Quinsey et al. 1986). Effective programs increase women's self-confidence, self-esteem and sense of control (Cohn, Kidder, and Harvey 1979; Kidder, Boell, and Moyer 1983; Ozer and Bandura 1990; Quinsey et al. 1986). Women who feel they can have control over a rape attack demonstrate more safety precautions than those who perceive it as an uncontrollable event (Heath and Davidson 1988).

The little systematic research about resistance to sexual harassment that has been conducted typically has been done through surveys of students, employees, and a cross-section of women (Livingston 1982). According to survey data, women rarely use formal mechanisms for reporting sexual harassment but more often verbally object, use avoidance tactics, or ignore the behavior (Livingston 1982; McKinney, Olson, and Satterfield 1988). Little information is available about the effectiveness of sexual harassment prevention programs in reducing harassment or increasing women's ability to cope with it (Livingston 1982). The work that has been done suggests that sexual harassment and responses to it are unlikely to change as long as the unequal distribution of power between women and men remains in work and educational settings (Livingston 1982).

The Literature on Self-defense against Sexual Coercion

Most self-defense and prevention programs concerning sexual coercion have not been evaluated or validated (Bateman 1986; Livingston 1982; Miller-Perrin and Wurtele 1988; Tharinger et al. 1988). Responding to immediate needs and with limited resources, most practitioners develop their programs on the basis of what they believe is effective. Although work on self-defense against sexual coercion is limited, it does suggest directions for theory, research, and practice. The variety of methods used in investigation and the diversity of groups and programs examined increase the validity of these ideas (Webb et al. 1966).

Four key ideas emerge from the work on child sexual assault prevention, self-defense against rape, and sexual harassment prevention programs:

1. Learning, observing, and practicing self-defense behaviors in varied and realistic situations is central to effective self-defense education.

2. Effective self-defense education emphasizes the learning and use of multiple verbal and physical strategies.

3. Women and children are more likely to learn and retain skills when the skills build on existing strengths, abilities, and inclinations.

4. Effective self-defense education fosters individual and group supports for self-defense, including self-esteem, self-confidence, and supportive emotional relationships.

Experiential Learning

A consistent theme emerging from research and critiques of prevention and self-defense is that programs in self-defense against sexual coercion must focus on the acquisition of experience, not the transmission of ideas (Conte et al. 1985; Ozer and Bandura 1990; Kraizer, Fryer, and Miller 1988; Leventhal 1987; Poche, Browwer, and Swearingen 1981; Telsey 1981; Wurtele, Marrs, and Miller-Perrin 1987). In a sexually coercive situation, women and children must weigh many complex factors, make decisions, and take action quickly. Their ability to use these behaviors in real-life settings can be maximized if they have the opportunity to practice in realistic and varied situations that are also psychologically and physically safe (Conte et al. 1985; Fryer, Kraizer, and Miyoshi 1987a; Harvey et al. 1988; Kraizer Brouwer, and Swearingen 1981; Wurtele, Marrs, and Miller-Perrin 1987). One woman commented that a course of experiential learning

> supported my efforts to change the behaviors I learned growing up: to be nice and polite, humble, get along, blend in. The training helped me in a very physical way to see how great the loss of my self has been. Experiencing this with my body is so different from thinking or talking about it. (Thompson 1990)

Multiple Strategies

Research as well as anecdotal evidence demonstrates that self-defense against sexual coercion involves multiple strategies (Bart 1981; Bart and O'Brien 1985; Caignon and Groves 1987; Kelly 1988). Sexually coercive situations are often ambiguous and emotionally stressful. Factors that contribute to this ambiguity and stress include the relative status and power of the defender and the attacker, the relationship of the defender and the attacker (a stranger, acquaintance, or family members), and the resources in the setting available for defense (Abarbanel 1986; Bateman 1986; Bart and O'Brien 1985; Gilgun and Gordon 1985; Livingston 1982). In any situation, an individual will have to weigh both the perceived risks and possibilities of self-defense. Given the range of possible circumstances, no one strategy or outcome can be advocated.

An effective self-defense program will acknowledge a continuum of outcomes, from minimization of an attack to prevention, and will therefore teach people multiple strategies, including acquiescence when the perceived risks outweigh the possibilities of active resistance. After completing a self-defense course, a woman described the multiple strategies and skills she had learned:

> I learned to fall, I learned to strike accurately—in the eyes, the head, the groin. I learned to respect my body as an instrument of power. . . . [This course] teaches women to say . . . no. It teaches women to use their natural wisdom, strength, and instinct to decide when to fight and then, how to fight. (Roth 1987: 3)

Self-defense courses cannot prepare people for every situation. An effective course will therefore offer no simple formulas but will encourage people to develop and practice knowledge, skills, and attitudes that will have applicability to a variety of circumstances.

Building on Strengths

To maximize the likelihood that people will learn and retain self-defense knowledge, skills, and attitudes, effective self-defense programs must build on what people can already do (Bateman 1986; Quinsey et al. 1986). Research and anecdotal evidence show that people who have not gone through formal self-defense training can defend themselves (Bateman 1986; Bart and O'Brien 1985; Caignon and Groves 1987). Building on existing strengths, inclinations, and abilities requires that instructors and students acknowledge the many ways in which women and children already resist sexual coercion and not narrowly define self-defense as physically stopping an attack. A woman described her joy in discovering that she could build on survival skills she had developed in her youth:

> As an incest survivor and especially as a survivor of ritual abuse, it was great to find that not all of the things I learned at such effort and cost to myself have had to be thrown away. I've known excellent coiling[1] since I was very small: coming totally into my body to be alert to whatever might

be required of me, relaxing completely and seeming compliant, seeming to cooperate without letting my spirit be broken, and staying deliberate no matter what. But now I can follow through with the kicks, bites, and yells that I've wanted to do my whole life. Now, when I hit that point of no return with someone else's violence, instead of leaving my body, I can fight like mad. (Thompson 1990)

Support

Sexual coercion undermines women's and children's sense of self-worth and encourages individual isolation. Self-defense education provides an opportunity to create a community of support that can restore and encourage high self-esteem and self-confidence (Kelly 1988; Smith 1986; Telsey 1981; Tesoro 1987). A woman described the importance of this support to her: "If you had said to me that within 24 hours I would be telling my story of incest and feeling comfortable with 14 total strangers, I would have thought you crazy. My class supported me emotionally more than any person in my entire life" (Anonymous 1989: 6). The support women receive strengthens their ability to see their own power: "By taking [this course], I was faced with a lot of different emotions: anger, fear, sadness, anxiety. But what the course gave me was empowerment and confidence. . . . I never before realized how much power I have within me, and how strong my will to survive is" (Thompson 1990).

Directions for Theory, Research, and Practice

My analysis of three distinct bodies of work—child sexual assault prevention, self-defense against rape, and sexual harassment prevention—suggests directions for theory, research, and practice of self-defense against sexual coercion.

Self-defense Theory

A theory of self-defense against sexual coercion must address a complex configuration of individual, situational, and societal factors, and it must also consider the process of how people acquire knowledge, skills, and attitudes that challenge the social values and patterns of relationships in the dominant culture (Freire 1968). We need to develop a theoretical foundation for explaining why self-defense education is effective when it focuses on learning and practicing multiple skills and strategies, builds on people's strengths, and builds psychological and social supports for self-defense.

A theory of self-defense against sexual coercion must also consider the limits of as well as the possibilities for self-defense against sexual coercion. Self-defense education increases women's and children's personal resources for resisting sexual coercion, but it cannot by itself alter societal values and patterns of relationships that justify and encourage sexual coercion. A theory of self-defense against sexual coercion must develop clear theoretical connections between individual and collective strategies for challenging sexual coercion.

Self-defense Research

An analysis of research in these areas reveals the need for multiple research strategies, the need to incorporate research about other forms of sexual coercion, and a research agenda. First, there is a need for multiple research strategies, each serving different purposes. Surveys will help document the extent of self-defense against sexual coercion. In-depth interviews and document analyses of police reports, social service agency files, and calls to crisis hot lines will help us understand women and children's actual experiences of sexual coercion and self-defense. Experimental evaluations will enable us to assess the effectiveness of particular programs.

Second, research design will be strengthened by considering research findings from other areas. For example, Conte, Rosen, and Saperstein (1986) identify a problem area in child sexual assault prevention programs: minimal information about how adults involve children in sexually coercive relationships. There is information available: feminist analyses of incest provide clues to the ways in which adults introduce children to and keep them in sexually coercive relationships (Bass and Davis 1988).

Third, to design effective self-defense and prevention programs, we need more knowledge about the strategies that work and why. For example, research suggests that people will learn and retain self-defense skills if they have opportunities to practice. What kinds of practice do they need? How realistic and varied should practice opportunities be? What are the ethical issues in simulating actual situations? How can practitioners create physically and psychologically safe learning environments? Of the multiple behavioral strategies possible for self-defense, which are the most effective and easily learned? How does the effectiveness and ease of learning differ by age, prior experience with sexual coercion, or cultural background?

Research indicates that effective self-defense courses build on existing strengths. How can we identify those strengths and determine which ones to build upon? How do we adapt these strengths to a course? How do strengths vary by age, experience, or background of participants? What kinds of support are most effective within a self-defense course? How much support is needed? How does an instructor create an environment of support? How does the kind and extent of effective support vary depending on the age, experience, or background of the participants?

Self-defense Education

Research and theory in self-defense are essential but will take time. While we investigate the limits and possibilities of self-defense against sexual coercion, women and children continue to be in jeopardy and need self-defense education now. I encourage people who teach self-defense or are considering taking such a course to consider the implications of the work summarized here. Whose perspective shapes the program? Does self-defense education vary depending on individual capabilities and situational power relationships? To what extent does a self-defense or prevention program give women or children an opportunity to practice self-defense skills in a safe environment? To what extent does a program emphasize the learning of multiple strategies? To what extent does it acknowledge and build on women and children's existing strengths? To what extent does it foster the development of psychological and social supports for self-defense? We need to develop and select programs based on the actual experiences of women and children and recognize the distribution of power in society, emphasize experiential learning of multiple strategies, build on existing abilities, and create safe, supportive environments.

Conclusion

Ideas about self-defense against sexual coercion exist in three separate bodies of literature—child sexual assault prevention, self-defense against rape, and sexual harassment prevention—that differ in their origins, programs, and issues. Collectively, however, they offer four key ideas around which to organize theory, research, and practice of self-defense against sexual coercion: experiential learning, multiple strategies, individual strengths, and individual and social support for self-defense.

This analysis suggests that a theory of self-defense against sexual coercion must be multifaceted and multidimensional, including attention to how people learn behaviors that challenge dominant social values and relationships. Research strategies will need to include surveys, document analysis, interviews, and program evaluations. Researchers must look to related areas for data and investigate what makes a self-defense program effective. Practitioners and women or children seeking self-defense education are encouraged to evaluate the extent to which existing programs are based on their experience, consider power relationships in society, emphasize learning and practicing multiple strategies, build on their abilities, and create supportive and safe environments. Effective self-defense education is vitally important for expanding individuals' resources and acknowledging women's and children's past experiences with sexual coercion and their resistance to it.

I started this chapter with a personal experience that at the time generated feelings of self-blame and helplessness. My own self-defense education and research have encouraged me to rethink that incident. I now recognize that my quick assessment of a potentially dangerous situation and my immediate action, not a miracle, probably prevented those four men from raping me. This represents one of the powers of self-defense education: recognition and affirmation of the myriad ways women and children already challenge sexual coercion in their everyday lives.

Note

1. *Coiling* is a term used in *Model Mugging* to describe the internal experience of waiting for an opening before physically fighting. A person's outward appearance indicates acquiescence while internally she is consolidating her psychological and physical resources for the moment of opportunity.

9
Vital Childhood Lessons: The Role of Parenting in Preventing Sexual Coercion

Andrea Parrot

There is no absolute protection against sexual assault and no way to know for certain who will be sexually coercive. The best prevention techniques for potential victims are awareness, information, assertiveness, learning avoidance strategies to diffuse potentially dangerous situations, learning how to get away from potential assailants, and perhaps fighting back. But assailants must stop committing sexual coercion for sexual coercion to stop. Men need to be socialized to believe that sexual coercion (child sexual abuse, sexual harassment, acquaintance rape, stranger rape, and others) is wrong. Prevention strategies can be implemented in childhood, but those who did not learn about child sexual abuse as children need to learn about it as adults. Because most people are victimized by someone they know, my primary focus is on sexual coercion in which the victim and the assailant know each other.[1]

Traditional Gender Socialization

Many males have traditionally been socialized as early as childhood to think that they have a right to sex, that they have to want sex at all times and should never say no, that sex is the goal, that heterosexual sex is the only "normal" option available to them, and that the only form of "real" sex is penis-vagina intercourse (Mahoney 1982; Mahoney, Shively, and Traw 1986). Boys and young men also learn to believe that women never mean "no" when they say "no"; they protest in a sexual situation because they are trying to protect their reputations.

Women and girls are socialized to please others and not embarrass themselves or others, which may cause them to ignore instincts indicating a situation is dangerous (Lewin 1985). A female who has been socialized to be passive has difficulty making her wishes clearly known if they are in conflict with another's. Also, it is unusual for assertiveness to be taught to children, especially females. Women and girls are traditionally taught to be passive, and boys and men are socialized to be aggressive (Tavris and Wade 1984). The very traits considered most feminine are considered most child-like (Kilbourne 1986). In addition, many girls are taught that they are fragile and do not understand that usually they will not suffer permanent damage if they are hit or knocked down. Thus, they are often reluctant to use physical self-defense when necessary because they are afraid of the consequences of physical reprisal.

These traditional messages are reinforced by advertisers who depict true femininity as the unrealistic and unattainable image of the perfect models in their ads. Women and girls may attempt to attain this goal by perhaps unwittingly wearing clothing considered seductive by many men or clothing that increases their vulnerability (such as spike heels and tight skirts, which make it impossible to run away from an attacker).

Alternative Parenting Strategies

Efforts to prevent sexual coercion directed at children must aim at replacing these traditional messages about gender and sexuality with healthier, child-centered messages and teaching parents more appropriate ways of dealing with their children.

Family systems theory postulates that if young people are clear about their values, are encouraged to be autonomous, understand appropriate uses of power, and are able to identify feelings of others, they will be able to act appropriately in social situations (Beavers 1977). If the family has done its job well in preparing children to deal with the world, young people will be able to be effective even in difficult or ambiguous situations. In our culture, family competence is closely related to encouraging individuals to be autonomous. The individual is given the opportunity to make decisions and is expected to act responsibly regarding the outcomes of these decisions, which results in children's being able to make good decisions autonomously in difficult situations. In addition, individuals from healthy families learn to assess the feelings of others and respect those feelings, and they usually exhibit consistent verbal and nonverbal communications patterns. Coercive control is not the kind of power employed by a member of a healthy family; rather he or she will express power through a coalition with others, stemming from mutual respect. Healthy families model healthy interpersonal interactions, which will prepare children to avoid child abuse because they will identify abusive behaviors as being different from the type of interpersonal interactions with which they are familiar. Healthy families will also help adolescents or adults avoid date or acquaintance rape or sexual harassment involvement by providing the family member with an ability to assess situations accurately and provide appropriate and consistent verbal and nonverbal messages.

Some perpetrators of child sexual abuse are children themselves, and unhealthy families perpetuate their involvement in child sexual abuse in a number of ways (Cantwell 1988). For example, parents of a young perpetrator may deny their child's unusual behavior and/or blame the victim for the assault. Many of these child perpetrators are never evaluated to determine if they had previously been victims. Their parents may not understand the serious consequences of the child's behavior and may deny him or her the opportunity to receive psychological treatment (Briere 1984). Many families severely punish children found in sexual interactions. The result is that victims remain silent, and perpetrators remain free to victimize, thereby perpetuating the cycle of abuse (Cantwell 1988).

Parents who raise their child to believe that the child deserves the negative experiences she or he has had and is no good and that if something bad happened that it is the child's fault may be raising a child who is ripe for victimization. In addition if a child is victimized by a parent or family member or if a victimized child does not receive any help from the parents, that child is likely to fall into a pattern of repeated victimization with others later in life. Sometimes these types of patterns develop if parents feel that a child is owned by the parents and therefore parents can do anything they want with their "property" (Herman 1981). Children must learn that their bodies are their own, and no one, even their parents, has the right to exploit or abuse them.

Above all else, educators, therapists, and parents must be armed with information about the factors that contribute to sexual coercion. Communication is the greatest enemy of child sexual abuse. When parents and other care givers learn about child sexual abuse prevention, their awareness levels and protective ability increase. When adults talk about child sexual abuse with children and inform and listen to them, uncomfortable feelings can be discussed that may help prevent potentially sexually abusive situations (Plummer 1986).

Although sexual abuse is never the fault of victims, some victims' personality factors and belief systems may increase the likelihood that they will be chosen as victims, and in some cases they may be victimized more than once by the same or different assailants. Parents should be aware of these factors so they will be less likely to blame victims, and they can help to socialize young people to reject these factors and belief systems (Sanford 1980). Victims as well as assailants may exhibit these factors and adhere to these belief systems. By trying to minimize them, we may be able to decrease sexual coercion by eliminating easy targets and by keeping potential assailants from victimizing. In fact, it is often difficult to draw a clear distinction between victims and assailants because some assailants have also been victims (Porter 1986).

Assailants obtain compliance through manipulation, coercion, threats, force, or physical violence.[2] Most of the time, coercion or manipulation is used in child sexual abuse. In rape cases where the assailant and the victim know each other, physical violence is rarely used. However, physical force, threats of force, coercion, and manipulation are common (Warshaw 1988; Parrot 1988). Stranger rape cases most often are associated with physical violence, force, or threat of force. Thus, potential victims need to learn to recognize and respond to a variety of verbal and nonverbal cues in order to help prevent sexual coercion.

Downer (1986) believes that children should be provided with nine messages about child sexual abuse prevention:

1. The child should know that it is acceptable to ask an adult for help if the child is touched without a good reason by an older person on the vulva, penis, or breast.

2. Children should know that it is their right to say "no" to an older person who touches their genitals or asks to be touched on his or her genitals for no good reason.

3. Children should understand that not all children have problems with unwanted touching, but children who do need to know that it is not their fault.

4. A child should know that unwanted touching is not the child's fault even if the child did not say "no" or tried unsuccessfully to say "no."

5. Children must know that unwanted touching can happen with anyone, even with someone they know well, including members of their own families.

6. Children should understand that they should tell someone if they do experience unwanted touching.

7. Children should know that it is never too late to tell someone about unwanted touching.

8. Children should be aware that most adults will not touch them inappropriately.

9. Children should know whom to tell about unwanted touching.

Children will be much safer regarding child sexual abuse if they are given these messages early in their lives. These messages may be reinforced by schools, religious organizations, and the media, but they should come from parents originally.

Parents need to discuss sexuality openly with their children to impart essential information about good touch and bad touch but also to impart values to their children. Parents are the primary sex educators of their children in the years before adolescence (Thornburg 1981). Therefore it is essential that parents provide children with strong skills and good information to counteract any inaccurate information or negative values or messages they may pick up from peers, other adults, school, or the media. If a child knows that discussing sex at home is normal, the child is more likely to talk with his or her parents about a sexually abusive event.

Parents should also allow their children to observe the full range of emotions in the home. If children learn to differentiate among the subtle variations of similar emotions (such as shame and guilt) at home, they will be able to utilize that understanding in relationships outside the home (Parrot 1986). They may be better able to understand when a situation is likely to become dangerous and may be able to leave before they are victimized. In addition, if they see that both men and women are permitted to experience a full range of emotions, they are likely to accept males who cry and females who are angry.

It is very important for parents to attempt to develop positive self-esteem in their children because children who feel good enough about themselves can stand up for what they believe and can withstand negative peer pressure. Parents should never reject the child (by saying something such as "You are so stupid. Can't you do anything right?"); rather they should reject the behavior but accept the child (such as, "Your grade on that spelling test wasn't good, but you are smart, and I am sure you can do better").

Parents may contribute to positive or negative messages children learn about sex. Parents who talk with their children openly about sex will relay the impression that healthy sex is not something dirty and secret; rather it is a normal part of life between two adults or young adults who love each other. It is not something of which to be ashamed or to be kept secret, especially from their parents. Many parents convey a negative message about sex by using negative terms when discussing sexual behaviors or body parts or by not discussing it at all. If adults are willing to talk about any other part of the body but not the sexual parts of the body, children learn to be embarrassed about those areas; they believe they cannot talk with their parents about any problems they may have with those parts of their bodies, which they consider dirty or disgusting.

Children will not be able to communicate openly about their genitals if they do not know the correct terms for penis, vagina, or breast. Parents may actually contribute to their childrens' negative self-esteem by implying that the sexual parts of the body are bad or dirty. This message may be transmitted when the genitals are referred to as "down there" or by a slang term with a negative connotation (such as *prick* for *penis*). Seldom do parents say that a child has a "beautiful vulva" or a "lovely penis" the way we may speak about "beautiful eyes" or a "beautiful smile." Perhaps parents should provide young people with positive messages about their sexual body parts and the notion that these parts are not something about which we should be embarrassed and therefore never discuss, even if we have a problem with them.

Children need to be taught assertiveness skills and that they have a right to their own bodies. They will be able to use those skills to get what they want out of social situations rather than going along with the crowd or being forced to do something sexually undesirable. One way parents can teach children these messages is to allow them to reject undesired social behaviors as children. For example, if Aunt Marge wants to kiss little Janey but she does not want to kiss Aunt Marge, she should not be forced. By forcing her, she is being taught to ignore her instinctual feeling of discomfort and to allow her body to be touched in a way that makes her uncomfortable. She learns that she does not have the right to control her own body. Another time when children receive this message is when they are being tickled and say "no" but the tickler will not stop.

If males are to be socialized to be sensitive to women's needs, boys need to be taught that they are not better than girls and that they do not have the right to do anything they want with a female. This message must be modeled by parents. They must not, for example, treat their son's football game as more important than their daughter's band concert or teach boys that "winning" (attaining their goal) is the most important outcome. Parents may do well to encourage their daughters to play physical sports to learn the limitations and strengths of their bodies. If young girls were taught contact sport such as soccer or football, they would gain the valuable knowledge that their bodies can be used to defend themselves.

Sexual behavior falls along a continuum from consensual sex to rape. There are many behaviors along the continuum that may desensitize the actor to more aggressive acts and allow him to move toward the rape end. Listening to sexist jokes precedes telling sexist jokes. Once a person becomes desensitized to sexist behaviors, it becomes easier to engage in objectifying behaviors, such as "rating" a woman based on her appearance (for example, saying, "She is a real dog; I'd give her a 3"). Exploitative behaviors include lying to a woman to get her to have sex (such as, "I have never said 'I love you' to anyone before") or getting a woman drunk to have sex with her. Legally, having sex with a woman who has passed out is considered rape, so there is very little difference between having sex with an intoxicated woman (exploitative behavior) or a woman who is passed out (rape). Of course, there are other, more violent and brutal forms of sexual victimization on the rape end of the continuum, which moves from sexist behavior, to objectifying behavior, to exploitative behavior, and finally to rape.

Parents need to understand the ease with which movement is made along the continuum and how desensitization to milder forms of inappropriate behavior can move a boy or man closer to rape, especially under the influence of alcohol and peer pressure. By not tolerating sexist behaviors of their sons, parents can better ensure that more coercive behaviors will be avoided. Boys must also be taught and encouraged to use peer pressure positively to discourage other boys from objectifying women. Parents need to teach their sons to hear and respect a "no" from a female.

The reality of the situation is that males know that if they exploit others sexually, they will probably not be caught and punished. However, there are several approaches we can use to get males to listen to the plea to respect others' sexual wishes about sex. First, we can tell boys that ignoring another person's sexual wishes and forcing him or her to do something sexually is exploitation, which is morally wrong. This approach will work only with people who have developed a strong set of moral values. If the moral approach does not work, we can tell them that they may be arrested, sentenced, and convicted for such behavior, because it is a crime in all fifty states. In fact, in 1990, a senior at an Ivy League university was convicted of first-degree rape for forcing sexual intercourse on a woman with whom he had previously had consensual sex. He will spend between two and twenty-five years in state prison for pushing her. Men and women are serving jail time in this country for committing incest, child sexual abuse, and acquaintance rape.

A final approach that may work if the other two do not is to ask the potential assailant how he or she would feel if someone forced his or her mother, sister, brother, girlfriend, or boyfriend into an unwanted sexual encounter. Many assailants find the notion of sexual assault of their loved one to be horrendous, but they do not necessarily feel the same way about the sexual assault of a stranger.

Parent-School Partnership

School-based child sexual abuse programs should include a partnership between the school and the community, build on parents' experiences and expertise, recognize that parents may be abusers, and include a discussion of appropriate intervention in an abusive family (Whatley and Trudell 1988). Children need to learn the difference between "good touch" and "bad touch" to understand what constitutes child sexual abuse; however, very young children may not be cognitively able to understand the difference (deYoung 1988b). Thus, programs for young children may have to present different concepts. They should reflect a child's conceptual approach to the world, not an adult's, and they should not instill fear in children. Rather, children should learn effective techniques to deal with potentially dangerous situations (Kraizer, Fryer, and Miller 1988). If school-based programs are to be effective, they must respond to the emotional as well as physical needs of the child.

All people have a right to keep from being victimized, sexually or in any other way. No one has the right to exploit or force others to do something sexual they do not want to do. If parents socialize their children to believe that they are worthwhile, to reject media images of the ideal, to understand that it is acceptable to discuss problems with sexual body parts and behaviors, and not to be embarrassed about their bodies, children will be better able to avoid sexual victimization.

Conclusion

Many of the suggestions appropriate for child sexual abuse prevention are also appropriate for acquaintance or marital rape prevention. Young people need to learn that no one has the right to force sex on another individual, regardless of the circumstances. Parents and schools can and should play an important role in sexual assault prevention education. However, before adults can educate appropriately about sexual assault prevention, they must understand the child-rearing practices and socialization messages that will help protect children from involvement in sexually coercive situations as victims or assailants and they need to know how to impart those messages effectively.

Traditional white female socialization does not prepare women psychologically or physically to avoid rape. Women would be best prepared with self-defense training, assertiveness training, and high self-esteem to know they have a right to avoid victimization and the willingness and tools necessary to keep an assault from becoming a rape.

The following suggestions are important for potential victims to consider (Parrot 1988):

- Feel good about yourself.
- If you have been victimized, get emotional help to avoid falling into a pattern of repeat victimization.
- Stay away from those who treat you badly.
- Mean what you say, and say what you mean.
- Try to avoid dangerous situations.
- Have a way out if you are trapped (even in your own home).

Victims must remember that even if they are sexually assaulted, the assault is the fault of the assailant, not the victim.

There are several important points potential assailants need to know about forced sex (Parrot 1988):

- Rape is a crime of violence motivated by the desire to control and dominate.
- One person never has the right to force another person to have sex, even if he thinks she or he has been "leading him on" and deserves it.
- Using force to get another person to have sex is a crime.
- Men do not always have to initiate sexually, and they can say "no" to sex too.
- If a person does not stop when a partner says "no" to sex, the actual act is rape.
- Alcohol consumption increases the likelihood of sexual assault involvement.
- It is wise to discuss sexual intentions honestly and openly with a partner prior to sex.

Assailants of sexual coercion can be men, women or children, and victims can also be men, women, or children. The recommendations made in this chapter apply to all three groups.

The most effective way to change sexual coercion patterns is to have parents, schools, and the media change socialization messages for young people about sex roles and sexual assault. Professionals need to share their ideas, research results, and failures regarding improvement in techniques and in the result of prevention efforts. Prevention programs that are securely funded, regularly given, and professionally monitored in every school in the country will present a formidable challenge to the dragon of sexual abuse (Plummer 1986).

Notes

1. The term *victim* will be used to indicate someone who has been forced to have sexual experiences against his or her will or without consent. Some professionals working with sexual assault victims prefer to use the term *survivor*. However, although victims may have survived physically, the victimization experience is likely to interrupt their psychological state and interfere with interpersonal relationships. Therefore, they are still being

emotionally victimized by the sexual assault. Until victims are able to place the blame for their victimization with the assailants (where it belongs) and put the assault in perspective in their lives, they are still being victimized. Because many victims of sexual assault do not seek help and because all victims experience some level of trauma after the assault, the term *victim*, rather than *survivor*, will be used.

2. Although all forms of sexual assault are violent by definition, not all have other types of physical violence associated with them. When the term *physical violence* is used, it is meant to imply beating, slapping, stabbing, shooting, and other similar actions.

10

New Approaches to Dating and Sexuality

Elizabeth Rice Allgeier
Betty J. Turner Royster

Shelley first noticed him over by the keg, talking to her friend Danny. He was in profile and had the body of a runner; she wandered over to talk to one of her girlfriends so that she could see his face. She liked the way his laugh dissolved slowly into a smile and decided that she would go over to the keg and get Danny to introduce them. By the time she made her way through the party crowd, Danny had gone, so as she approached the keg, she glanced at him briefly and licked her lips. She flicked her hair back over her shoulder with her hand, smiled more directly at the stranger, and reached for the pump. He smiled back and said, "Let me give you a hand with that." She thanked him, and after her plastic cup was filled, he said, "What's your name, anyway?"

Shelley and Mike spent most of the evening talking, and when the party began to wind down, Mike offered her a ride home. She grinned at him and said, "I'd *really* like to accept, but I have my car and promised to give my roommates a ride home." He replied, "That's too bad; I'd like to continue our conversation. Maybe we could meet somewhere after you've dropped them off." Shelley smiled at him again: "I wish I could, but I have an exam tomorrow morning, so I'd better get some sleep. Maybe you could give me a call, and we could get together Friday or Saturday night." He asked for her phone number and called her later that week. Over the next month, they saw each other several times a week.

They were sitting in her apartment one night when her roommates had gone home for the weekend. They had a videotape on but had gotten so involved in kissing and cuddling that they lost track of the plot. He started to play with her breasts, by now both of them sexually aroused. In a husky voice, Mike said, "Oh, Shelley, I love you." She nibbled on his ear, murmuring, "I love you, too, Mike." But when Mike tried to unbutton Shelley's jeans, she took his hands and moved away from him on the couch, saying, "Oh, Mike, you know how much I care about you, but I'm just not ready to go any further right now." Actually one part of Shelley wanted very much to continue and to make love with Mike, but she thought that they needed to talk about their relationship; moreover, she was not on the pill and did not want to get pregnant. Mike, however, could not tell whether she wanted him to persist or whether she really did not want to have sex with him yet (or at all), so he stood up and said, "Well, I think I'd better be going," hoping that she would stop him. She didn't but said, "Ok. I'll give you a call tomorrow." They kissed demurely at the door and said good-night. After they parted, each felt a little rejected and confused. He wondered why she had put him off after all the necking and petting they had been doing the past few weeks, but he did not want to get into a position of pushing her into something she didn't want. She wondered why he left so abruptly.

Shelley and Mike will provide us with a means of comparing stereotypes about dating and sexuality to what contemporary observations have indicated actually goes on in heterosexual courtship. We will return to their relationship later.

Accompanied by an increase in the economic and social status of women as a group, considerable change has occurred in the past few decades in the patterns of dating and sexual interactions between women and men. We will review traditional courtship patterns and discuss the concept of equality between romantic partners, describe research on contemporary dating and courtship negotiations, and address the issue of attempts by one person to use verbal and nonverbal methods to have sexual relations with another person who does not currently want increased intimacy. We conclude with models for giving and receiving informed consent before agreeing to become sexually intimate.[1]

Shifting Courtship Patterns

Meeting, dating, and courtship rarely follow an idealized "man and woman meet, date, fall in love, marry, and live happily ever after" pattern. The process involving meeting, marrying, and mating can have numerous glitches, starts and stops, and misunderstandings. Furthermore, when all three events do occur, they now usually occur in a different sequence: meeting, mating, and marrying. That is, most contemporary couples engage in sex before marrying.

The traditional dating scenario placed the man in the role of initiator. He selected the woman, initiated the relationship, asked the woman out, planned the activities, and provided resources (money and transportation, for example) for dates. The traditional woman was expected to assume a passive, receptive role, which included waiting for the man to ask her out. He was expected to provide the transportation and to pay the dating expenses.

Dating and mating behavior has changed in the past few decades, and these shifts may reflect changes in gender role expectations and the status of women in Western society. The 1960s marked the beginning of the modern movement toward women's achieving increased economic, social, and legal independence; during the 1960s, most women's status, life-style, and financial resources were still heavily determined by their husbands. By 1990, employment of women outside the home regardless of their family status (single, married, or mothers of young children) had become the norm, although women still earned less than their male counterparts. Nonetheless, women's increased opportunity to achieve their own social status and economic well-being independent of their spouse's social standing and economic achievement has provided women with increased freedom to select mates on the basis of love rather than on the basis of a man's potential capacity to provide them with assets that women formerly could acquire primarily through marriage. In the 1960s, less than a quarter of women would refuse to marry a man who had all the qualities they wanted in a spouse even if they did not love him (Kephart 1967); the vast majority of women now require love in a potential spouse (Allgeier and Wiederman 1990; Simpson, Campbell, and Berscheid 1986). Stated another way, some of the rules of courtship and mate selection may be changing, with the trend toward increased equality between potential partners. It is unlikely that two individuals, however, will have precisely the same degree of power or resources in their interactions or in the world beyond their relationship.

Power and Initiation in Courtship

The concept of power in the realm of dating and courtship relationships has a variety of dimensions (Frieze et al. 1978; Richardson 1989). Two people may differ in power in their social status, professional status, economic well-being, age and relative experience, and desire to establish a relationship with one another. And in the case of assault, power can differ physically or psychologically, resulting in one person's coercing another to engage in unwanted sexual contacts.

The concept of power is important in evaluating relationships, partially because the person holding more relative power is more likely to have his or her needs met than a person holding less power. Further, a person having less power may be unable to grant true informed consent to engage in a relationship. The relative value of the relationship for each of its members is also of crucial importance as a measure of power. Observers of social behavior have consistently concluded that the individual who is most desirous of maintaining a relationship (or who values the relationship most) is the one who possesses least power in the relationship (Blau 1964; Hatfield 1983; Peplau, Rubin, and Hill 1977; Richardson 1989; Sprecher 1984; Waller 1938). One measure of the value an individual assigns to a romantic relationship is his or her avowed level of commitment or love involvement. In one study of factors that affect perceptions of egalitarianism in dating relationships, it was found that "an imbalance of love involvement and perceived intelligence is related to an imbalance of power in dating relationships for women" (Grauerholz 1987: 568).

According to Frieze and coworkers (1978), males have higher status by virtue of their gender classification. That is, "masculine" attributes (such as leadership and aggressiveness) are more highly valued in our society than are "feminine" attributes (such as nurturance and yielding). Thus, a man's standing in his social network, in addition to his use of the masculine prerogative of date initiation, make him more likely to perceive his relative power. In some cases, a power imbalance is strengthened by the additional power accrued to men who initiate dates, pay for dating expenses, and provide transportation. A woman, on the other hand, may perceive herself to have less freedom of choice and power and thus may be more likely to attribute greater relative value to "the bird in the hand," particularly if she believes that she must either passively wait for a man to initiate or for a new relationship to develop. As we shall see, however, recent research indicates that women have considerably more freedom of choice than current stereotypes would suggest.

At the beginning of this chapter, in reading about how Shelley and Mike met and began their relationship, you may not have noticed anything discrepant with your own experience. But if you return to that description and compare it with the stereotype of male-female courtship, you will notice a number of important discrepancies. First, who did the selection? There was Mike, drinking his beer and minding his own business. Shelley, however, noticed him, and she liked what she saw. She then selected him and signaled her interest in him. Having gotten the signals, he responded with interest, offering to help her get beer from the keg, asking her name, continuing the conversation, and offering her a ride home.

That description varies from the commonly held stereotype that it is males who do the selecting of females. A decade ago, scholars began to question this stereotype using a variety of different research approaches in their examination of various phases of the courtship process: selection, initiation and escalation of a relationship, and seduction and rejection strategies (McCormick 1979; Moore, 1985; Perper 1985; Perper and Fox 1980; Perper and Weis 1987). This line of research was begun in the late 1970s with the work of Timothy Perper and his colleagues.

Perper spent almost a thousand hours in singles bar settings. He and Susan Fox (1980) watched the process that sometimes culminated in a man and woman, initially strangers to one another, leaving the bar together. Perper (1985) concluded that it was the woman, rather than the man, who did the selection of a partner. His conclusion was based primarily on visual observations of nonverbal behavior, but he and Fox also subsequently interviewed some of the people they had observed leaving the bar together on previous evenings. The common wisdom is that the primary role of women is to be receptive or rejective—that is, they may accept or reject a man's approach. In contrast, Perper and his colleagues concluded that women are proceptive—active in their selection of a potential partner. Essentially they found that the women whom they interviewed were very aware of being proceptive and of what they had done to select a partner and to initiate a relationship. In contrast, the men who were interviewed were relatively unaware of the woman's proceptive behavior or who was responsible for the increasing intimacy between them and their partner. In other words, the women quite deliberately selected a target male and signaled their interest, and the man then either did or did not respond to their interest. Further evidence of women's proceptive power was documented by Monica Moore's (1985) research demonstrating a very strong correlation ($r = .89$) between the number of signals a woman directed at a man in various settings (singles bars, snack bars, and so forth) and the man's subsequent approach to her.

What happens after a woman has selected and signaled a man and he has approached her? Perper (1985) hypothesized a sequence of behaviors leading to sexual intimacy. Specifically, he concluded that following the man's approach, the woman chooses either to escalate or deescalate the relationship depending on her evaluation of him. If the relationship is maintained and escalated, Perper hypothesized that at the point that a couple (or at least the man) is ready to engage in sexual intimacy, a transition in power takes place in which the man takes over the responsibility for initiating sexual contact. In support of Perper's hypothesis, Gaulier, Travis, and Allgeier (1986) found that although women are more likely than men to report engaging in behaviors designed to initiate the onset of a relationship, men are more likely than women to describe themselves as attempting to move toward greater sexual intimacy and to arouse the partner.

At this point, it seems quite clear that it is females, rather than males, who select partners. However, we should note that women are expected to do so in a relatively indirect fashion; most women do not walk up to a man and say, "I think you look interesting, so you may approach me for conversation while I check you out." Nonetheless, although the prerogative of males' selecting females may be considered outmoded, male initiation of dates still appears to be operative on the first date after meeting, as is the expectation that the man will plan and pay for the date (Komarovsky 1985).

Some research on changing trends, however, suggests that the acceptance of female initiation for at least one of these responsibilities has occurred (Muehlenhard 1981). When undergraduate men were asked to indicate the extent to which they would be disturbed by women's initiating dates, they reported that they generally preferred a woman to hint rather than to initiate a date outright. More important than the men's preference for direct versus indirect strategies in initiating dates was how much they liked a particular woman. On the basis of her data, Muehlenhard noted that "if a woman takes the initiative, the man will accept if he likes her and will not accept if he does not like her" (p. 691). McCormick and Jesser's (1983) research with college students indicated that the rules of courtship still follow gender role stereotypes: "Men are more likely to influence a date to have sex; women are more likely to refuse sex" (p. 85).

Current trends in premarital sexual behavior and expectations related to such behavior seem to be dependent on the stage of development in the dating relationship (Roche 1986) as well as on gender role stereotypes. Roche conceptualized the progress of a dating relationship as a progression through five stages:

Stage 1: Dating without affection.

Stage 2: Dating with affection.

Stage 3: Dating individuals consider themselves to be "in love."

Stage 4: Dating only the loved person.

Stage 5: Couple becomes engaged to marry.

When male and female college students were asked what they considered to be proper sexual behavior during these five stages, there were considerable gender differences in judgments about proper behavior during the first three stages. In those stages, men condoned greater permissiveness and reported that they engaged in significantly more petting than did women. In the last two stages, these differences essentially disappeared. There was agreement between men and women about the appropriateness of light and heavy petting and intercourse during stages 4 and 5, and large numbers of both men and women reported engaging in sexual intercourse during those stages. The only gender difference to emerge for later stages involved oral-genital sex. A large majority (86 percent) of the men indicated that oral sex was appropriate at stage 4. Although 71 percent of the women endorsed oral sex at stage 4, 20 percent indicated that this practice should occur only after marriage. It is important to note that both men and women reported greater permissiveness in their actual behavior than in their definitions of proper behavior.

Strategies Employed to Increase or Reduce Sexual Intimacy

When young men and women were asked by McCormick (1979) to indicate how they would attempt to have sex with a person to whom they were attracted, both preferred using indirect strategies, such as sitting closer, holding hands, and so forth. McCormick concluded that of the ten strategies reported by men and women, both men and women preferred the use of seduction over the others. By her definition, seduction involved a definite plan for getting a date to have coitus by focusing on sexually stimulating the date. This strategy was a relatively indirect one compared to others that she measured, such as telling a date directly that sex was desired or using rational arguments to convince a date to have intercourse.

Perper and Weis (1987) obtained essays from college women in Canada and the United States on how they would influence a date to have sex and how they would avoid sex. The strategies that women most commonly reported using to indicate sexual interest included situational strategies (dressing in a seductive fashion and/or creating a romantic ambience), indirect or direct verbal indications of interest (compliments, sexy romantic talk), and nonverbal cues (eye contact, touching, kissing). The rejection strategies formed two categories Perper and Weis (1987) labeled Avoid Proceptivity and Incomplete Rejection. In the case of Avoid Proceptivity, the woman sends no proceptive signals, ignores any such signals sent by the man, and avoids placing herself in an intimate setting with the man. When using the Incomplete Rejection strategy, the woman indicates some interest in the man and, simultaneously, a desire to postpone greater intimacy. The response of Shelley to Mike's attempt to become more physically intimate is an example of the Incomplete Rejection strategy; it leaves the door open for future sexual negotiations. Perper and Weis discussed both the utility and the potential for abuse that may accompany use of the Incomplete Rejection strategy. On the one hand, such a strategy may allow a woman to assess her partner's potential for the kind of sensitivity needed in a long-term caring relationship. If he is willing to wait until she is ready to become more intimate, perhaps he will be sensitive to her needs in other areas as well. However, such a strategy can be problematic when used with a man who believes that a woman's stated reluctance to have sex is merely a smokescreen to avoid the appearance of promiscuity. Such a man may escalate his attempts to have sex, and date rape may result. Hence, Perper and Weis construed this strategy as both a sensitivity filter and a potential precursor to sexual coercion.

The difficulty facing men who receive an incomplete rejection message is in interpreting it. Does the woman mean precisely what she is saying—"I'm not yet ready"—with the implication that she will desire intercourse later?

Because of their socialization to be nurturant and supportive, some women use the same words and engage in the same behavior, but their words do not always have the same meaning. Some of the female members of our research group have reported that they are aware of having done and said the same thing but with three different kinds of motivation: (1) when they do not want to be perceived as being a "slut" or too "easy"; (2) when they are feeling mixed emotions but definitely want to become sexually intimate in the future; and (3) when they are not in the least interested in further sexual intimacy but do not want to hurt the man's feelings. Thus, the man in the situation is faced with the task of interpretation. Does the message mean "I'm resisting, but please persist," "Give me a little more time," or "Back off, buster! Can't you take the hint that I'm not interested?"?

A particularly direct example of motivation 1 by a woman and an accurate interpretation (1) by a man appeared in research in which college men and women were asked to provide written descriptions to questions about the circumstances surrounding their first experience of sexual intercourse with their most recent (or only) intercourse partner (Allgeier 1989). One young woman reported that she and her boyfriend were kissing romantically and that he kept trying to have intercourse but that she kept saying no. "Finally, he just sort of forced it in" (p. 7). She said that she had decided to have sex with him earlier but "wanted to wait awhile and play hard to get. . . . I've always wanted 'sex' from my boyfriend but I said no so he'd respect me" (p. 8). When asked to compare that experience with previous sexual encounters, she said that her previous boyfriend was

> extremely loving, understanding, and fun. My ex-boyfriend would have never forced himself on me! But weirdly enough, I liked that forcefulness from my [present] boyfriend because I knew it was out of love. . . . Now my boyfriend and I laugh at it, because he stated that it was an extremely mild form of date rape. (p. 8)

What we described as motivation 1—wishing to avoid being perceived as a slut or too easy even when they do wish to have sex—is also known as the "token no." Charlene Muehlenhard and her colleagues have done a considerable amount of research on this topic. They found that women do in fact report sometimes using the token no and that men are more likely than women to believe that women really mean "yes" when they say "no" to sex (Muehlenhard 1988a, 1988b). Traditional males have sometimes used this rationale to justify continuing sexual advances despite the protests of their female companions. The woman's protest was considered to be a token response geared toward presenting herself in a nonpromiscuous light (Check and Malamuth 1983).

Stated another way, sometimes when women's "no" is due to motivations 2 ("not yet") or 3 ("never"), men mistakenly use interpretation 1 ("I'm resisting, but please persist"). The disjuncture between women's motives and men's interpretations sets the stage for one of the circumstances under which sexual coercion may occur on dates. It is important to realize that date rape is generally traumatic for the victim rather than leading the couple subsequently to "laugh at it . . . because it was an extremely mild form of date rape," as the young woman above described.

Date rape cannot be excused on the grounds that women sometimes use the token no. When a woman actually uses a token no and her partner accurately perceives it as such, no one is violated. Problems with the token no arise because many women report that their "no" reflected their true wishes. If a man errs in his interpretation of a woman's rejection of sexual intimacy, it is preferable for him to err on the side of constraint rather than to risk violating the wishes and body of a person who truly does not wish to become more intimate.

Although the token no and incomplete rejection strategy hypotheses offer potential explanations for the occurrence of some sexual coercion directed toward women by men, they are not as easily applied to sexual coercion of men by women. Surveys indicate that although sexual coercion of women by men is more common, sexual exploitation of men by women is also a problem (Aizenman and Kelley 1988; Muehlenhard and Cook 1988; Struckman-Johnson 1988). Of the 400 men in Aizenman and Kelley's survey, 14 percent reported being coerced into having sexual intercourse against their will and 17 percent said that they had engaged in other sexual contact against their will. Of the males in Struckman-Johnson's survey, 16 percent reported that they were pressed by dating partners to have sex when they did not want to do so.

Heavy drinking and abuse of other drugs has been implicated in sexual coercion among acquaintances in a number of studies (Ageton 1983; Levine and Kanin 1987; Struckman-Johnson 1988). Presumably the impairment produced by alcohol and drug use would be likely to interfere with clear, direct communication of one's sexual desires, motives, and interpretations.

Methods of Increasing the Pleasure of Romantic and/or Sexual Relationships

A decided trend toward the relative valuation of honesty and intimacy above traditional values was observed in a sample of more than 200 dating and cohabiting couples by Rubin and coworkers (1980; see also Peplau, Rubin, and Hill 1977). The couples in their sample—some of them sexually intimate—reported a high level of self-disclosure of their feelings. The openness of these couples may not be representative of the larger population of dating couples, however, in that they were selected to participate (and volunteered to do so) after having been dating for an average of three months or more. Presumably couples experiencing sexual coercion would either not still be intact or would decline to participate.

The clarity of communication about one's current disinterest in increased intimacy appears to be an important determinant of the extent to which the recipient of the message responds to it (Bart and O'Brien 1985; Kanin 1985). Perceptions of students tended to be more lenient toward the perpetrator of rape and less favorable toward the victim when there was ambiguity in the victim's desire for intercourse, with the effect more pronounced for male than female respondents (Johnson and Jackson 1988).

Both women and men may feel themselves to be in a double bind in communicating their real sexual feelings, although for different reasons. Women sometimes may feel pressed to give the token no for reasons already described when they want to become more sexually intimate and may be communicating those feelings nonverbally. In contrast, because of gender role stereotypes suggesting that "real" men always want sex, some men may respond positively to an opportunity for sex when in fact they would sometimes prefer to postpone or avoid sexual involvement (Muehlenhard 1989; Struckman-Johnson 1988).

Muelenhard and her colleagues have been involved in an extended research program to increase knowledge of ways to strengthen women's ability to resist sexual coercion attempts by eliminating any ambiguity in the victim's desire for intercourse. Their dual approach hinges on first developing a means of identifying characteristic patterns of vulnerability to sexual coercion and then teaching those who may be particularly vulnerable how to avoid or refuse unwanted sex as well as how to initiate wanted sex (Muehlenhard et al. 1989).

The first aspect of their approach was accomplished through the development of the Sexual Assertiveness Questionnaire (SAQ) (Muehlenhard and Linton 1985), the Sexual Assertiveness Role-Play Test (SARPT) (Flarity-White and Muehlenhard 1988), and the Sexual Assertiveness Self-Statement Test (SASST) (Muehlenhard et al. 1989). The SAQ is a self-report measure that assesses a woman's ability to refuse undesired dates and sexual behavior. The SARPT is an innovative supplement to the SAQ. It consists of a videotaped set of extended interactive role-play situations of potentially coercive situations. Women are asked to stop the tape at appropriate places and to respond verbally and physically as they would if the situation were real. The SASST was designed to assess women's positive and negative self-statements about unwanted sex. The rationale for the development of this measure was the reported phenomenon of the common failure of victims to label sexual coercion on dates as rape (Koss et al. 1988). Muehlenhard and her colleagues asserted that effective assessment can lead to strategies to deal specifically with areas of weakness in resisting sexual coercion.

The second focus was the development of a cognitive-behavioral treatment program geared toward improving the rape resistance skills in college women (Carlson, Julsonnet, and Muehlenhard 1988). This program had three components:

1. A didactic component in which assertive behavior is defined and effective rape avoidance strategies are discussed.
2. A cognitive-restructuring component that includes a discussion of negative self-statements and women's sexual rights.
3. A behavioral rehearsal component that includes behavioral role playing of potentially coercive situations.

Giving and Receiving Informed Consent: A Model

The approach used by Muehlenhard and her colleagues is designed to reduce the likelihood of sexual coercion. Now we will focus on an approach designed to increase the likelihood of healthy sexual interactions' occurring only when both members of a couple feel mutually ready for consensual sexual contacts.

The concept of informed consent widely used in the context of behavioral research, refers to providing potential research participants with enough information about a particular study so that the individual can make an informed decision before giving consent to participate in the research. As we will be using the term, it refers to potential participants in a romantic and sexual relationship giving one another enough information about themselves, their past, and their motivations for the relationship so that each can make an informed decision before giving consent to participate in physical intimacy with one another.

When we left Shelley and Mike at the beginning of the chapter, Mike had nonverbally indicated an interest in becoming more physically intimate with Shelley by attempting to unbutton her jeans, but Shelley told him that she did not want to become any more intimate at that point. They had not discussed their motives for the relationship, their plans for dealing with potential pregnancy or sexually transmitted diseases, or the risks that their past relationships might pose to one another. Unfortunately, neither Shelley nor Mike indicated directly that they wanted to discuss these issues with one another. Before discussing these issues with another individual, a person needs to know his or her own feelings and policies.

Acknowledging One's Own Policies and Desires to Oneself

The idea of having a sexual policy may sound foreign in a culture in which we are told to "just say no" to a variety of things (drugs, premarital or nonmarital sex, and so forth). However, most of us do have sexual policies even if they are somewhat vague and inconsistently applied. For example, some people have a policy that they will not kiss on a first date or that they will not have sex until they have been dating someone for a particular length of time or number of dates. Others have policies that they will not have sex with married people or with anyone but their spouses. Some individuals are unaware of having policies about the conditions under which they will express their sexual feelings, believing that sex should be spontaneous and that planning for it will ruin the romance and spontaneity of a relationship. Even this approach—the idea that sex and romance should not be planned—is a form of sexual policy, although this particular policy is less likely to lead to mutually satisfying experiences than is overt discussion of the conditions under which sexual intimacy is acceptable and desired by both persons.

Communicating and Negotiating Sexual Behavior with a Potential Partner

As soon as one person is aware of having sexual feelings toward another person and thinks that he or she would like to act on those feelings in the future, it is appropriate to begin discussing issues relevant to their motives and the risks and benefits of sexual intimacy. Depending on the individuals and their particular policies, such a discussion might be appropriate the day they meet, after their first date, or after several weeks or months. Such discussions are best held in relatively public settings or at least in locations in which others are nearby should one of the people attempt to coerce the other.

Among the topics that should be discussed are each person's policies and motives for sexual involvement. For example, both people may perceive each other as an SO. But SO may stand for "significant other" to one of the people and for "sex object" to the other. If their motives are very different, it may not be wise for the person who is expecting more of the relationship to invest in it sexually, at least at the present time.

Risks posed by past relationships need to be addressed. The greater the number of sexual partners a person has had, the higher the likelihood that the person has contracted a sexually transmitted disease (STD), and many STDs are asymptomatic but may still be contagious. If both people have had STD screening tests after their last sexual liaison, then they are in a better position to give factual information to their new (potential) partner. Further, both parties have the right to know if their new partner is romantically involved with anyone else—both because of the risks of STDs and because of differences in motives or expectations for the relationship. Of course, if a person is dishonest the receiver cannot be fully informed and thus cannot give informed consent.

Plans for dealing with the possibility of pregnancy should be considered. There are no totally effective contraceptives, but the risk of unwanted pregnancy can be sharply reduced by the use of condoms, diaphragms, and oral contraceptives. Because pregnancy could still occur, the couple should discuss what they would do in the event that they conceive.

Discussion of sexual preferences is also appropriate. No two people have precisely the same attitudes, and if a couple shares with each other their feelings about coitus and various coital positions, oral sex, mutual masturbation, and other sexual behaviors, they will be in a better position to give and receive pleasurable stimulation. Attitudes can change, of course, so if the man or woman indicates a desire for the woman-above coital position, for example, and the other partner is uncomfortable with that position, the couple can engage in other sexual activities. Knowing that one's partner would like to try something different allows the other person to accept or even to initiate that activity at some point in the future.

In summary, it is important that potential partners give and receive information that is relevant to their individual and mutual well-being before consenting to becoming sexually intimate. In discussing these issues with our students, we have been nonplussed by two reactions. One is best summarized by students who tell us that they think they have become pregnant and want advice on where to go to get tested. When asked what kind of contraceptive was used, some of the students say nothing; they did not want to talk about contraception with their partners because it was too personal. Our surprise stems from the fact that they found talk about such issues too personal but could still engage in the very personal behavior that sometimes involves penetration of their bodies, exchange of body fluids, and so forth.

The other source of surprise comes from the fact that when pressed about why they did not talk about these issues, they say that they think that such discussion will take the spontaneity and romance out of the relationship. Sexual interaction, particularly intercourse, is never utterly spontaneous in our culture. A couple needs to find a private location, get their clothes off, and so forth, and these activities involve two people to make decisions, even if they are not acknowledging the decisions to themselves. As far as romance is concerned, it is deepened by the intimacy engendered by sharing the kind of personal information with one another that is needed for true informed consent.

Let us return to Shelley and Mike, to several weeks before they were ensconced on the couch watching the VCR and necking.

After going to a movie one night several weeks after they met, Mike and Shelley decided to go to a quiet bar to share a few beers and talk about a camping trip they were planning to take during spring break. They discussed the movie, and Mike said that he'd like to have the kind of relationship portrayed by the lovers in the movie. Shelley agreed but said, "Don't you think that it's weird the way they just started having sex without ever talking about birth control or anything else?" Mike replied that maybe the guy thought the woman was on the pill, to which Shelley responded, "Yeah, but he never asked her."

Mike (taking Shelley's hand): Well, maybe I should ask you.
Shelley (laughing): About what?
Mike: About the pill. I've done nothing but think about you ever since we met, and I really want to get closer. (Mike reaches up and strokes her cheek.)
Shelley (nuzzling his hand between her cheek and shoulder): I've been thinking about you, too, Mike, and I want to get closer, but we have some things we should talk about. I'm not on the pill, so that's one of them.

They have a discussion of the birth control options open to them, and Shelley said that one of her roommates had gotten chlamydia, and she did not want to get an STD. On an earlier occasion, they had talked about their previous relationships, and Mike said now that he was pretty sure that he did not have any STDs. Shelley pointed out that many STDs have no symptoms but that she had been screened for STDs by Planned Parenthood the last time she had her annual pelvic exam, which was after she and her last boyfriend had broken up. She suggested that Mike could have himself tested at Planned Parenthood, too, to make sure. Mike said that he cared enough about her that he'd be willing to be tested and that he really wanted to make love to her.

Shelley: I feel that way, too, Mike. In fact, what I would really like to do right now is to go back to my place with you and take a bubble bath and light some candles and go to bed together. Unfortunately, my roommates are there, and I think . . .
Mike: Well, there's no one at my place right now . . .
Shelley: Yeah, well even though I want to make love, I don't want this to be a one-night stand, so I want to make sure that everything is right between us. Also, we've been drinking, and I want to think about this by myself with a clear head.
Mike (interrupting): Shelley, this wouldn't be a one-night stand for me. If I'd felt that way, I'd have made moves on you the first night.
Shelley (grinning and stroking his hand): Well, Mike, you *did* try to get me to meet you after the party the night we met.
Mike: Sure I did, but I didn't say I wanted to have sex that night. . . . Well, I wanted to, but I also wanted to get to know you better, and I haven't made any heavy moves since then, have I?
Shelley (leaning over and kissing him): No, you haven't, and I really appreciate the lack of pressure. I need to be getting home, but let's think about what we're going to do about birth control and why don't you get yourself tested.

Maybe by the time we go on our camping trip, we'll be all ready to make love. I'd really like that.

Mike took Shelley home, and they kissed goodnight at her door. Mike was tested during the next week, they agreed to use condoms, and they had a wonderful time on their camping trip. Some time later when Shelley's roommates were gone for the weekend and Mike and Shelley were watching a movie on the VCR, Mike started to unbutton Shelley's jeans. Shelley stopped him, smiling, and said, "Here, let me help you with that."

Note

1. The conclusions regarding dating and courtship in this chapter apply almost exclusively to white, middle-class, heterosexuals. Investigations of the courtship patterns of gays, and of members of other ethnic groups is badly needed.

11
Educational Reforms

Janet Lynne Enke
Lori K. Sudderth

T here has been a growing awareness of the need to educate young people about sexual coercion, particularly child sexual abuse and rape. This chapter combines a review of programs in the educational system with research on the cultural context of primary and secondary schools to make the argument for a multilevel, comprehensive approach to educational reforms that both changes sexually coercive attitudes and behaviors and prevents sexual coercion from developing in social interaction.

Current Programs and Reforms in Schools:
A Review

Several studies have examined kindergarten and elementary school programs designed to prevent the sexual abuse of young children (Borkin and Frank 1986; Conte, Rosen, and Saperstein 1986; Trudell and Whatley 1988). Model programs for the prevention of child sexual abuse have been implemented in many schools and communities using workshops, theater, and self-defense classes for children. These programs usually focus on the right to say "no" to any unwanted touch, whether by a stranger or someone the child knows. Emphasis may also be placed on distinguishing between comfortable and uncomfortable touch and encouraging children to come up with strategies for dealing with potentially threatening situations (see Nelson and Clark 1986 for a listing of programs).

Information about sexual coercion at the secondary level is contained, if at all, within the general sex education curriculum, but most of these programs are inadequate in terms of dealing with sexuality and tend to reinforce traditional gender expectations (Jackson 1978; Pollis 1988; Szirom 1988). In schools where sex education is implemented, the focus is on reproduction and the prevention of unwanted pregnancy and disease, with little attention given to women's sexuality, gay and lesbian issues, or sexual coercion. At a time when teenagers are beginning to explore their sexuality, the educational system ignores or condemns female sexual desire while presenting male desire as a biological, heterosexual phenomenon (Fine 1988). Furthermore, female sexuality is linked to victimization, depicting females as vulnerable to the male sex drive, thus reinforcing women's status as victims without providing a climate conducive to reporting coercion.

Informational sources are available to parents (Adams, Fay, and Loreen-Martin 1984) and teenagers (Ageton 1985) on how to deal with sexual assault and adolescents' attitudes toward date rape (Maxwell 1990), but this information is typically not taught as part of the curriculum of most schools. Among the few programs set up to deal with rape myth acceptance among adolescents in secondary schools is the Teen Acquaintance Rape Project developed in 1983 by Alternatives to Fear in Seattle, Washington. This program targets teenagers, parents, teachers, and youth leaders. Participants in the workshop are asked to differentiate between acceptable male-female interaction and acquaintance and date rape. They are then encouraged to think about ways to communicate their needs clearly regarding affection and intimacy within a sexual interaction.

Several programs have been set up around the country to deal with student attitudes about rape and sexual coercion in an attempt to change behaviors within college and university settings. Washington State University, in coordination with a local task force and the police department, has set up a rape awareness program designed to raise consciousness, foster communication about rape, explain state laws on rape, and assist victims in legal matters as well as emotional recovery. In addition to the workshops, the local police allow victims or third parties to report rape anonymously, ensuring confidentiality for the victim. Although it is still rare for acquaintance rape to reach the courtroom, the rate of reporting has increased since the implementation of the project (Project on the Status and Education of Women 1985).

The Rape Prevention Education Project developed by the Mid-Missouri Men's Resource Group, focuses on teenage and adult men. The two-hour workshop, conducted by male volunteers, consists of four parts: a discussion of the myths and facts about rape, a narrative about the experience of rape to help participants empathize with the victim, a guided fantasy in which participants imagine a date rape situation and discuss their feelings, and overall responses to the workshop. The program has been used in a variety of settings, and in one study of twenty-four undergraduate men, the workshop was effective in changing participants' attitudes about rape (Lee 1987).

The best guide for universities, colleges, and secondary schools in setting up a rape awareness program is *Stop Date Rape: How to Get What You Want, But Not More Than You Bargained For,* a manual developed at Cornell University by Andrea Parrott in 1987. The manual contains information on presenting workshops on acquaintance and date rape, including suggestions for publicizing the issues, leading discussion and group activities, coordinating with mental health and law enforcement officials, and evaluation of programs. The workshop uses a video or live drama presentation with discussion led by a male and female team of specially trained students.

One workshop modeled after the Cornell program has been established at Indiana University through the Personal Safety Commission and the Office for Women's Affairs. "Student to Student: Straight Talk on Dating" is presented by a male and female team of students and is designed to facilitate discussion about dating, sexuality, and rape. Typically a video of a date or acquaintance rape scenario is shown, and then peer presenters encourage students to share their thoughts and feelings on the issue. The program has also been used to sensitize residential advisers to issues surrounding rape, from recognizing the signs that a woman has been raped to counseling techniques specific to sexual assault victims. Although the workshop is not mandatory, the peer presenters reach one thousand to two thousand students a year.

Several other programs have been set up at universities and colleges around the country, but because these programs are relatively new, few studies have addressed the effectiveness of this format in terms of attitudinal and behavioral change. Most programs implemented on the university, college, or high school level are not mandatory. If an interested party wants to sponsor a program on date rape, it is possible if such a service is available on campus, but discussion of acquaintance and date rape issues is not required of staff or students. Maxwell (1989) points out that it is difficult to assess the generalizability of studies on the effectiveness of rape awareness workshops because the samples are based on students who volunteered to participate in the program.

The Cultural Context of Schools

While changes on the university and college level are vitally important, it is essential to begin counteracting rape myths and sex stereotypes in the educational system as early as possible (Swift 1985). Several studies have focused on how the educational system reinforces traditional gender role expectations (Kessler et al. 1985; Eder and Parker 1987), but few have examined how this system contributes to the development of sexually coercive attitudes and behaviors.

Because children and teens are given little information about sexuality and few outlets for discussing sexual feelings within the educational system, they often turn to each other to interpret cultural messages. Young people attempt to make sense of the conflicting and ambiguous messages from the adult world within the context of peer groups and interpersonal relationships (Corsaro 1985). In the process, they produce a peer culture that often reproduces the attitudes and behaviors associated with sexual coercion in the adult world. Kanin (1984) found that peer group socialization in high school was a critical factor in explaining the behavior of date rapists in that these men had been part of peer groups that viewed women as sexual conquests.

Educational practices influence and constrain the social and sexual experiences of children and adolescents. Within the structure of most schools is a system of rewards for gender-appropriate behavior that imparts very narrow definitions of masculinity and femininity, polarizing the two concepts rather than seeing them as a continuum of behaviors, attitudes, and preferences. By emphasizing the differences between women and men, schools set up models for male-female interaction that are simplistic and narrowly defined and obstruct honest communication. This may also create adversarial relationships between men and women, which may be correlated with greater acceptance of a rape supportive ideology.

This process begins as early as primary school with gender segregation in the classroom and playground. Boys learn the importance of toughness, achieving, and competing, while girls learn social and nurturant values and skills (Lever 1978; Best 1983). Children also learn different sexual scripts and patterns of bonding within these gender-segregated groups. Boys learn to talk dirty and to associate arousal with group rule breaking, while girls are immersed in best friend relations and are learning about self-disclosure and intimacy. Thus, the stage is set for boys' primary commitment to sexual behavior, while romance and emotions come first for girls (Thorne and Luria 1986). Cross-sex interaction at this age is characterized by sexual and romantic overtones, teasing, chasing, and pollution themes (such as girls being contaminating and having "cooties") (Best 1983; Thorne 1986), although relaxed interaction between boys and girls can take place if adults set it up and legitimize the interaction (Thorne 1986).

In middle school and high school, extracurricular activities continue to structure the social world of teenagers. Male athletic activities are the main cultural events of secondary schools, providing male athletes with considerable status among their peers (Coleman 1966; Spreitzer and Pugh 1973; Eitzen 1975; Eder and Parker 1987). The importance of athletics for peer status is underscored by the structural and financial support male athletic programs receive, especially in comparison to girls' athletics, boys' minor sports, music, drama, art, and academic clubs. The implicit message to students is that males are to be supported and cheered on in their athletic activities, particularly in sports such as football and basketball, and females are to be supportive and decorative, despite women's increased participation in active roles like sports. The effect is twofold. First, females are objectified, reinforcing the stereotypical association of femininity with a concern for appearance, social relations, and secondary status. Although women are receiving legitimation to achieve in other realms, they are still expected to be concerned with their appearance and social relations. Second, males are rewarded for a narrow conception of achievement, reinforcing the stereotypical association of masculinity with athletic prowess, strength, and male authority. The structure of athletics is such that boys are set up for failure because self-affirmation and group intimacy are undermined by the emphasis on competition and winning (Messner 1987). Homophobia further inhibits men from developing emotional relationships with male peers (Lehne 1976).

The sexual aspect of this message is that women are supposed to attract men, but it is not clear how far that attraction is supposed to go. This ambiguity about female sexuality is exacerbated by the media, which associate female happiness and success with being attractive and alluring. Furthermore, women are at risk of being negatively evaluated by peers if they are not in a steady relationship with one man. The label "slut" becomes a means of structuring young women's lives and controlling female desire and sexuality (Lees 1986; Fine 1988). As a result, women learn to be coy, manipulative, and subtle in social interaction rather than learning how to identify and directly state their desires and needs.

Conversely, for men, sexual activity becomes a means for achieving (Beneke 1982) and proving one's masculinity to both self and peers, particularly since the number of males who can acquire status through athletics is limited. Given these status concerns, young men may feel pressured to engage in sexual activity and to perform sexually, perhaps before they are ready. This association between masculinity and sexual activity is further supported by the media's portrayal of men's sexuality as a biological drive that is always present and in need of gratification. The right to have that need met becomes legitimated through media images, even when the physical contact involves coercive means. Not surprisingly, associating sexual activity with physical release and status alienates young men from their feelings and the emotional aspects of sexuality.

Cultural models of interaction are thus based largely on male power and authority and female passivity and dependency. If a man "comes onto" a woman, it means she is attractive, and thus her worth is legitimated (Sidel 1990). However, while trying to attract the attention and affection of male peers, young women may be confused as to what is appropriate behavior and how to communicate their feelings to boyfriends, dates, or friends who are pressuring them sexually. Women internalize this notion of the biological male sex drive and thus feel responsible for men's pleasure, making it more difficult to say "no" (Kelly 1988). This is compounded by women's drop in self-esteem during adolescence (Simmons, Rosenberg, and Rosenberg 1973) and their increased sensitivity to others' opinions (Rosenberg and Simmons 1975). In general, young women emerge from adolescence ill equipped to respond clearly and assertively to the demands of males.

These patterns of interaction lay the foundation for the development of sexually coercive attitudes and behaviors, both verbal and physical. It is difficult to become conscious of patterns without access to information or the opportunity to learn new skills. Students fortunate enough to go to college may be exposed to new ideas and alternative ways of thinking regarding the nature of sexuality and gender roles; however, studies examining student attitudes about rape have found an alarming level of acceptance of rape myths among college students (Gilmarten-Zena 1988; Goodchilds et al. 1988; Carmody 1989). The acceptance of rape mythology is disturbing not only in terms of contributing to the likelihood of sexual aggression but in that it allows men who rape to justify their actions with culturally sanctioned beliefs (Marolla and Scully 1982; Burt 1983) and discourages victims from reporting rape (Russell 1975).

The attitudes conducive to sexual coercion are already established by adolescence. Both males and females in a sample of 14 to 18 year olds consider nonconsensual sex to be rape only when a certain level of force is used and if the victim and assailant are strangers to one another. If the two people involved knew each other, forced sex was considered acceptable by adolescent males depending on duration of time together, how excited the male was, how much money the man had spent on his date, or if the woman was stoned, drunk, or had previously indicated that she wanted to have sex (Goodchilds et al. 1988). Szirom (1988) found similar attitudes among the high school students she interviewed in Australia; male students did not see the idea of pressuring young women into having sex as problematic. Reforms to counteract these attitudes must begin earlier, when children begin to explore sexual feelings and values. Programs need to be developed and implemented on all levels of the educational system, including child care facilities for preschoolers, primary and secondary schools, and university and colleges, if we hope to change the patterns that underlie sexually coercive attitudes and behavior.

Educational Reforms: A Multilevel, Comprehensive Approach

The programs discussed in the first part of this chapter focus on two critical populations, children and college students; they are limited in focus and scope. First, few reforms for children address peer relations, yet children can be coerced by siblings and peers as well as adults. Second, the educational system implicitly supports cultural stereotypes and coercive attitudes and behaviors at the secondary level through its practices and silence about teenage sexuality. This is the age period when romantic and sexual relations become more salient, yet few reforms address the needs and concerns of adolescents. Finally, most of the programs aimed at college students focus on generating awareness about rape. Although these programs are important, a multifaceted approach to rape and violence on campus is needed.

We argue that a comprehensive, multilevel approach to educational reforms is needed—one that targets children, adolescents, and young adults. Any reforms aimed at schools must examine the social world of young people and take the cultural context of schools into account. Moreover, educators need to be sensitive to racial, ethnic, social class, and environmental differences (for example, rural or urban) when designing and implementing specific programs in schools. Education can be reconstructed as an empowering context—one in which students develop their capacities as human beings, men and women, and sexual beings.

A different agenda must be established for social interaction that is based on equality, respect, and sensitivity to other people rather than status, inequality, and power over others. Children must be taught skills that will enable them to state their needs clearly and directly so that manipulation and coercive behaviors do not have to be used to get one's needs and desires met. This process should begin with preschoolers in child-care facilities, with teachers serving as role models as well as facilitators. Young children must be taught the connection between their feelings and their bodies (for example, "I feel happy when my mom hugs me"). Such messages can help to instill a sense of trust in their own perceptions and bodily responses, which can help them distinguish appropriate and inappropriate touch. Rather than rewarding children for gender-appropriate behavior, teachers can encourage children to play with any toys and engage in any activities, enabling both boys and girls to develop masculine and feminine qualities.

Primary school teachers continue to have an important influence on the lives of children. One of the simplest yet most effective ways they can begin to have an impact at this age level is no longer segregating children by gender into play and work groups, a practice that reinforced differences between males and females that support cultural stereotypes. Children need many opportunities for cross-sex interaction and friendships that are not dominated by sexual and romantic overtones. If mutual interests and activities, rather than gender become the basis of friendships, children will learn how to relate to peers as human beings first and sexual beings second. Teenagers will be more likely to view sexual activity as a deeper way of relating to the other sex rather than being the only way if they have friendship experiences with peers beginning at an early age. In addition, if children can learn how to communicate effectively with peers before entering adolescence, they will be more prepared to deal with sexual and romantic feelings and to cope with potentially coercive situations. Teachers can legitimate this interaction and intervene if students are teasing or taunting their peers for playing with the other sex. Also, children should be encouraged to participate in a wide variety of activities within the school. It is critical for children to begin building self-esteem that is based on both individual achievement and cooperation with others. These reforms can provide a supplement to the programs already in existence for child sexual abuse.

Secondary schools must begin promoting healthier and broader conceptions of sexuality and gender identity. They can provide multiple ways for students to explore their masculinity and femininity through a restructuring of the school curriculum and extracurricular activities. Although there are opportunities for women to participate in more active, achievement-oriented roles, these activities are not highly valued within the peer culture. Similarly men do not receive peer support for participating in activities that stress the development of nurturant, dramatic, or artistic skills. The school can legitimate these activities by allocating more money and resources and providing more schoolwide support for them.

Sex education programs in secondary schools need to be expanded greatly to include more information about female desire (Fine 1988), sexual response, heterosexuality, lesbianism, homosexuality, masturbation, birth control, sexually transmitted diseases, and sexual coercion. The curriculum should address the discourse and ideology surrounding sexuality in our culture, which includes fear, victimization, violence, compulsory hetero-sexuality, the negative labeling of women, and silence (Fine 1988). We need to empower young women to be participants in their own experiences. Similarly, men need to learn how to be more interactive in their relations with women and peers. Adolescents should have the opportunity to discuss their ideas, values, and feelings. They should be able to explore their sexual feelings without guilt, fear, or ignorance. The key is to teach students responsible sexual behavior while encouraging them to develop their sexuality at their own developmental pace.

In addition, schools must teach a more holistic conception of sexuality. In our culture, we tend to equate sexuality with sexual activity, especially sexual intercourse. Although there is certainly a behavioral component to sexuality, sexual energy and sexual feelings can be expressed in a variety of other ways. If we can teach children the interrelationship of their bodies, minds, and feelings, they can learn to express their sexuality through dance, the arts, drama, music, and other forms of activity.

Sexual coercion could be discussed within the context of a health or sex education class or as a separate course. It is important to address the implicit bargains in dating relationships, how students believe the bargain changes by the duration of the relationship, as well as attitudes and beliefs about the sexual response of both males and females. It should be clear that there is a supportive environment in which adolescents may report rape and harassment, as well as learn techniques of resistance, both verbal and physical. Furthermore, schools need to teach young people, particularly women, to be survivors rather than victims of coercion.

Programs on sexual coercion should focus on both male and female students. The peer facilitator program used at colleges could be expanded to include secondary schools. Since peers are highly influential at this age, it would be helpful if presenters were as close to the students' ages as possible, although adults could supervise the program and be available for guidance. For example, college students could talk with high school students and high schoolers with adolescents in middle school. These facilitators could provide concrete information and also act as a role model for younger students. While the overall presentation should be to large groups of female and male students, it might be helpful to break down into smaller groups in terms of facilitating discussion.

One method for modeling appropriate behavior is using a theater presentation in which the performers play out a scene that ends in date rape. The performers then answer questions from the audience from the perspective of the character they are playing. A male-female team of facilitators asks for suggestions as to how the performers could respond differently to the situation. The performers then redo the scene incorporating the suggestions of the participants (Parrot 1987). This approach could be applied to other forms of coercion and inappropriate touch and could be used with children, adolescents, and young adults.

Other tools schools can use for working with children and teens include novels, magazines, films, and videotapes. If adults become sensitized to what is salient within the peer culture of a particular school and community, they can work with teenagers by drawing on elements of that culture to disseminate information. In addition, schools could draw on a growing national community-based movement, the Peer Assistance and Leadership Program (Leslie et al. 1988), to provide another outlet for students to talk about sexuality and coercion.

One obvious barrier to implementing the reforms we have suggested is school boards and parents. Many adults may endorse the widely held belief that giving information about sexuality to teenagers encourages sexual relations. Further, parents may believe that such matters should be discussed only within the confines of family or religious organizations. It should be remembered, however, that discussing sexuality in the classroom does not exclude talking about such matters in other contexts and could even promote discussion in families and religious groups, and as long as sex or sexuality cannot be discussed in the classroom, sexual coercion will continue to be a problem as adolescents act on the cultural stereotypes and assumptions they have learned.

Many adults may be uncomfortable with their own sexuality and thus find it difficult to acknowledge sexuality in young persons. Programs could be set up to educate both parents and adults who work with children and adolescents. These programs could provide information and opportunities to discuss issues related to sexuality—whether their child's or their own. A theater presentation could be used to model ways for parents to approach and talk with their children about sexuality, with support groups established for parents who want to discuss and share experiences with other parents, perhaps in combination with other concerns, such as drug and alcohol use. Adults must become clearer about their own sexuality and attitudes regarding sex, gender, and sexual coercion if they are to give young people clear, direct, and healthy messages.

Because a number of factors underlie violence on campus, it is important to take a multifaceted approach to preventing or stopping it (Roark 1987). Although Roark's suggestions are directed specifically at universities and colleges, these proposals may be applied to any educational community seeking to create a safer environment. Any institutional effort to prevent sexual coercion must begin with an understanding of the student population and the educational environment, as well as a familiarity with the range of sexual violence. This could best be achieved by encouraging the involvement of student groups, campus administrators, faculty members, staff, local police, and mental health professionals in the implementation of the program.

Roark suggests three interrelated levels of reforms. First, there should be support services for those who are victimized: medical, legal, protective, and emotional support to guide the victim through the recovery process, with family and friends included in the outreach. Because many victims are hesitant to report rape or sexual assault, efforts should be made to ensure confidentiality, provide more than one place to report the crime, and publicize the supportive environment. Second, rape awareness should be integrated into the school system at large. Policies and procedures concerning the definition of rape, sexual assault, and sexual coercion must be updated and clarified. This should be a public process and should be enforced once established. Discussions regarding rape, sexuality, gender roles, and sexual coercion can be integrated into the curriculum in a variety of fields, such as sociology, psychology, or health or into single-issue courses. Third, measures should be taken to prevent sexual coercion. Rape awareness and prevention training should be mandatory for all staff members dealing with students. Counselors should be available to talk with staff members who may have personally experienced coercion or rape. The physical environment can be altered by providing well-lighted walk areas and parking lots, increased security around high-risk areas, and the establishment of more transportation services. Workshops on a variety of skills and attitudes should be offered to change attitudes and provide self-defense and coping techniques. Facilitators should be aware of the likelihood that both victims and perpetrators of rape will be in the workshop; therefore it is important for mental health professionals to be available to all participants.

Future studies should focus on attitudes about sexual coercion among teachers as well as their students. Studies on the effectiveness of education on attitudes concerning sexual coercion for the purpose of developing recommendations for programs throughout the country would be helpful. Studies that examine teachers' attitudes and how they influence beliefs about sexuality through classroom practices also would be useful for educators.

Our growing awareness of the extent of sexual coercion must be accompanied by appropriate reforms in the educational system. Without an institutional response to the problem, sexually abusive behavior will remain the burden of individuals rather than a societal responsibility, and the attitudes and behaviors that contribute to sexual coercion will be reproduced by another generation. Reforms in the educational system are certainly not the only change needed to counteract the epidemic of sexual aggression, but they are a step in the direction of a safer, healthier society.

12
Feminist Reforms of Sexual Coercion Laws

Jo Dixon

L aws are one of the major sources of our thinking about sexual coercion. Prevailing legal discourses about sexual coercion serve as "the embodiment of reason and universal truth" (Mensch 1982: 18), as well as "the commonplace reality that ordinary people carry around with them for use in ordering their everyday" sex lives (Gordon 1984: 109).

An irony of sexual coercion laws is that they have been a source of both oppression and liberation for women. Because laws concerning sexual coercion have reflected and had an impact on the world, they have been constitutive and derivative of social and political change. "The world is different when laws change and laws change because the world is different" (Eisenstein 1988: 46). Nowhere has the relationship between social and political changes, legal reform and female disadvantage been more apparent than in the history of legal reforms in sexual coercion.

Each type of sexual coercion has had a unique legal history. Because the various categories of sexual coercion have not been treated as a single legal category, the laws, legal practices, and reforms for each form of sexual coercion (rape, sexual harassment, child sexual abuse and prostitution) have varied. In this chapter I focus solely on rape and sexual harassment; however, issues surrounding legal reforms of these forms of sexual coercion are pertinent to other forms.

Traditional Laws and Legal Practices

Rape: The Common Law Tradition

Criminal laws in the United States regarding rape derived from English common law, which defined this crime as "illicit carnal knowledge of a female by force and against her will" (Black 1968: 1427). Under common law, there were four conditions necessary for establishing a behavior as rape: (1) it had to be sex specific, (2) it had to be extramarital, (3) it had to involve penetration of the vagina by the penis, and (4) it had be forcible (Tong 1984).

According to common law, only men could be perpetrators of rape and only women could be victims. Thus, homosexual rape and marital rape were not prosecuted. The exclusion of marital rape was based on the arguments of Lord Chief Justice Matthew Hale, who submitted that "a husband cannot be guilty of rape committed by himself upon his lawful wife, for by their mutual matrimonial consent and contract the wife hath given up her self in this kind unto her husband which she cannot retract" (Hale 1678: 628). Because of the preoccupation of common law with vaginal penetration by a penis, oral and anal intercourse were excluded, as were penetration by the tongue, fingers, toes, or artificial instruments.

The common law tradition treated forced intercourse by a stranger against a chaste woman as the "ideal" type of rape. Hence, coercive sex departing from the ideal type was often socially and legally denied, viewed with suspicion when acknowledged, and frequently unpunished (Clark and Lewis 1977).

Inherent in the common law definitions and punishments for rape were gender, class, and racial biases. Even when the ideal type of rape occurred, punishments were often directed toward victims or other women rather than perpetrators. In some circumstances, rape victims were required to marry their assailants, and in others the fathers of rape victims were granted permission to rape the wife or sister of the assailant (Rhode 1989). In early English laws, the grading of offenses rested more on the class or status of victims than on the degree of injury. For example, the punishment for the rape of nuns, wives, or widows was considerably less severe than the castration or death penalty punishments prescribed for offenders who raped propertied virgins (Luria, Friedman, and Rose 1987; Rhode 1989). Rapes of black women by white men were trivialized, but rapes of white women by black men resulted in extremely harsh punishments, including lynching. Between 1945 and 1965, blacks convicted of raping white women were eighteen more times more likely to receive the death penalty than any other racial combination (Rhode 1989; Wolfgang and Riedel 1977).

Given the gender, class, and race biases in the common law tradition, it is not surprising that rapes deviating from the ideal type have been characterized by low reporting (Russell 1984) and high attrition rates from complaint to conviction (Galvin and Polk 1983; Schur 1988; Estrich 1987).

For rapes that deviated from the ideal type (chaste victim and violent stranger), legal practices under common law reflected the same sexism found in definitions and punishments. The requirements for proof under common law were excessive. Although rape had a low reporting rate, the common law legal tradition was permeated with an extensive fear of false accusations of rape (Largen 1988).

Some of the difficulties in obtaining rape convictions under common law stemmed from evidence rules that assumed women to be liars. Reinforcing this misogynist image of women were corroboration rules, cautionary instructions, inclusion of the victim's prior sexual history, and standards of proof of resistance and/or nonconsent (Tong 1984). The justification for these requirements came from several influential jurists. Matthew Hale stated that "rape is an accusation easily made, hard to be proved and harder to be defended by the party accused though ever so innocent" (Hale 1678: 635). In a similar vein, John Wigmore used psychoanalytic theory to substantiate the view that "most women entertain fantasies of rape. Hence, it is easy for neurotic women to translate their fantasies into actual beliefs and memory falsifications" (Wigmore 1934: 329). His ideas were later used to justify giving lie detector and psychological tests to rape victims.

Rape is the only crime for which corroboration of victim testimony has been required. In fact some states required corroboration of identification, penetration, and lack of consent (Batelle Law and Justice Study Center 1978). In order to prosecute rape under common law in some states, the prosecution was required to produce evidence of an eyewitness to some phase of the attack or verifiable recollections of details of the defendant's possessions. In corroborating penetration, victims had to produce vaginal tears, sperm, or pregnancy. Finally, body bruises, a weapon, torn clothing, hysteria, or flight were often necessary for corroborating a lack of consent (Tong 1984).

The prosecution difficulties created by corroboration rules were exasperated by cautionary instructions given to juries in rape trials. A typical cautionary statement came from the writings of Matthew Hale: "A charge such as that made against the defendant is one which is easily made and once made, difficult to defend against even if the person accused is innocent. Therefore, the law requires that you examine the testimony of the female person with caution" (Hale 1678).

In addition to corroboration rules and cautionary instructions, common law practices allowed the prior sexual history of victims to be used to discredit the testimony of the victim and to establish consent. Prior to the 1970s, many judges instructed jurors that evidence of unchaste character was relevant in assessing credibility and consent. Since studies of the attitudes of jurors have found that respondents attribute provocation to rape victims if they have been unchaste, drinking, or wearing seductive clothing (Kalven and Zeisel 1966; LaFree 1989), the burden of proof has often rested with the victim. Given the emphasis on consent, resistance by victims became an objective standard for testing nonconsent by victims. Although resistance standards varied from state to state, they focused attention away from the actions of the perpetrator and toward the actions of the victim.

Sexual Harassment: The Criminal and Tort Tradition

Unlike rape, sexual harassment law has had no long history of evolution from common law definitions. Historically no definition of sexual harassment per se existed. It was not until the 1970s that the first litigation of sexual harassment occurred. Prior to that time sexual harassment offenses were prosecuted within standard criminal and tort categories such as battery, assault, or the intentional infliction of mental and emotional disturbances. Although sexual harassment involving annoying and offensive behavior was recognized by law, most cases were confined to those involving getting a woman to engage in sexual intercourse. And as was the case with rape, sexual harassment complaints were usually rebuffed, met with doubt, and seldom met with punishment for the perpetrator.

Regardless of the legal avenue employed, most traditional prosecutions involving sexual harassment required four major elements:

1. an annoying or unwelcome sexual advance or imposition,
2. a negative response to the advance or imposition,
3. the presence of intimidation or coercion when the sexual harasser held more power than the person sexually harassed, and
4. the suggestion that inappropriate rewards or penalties would result from compliance or refusal to comply (Tong 1984: 67).

Legal definitions and punishments were wrought with gender, class, and racial biases. Constructions of sexual harassment as sexually coercive and illegal were hampered by adherence to traditional gender expectations. The gender biases that historically precluded the legal prosecution of sexually harassing behavior were expressed in Phyllis Schlafly's statement that "harassing behavior has not been a problem for virtuous women except in the rarest of occasions. When women have conformed to appropriate standards of feminine decorum, they have not needed to worry" (Schlafly 1981: 13). Historical research has documented the gender and class biases found in early sexual harassment laws. For example, laws were enacted to discourage the sexual harassment of women who traveled on the railroad. One law in the nineteenth century entitled female railroad passengers to a ride in which "they would meet nothing, see nothing or hear nothing that would wound their delicacy or insult their womanhood" (Rhode 1989: 231). On the other hand, there were no legal protections for female domestic servants, factory workers, or other working women (Bularzik 1978). Black women's least advantaged position in the economy coupled with the legacy of slavery made them particularly vulnerable to harassment. In addition, any complaints they waged were met with extreme skepticism.

The earliest legal responses to sexual harassment involved criminal proceedings relying on harm principles. Because this type of prosecution was appropriate only when the sexually harassed woman was a victim of rape, indecent assault, common assault, assault causing bodily harm, threats, intimidation, or solicitation, it was seldom employed (Tong 1984). If the victim was seriously harmed, the prosecutor was likely to bring the offender up on criminal charges of rape or assault rather than sexual harassment. Conversely, if it was hard to establish serious harm, prosecutors were unlikely to press criminal charges. As a result, most sexual harassment proceedings involved civil torts based on a combination of harm and offense principles.

The legal practices involved in traditional prosecutions of sexual harassment under tort law reflected the same sexism found in the criminal prosecution of rape. The requirements for proof of intent or victim injury were excessive. Like rape, sexual harassment had a low reporting rate but invoked rules that assumed large numbers of false accusations.

Tort prosecutions of sexual harassment were traditionally carried out under tort categories of battery, assault, and the intentional affliction of mental or emotional disturbance (Tong 1984). When sexual harassment was prosecuted under battery and assault, the harasser was liable for his actions only if the women failed to consent to his sexual advances and if his conduct would be considered offensive to a person of ordinary sensibilities. As in rape, the victim's resistance emerged as the standard for testing consent. Given this standard, sexual harassment actions focused more on the actions of the victim than on those of the harasser. Furthermore, the test of ordinary sensibilities usually regarded the sensibilities of the ordinary man as the reference point.

Tort prosecutions alleging the intentional infliction of mental or emotional disturbances were often used because they employed a consequences approach that did not require the victim to prove her lack of consent. However, these cases did require extensive proof of the harm suffered by the victim. Generalizing from their own experiences, many male judges and jurors found it impossible to believe that sexual overtones could cause serious psychological or physical injury. In a class action suit filed by a male assistant professor and five women students at Yale, it was argued that the offensive behavior of several male professors resulted in physical and emotional harm. One university official dismissed the injuries and went so far as to blame the harassing behavior on the lack of intelligence of the victims. According to this official, "There is a stronger argument that if women students aren't smart enough to outwit some obnoxious professor, they shouldn't be here in the first place. Like other institutions, Yale has its share of twisted souls" (Backhouse and Cohen 1982: 34).

Prior to the 1970s, some attempts were made to reduce the patriarchal customs embodied in traditional legal practices, but it was not until after the women's rights movement in the 1970s that systematic changes transformed traditional rape and sexual harassment laws. The legal definitions, punishments, and legal practices that emerged no longer reflected the traditional forms of patriarchy. Rather, a liberal legalism evolved that gave women the same formal legal rights as men.

Liberal Reforms of Traditional Laws and Legal Practices

Because the rise of the contemporary women's movement coincided with the rise of the liberal state, reforms of rape and sexual harassment laws were completely intertwined with liberalism. Because liberalism emphasized a gender-neutral humanism over a sex-specific feminism, women were viewed as individuals rather than women classified by their sex. Given liberalism's stress on the autonomous individual and choice, sexual coercion came to be viewed as individual and gender neutral rather than institutional and sex specific. Moreover, its violent rather than its sexual aspects were emphasized. According to liberals, coercion consists of force or threats of force that violate natural human rights. Because liberalism established that women should be treated as individuals, not as women classified by their sex, legal standards of objectivity determining whether coercion existed in any circumstance regardless of sex were preferred to the gender-biased standards adhered to in traditional legal practices.

Liberal reformers criticized traditional legal practices for stripping women of their natural rights and lobbied for legal reforms granting women the same rights and opportunities as men. Maintaining that the natural rights of women were pregiven and needed only to be realized in the context of a neutral legal system, liberal reformers advanced formal legal equality between the sexes through the establishment of a sex-neutral set of legal definitions and practices.

Early legal reforms established uniform standards for men and women in the public sphere, such as voting, education, and employment. With the rise of the equal rights revolution in the 1960s and 1970s, feminists continued to argue for equal rights for women in the public sphere (Friedan 1974); however, they increasingly argued for objective standards for laws governing the behavior of men and women in the private sphere (Friedan 1981). Movement activists organized and developed an agenda to reform laws concerning rape and sexual harassment.

The legal reforms of rape following the equal rights revolution radically departed from the legal theory and traditions of the past. Because reformers chose the legislative rather than the common law process for pursuing reforms, citizens were permitted greater participation, and changes were more revolutionary. The legislative reform movement was successful in generating a large number of liberal reforms of traditional rape laws and legal practices. Because the compromises of different interest groups varied across states, the uniformity found in the common law tradition of rape was replaced by a complex array of differing state laws (Largen 1988). Nonetheless, a number of successful liberal reform features were adopted in most states.

About half of the states repealed the common law definition of rape. In some states that retained the common law formulations, the range of prohibited criminal acts was broadened by adding new offenses to existing carnal offense statutes. Unfortunately a number of states unified former common law offenses but made few changes in the requisite elements or punishments of each offense (Largen 1988).

A small number of states made revolutionary changes in the common law definition by adopting a sexual assault and battery approach. Focusing on the violent rather than sexual aspects of rape, these states defined rape statutes in gender-neutral terms. While force requirements were usually lowered in these states, statutes were broadened to include sexual contacts that did not involve penetration by the penis.

In addition to changes in the definition of rape were changes in the corroboration rules and cautionary instructions. Corroboration requirements were relaxed in many states though still necessary in many cases to convince the jurors of the victims' version of the rape. Many states eliminated or made voluntary the use of cautionary jury instructions. However, many states that eliminated the cautionary instructions replaced them with psychiatric and lie detector tests for the victim.

Less successful were reforms aimed at eliminating marital immunity, prior sexual history evidence, and consent standards. Only 25 percent of the states abolished the spousal exemption, and most states maintained a resistance standard for proof of nonconsent (Largen 1988). Reforms aimed at eliminating the use of prior sexual history were initially opposed because they posed threats to the Sixth Amendment rights of defendants. As a resolution to this conflict, most states adopted a practice whereby closed hearings were held to determine the degree to which the prior history of the victim was crucial for a defendant's defense (Batelle Law and Justice Study Center 1978).

The rape reforms that most reflected the ideology of liberal legalism and liberal feminism were those introduced into the 1974 Michigan criminal sexual conduct statute. The new law defined rape as a sex-neutral crime of violence. More specifically, it provided four proposals:

1. a specification of degrees of criminal sexual assault that reflected a continuum of violence represented by these crimes,

2. prohibition of sexual history evidence,

3. elimination of resistance and consent standards, and

4. extension of the law's protection to homosexuals.

Critical of the tort approach to sexual harassment, liberal feminists also advanced reforms that defined sexual harassment as an act of coercion rather than a set of offensive behaviors. Since sexual harassment was an offense that had not been prosecuted or even acknowledged in the past, the liberal movement involved more development than reform of sexual harassment laws and legal practices.

The judicial decisions from the earliest sexual harassment cases were inconsistent because liberal reformers began imploring the use of an antidiscrimination approach over a torts approach. As Rosemarie Tong (1984: 77) notes:

> Whereas tort law views sexual harassment as an outrage to an individual woman's sensibilities and to a society's purported values, antidiscrimination law casts the same act as either economic coercion, in which the material survival of women is threatened, or as one of intellectual coercion, in which the spiritual survival of women in general is similarly jeopardized.

The antidiscrimination approach argued that sexual harassment is coercive rather than offensive. At first glance this change appears to define the coercion in harassment as institutional; however, the legal practices liberals advocated for determining discrimination reiterated their individual approach to sexual coercion. Maintaining that sexual harassment involves violence and power, liberals married an institutional antidiscrimination approach with objective and sex-neutral standards of proof.

Given this uneasy marriage of a definition suggesting institutional coercion and a set of legal practices reflecting individual coercion, it is not surprising that early attempts to apply discrimination law to sexual harassment were unsuccessful. However, the ruling for an appeal of *Barnes v. Train* paved the way for major court reforms that placed sexual harassment under the jurisdiction of discrimination law.

Liberal reformers developed a differential treatment interpretation of sex discrimination. The basic question posed by this liberal approach was, Would a person of the opposite sex in the same position be treated the same? Advocating this sex-neutral definition that perceived sexual harassment as a show of power rather than an expression of social inequality, liberal reformers maintained that men as well as women could be victims of sexual harassment. As a result, liberal reformers argued that rigorous applications of neutral standards provided the best test for sexual harassment.

As McKinney and Maroules state in chapter 3, the most successful feature of liberal reforms occurred in 1980 when the Equal Employment Opportunity Commission (EEOC) issued a revised set of guidelines proclaiming sexual harassment a violation of Title VII of the U.S. Civil Rights Act, which banned discrimination on the basis of sex. Another victory occurred when the first Supreme Court decision on this issue (*Meritor Savings Bank, FSB v. Vinson*) supported the EEOC rules. In addition to upholding the EEOC guidelines, the Court supported the addition of quid pro quo harassment (sexual advances or related conduct where the response affected employment decisions) and work environment harassment (conduct that unreasonably interfered with an individual's work performance or that created an intimidating, hostile, or offensive work environment) (Rhode 1989).

The Supreme Court ruling would have been considered a major victory had the justices not simultaneously ruled that sexually provocative speech or dress were relevant to whether the conduct was offensive (Rhode 1989). Despite its drawbacks, the ruling in this case gave the authorities in the workplace or the academy liability for protecting employees from sexually harassing behavior. Even so, cause for judicial actions against organizations was justified only if organizations failed to take prompt remedial actions upon received complaints. Given this restriction on just cause, organizations typically used remedial rather than punitive measures in dealing with sexual complaints, a constraint that discouraged many women from pursuing legal routes. In fact, some have argued that women are better off avoiding internal grievance procedures and complaints if they must be made directly to management (Backhouse and Cohen 1982).

Future Reforms of Liberal Law and Legal Practices

From the perspective of liberal feminists, liberal legal reforms have been a success. According to liberals, these reforms have reduced gender inequality by promoting legal practices characterized by equal rights and equal treatment under the law. Within the current liberal legal tradition, rape and sexual harassment have been defined as sex-neutral acts of violence involving individual coercion. Given this sex neutrality, liberal laws have played an active role in creating formal legal equality between the sexes. However, the lack of decreases in violence against women suggests that they have played a relatively passive role in creating greater gender equality. In fact, some suggest that the vocal male referent stated in traditional laws has been transformed into a silent male referent obscured by abstract rights and sex-neutral objective standards.

Recent critiques of liberal legal reforms have pointed to the contradictions and limitations of reforms presuming equality and objectivity while continuing to operate in a society that treats men and women unequally. Turning their attention to liberal reforms where there have been equal legal rights but for women disproportionately unfavorable legal results, they cast doubts on liberal legal reforms of rape and sexual harassment centered on equal rights and equal treatment. Maintaining that sexual coercion is institutional rather than individual, recent reformers have turned to a focus on "treatment as an equal rather than equal treatment" (Dworkin 1977: 227). According to Dworkin, treatment as an equal refers to "the right not to receive the same distribution of some burden or benefit but to be treated with the same respect and concern as anyone else" (p. 227).

While the departure from traditional forms of law based on sex differences reduced many forms of sexism, liberal laws based on sameness and sex-neutral rules have given birth to new forms of patriarchal legal practices. While traditional laws and practices concerning rape and sexual harassment brazenly exhibited gender hierarchy and inequality, liberal laws are characterized by a silent male referent that masks rather than eliminates sexual hierarchy and inequality (Eisenstein 1988).

Various criticism have been lodged against the rape and sexual harassment reforms enacted in the past few decades. Estrich (1987) argued that the Michigan reforms defining rape as a violent rather than a sexual crime made it harder for the prosecution of rapes lacking physical violence, such as date rape and marital rape. Similarly, sex-neutral definitions have divorced rape from sex and created the illusion that rape is as much a problem for men as for women.

One of the most vocal critics of liberal legal reforms of sexual coercion that define sexual coercion as individual rather than institutional has been Catherine MacKinnon. MacKinnon posits that sexuality itself is violence that constitutes the meaning of gender. Hence, rape laws that have divorced sex from violence on the basis of objective standards of consent have evaded the institutional basis of rape.

MacKinnon (1970) criticized sexual harassment reforms along the same lines. Uncomfortable with the temporary presumption of sex equality used in establishing the disparate treatment approach to discrimination in sexual harassment cases, MacKinnon offered an alternative to sex discrimination based on "disparate impact" (MacKinnon 1979). This question of import from the disparate impact perspective asks whether the pattern or practice has an adverse impact on women.

The conceptualization of sexual coercion as institutional rather than individual has two consequences for future reforms. First, it suggests that the focus of inquiry in rape and sexual harassment cases should change from intent to injury. Second, it suggests that the burden of proof should be moved from the victim to the perpetrator and the cultural forces that produced the behavior.

Focusing on gender disadvantage, Rhode (1989) and Eisenstein (1988) propose future legal reforms based on radical pluralism. Both recommend that liberal discourses in law be replaced or reconstructed such that current preoccupations with abstract formal legal rights and/or gender differences be replaced with discourses that examine how difference constitutes the meaning of equality. This approach assumes that "differences and plurality constitute society but understand that hierarchy and unequal relations of power presently structure those differences" (Eisenstein 1988: 222). Unlike previous approaches, this one acknowledges the similarities and differences among men and women, as well as the similarities and differences among women. Hence, it provides a framework for reforming gender disadvantage without obscuring the racial and class differences among women. As long as legal discourses center on the degree to which women are similar to or different from men, it privileges men by putting them at the center of the discourse. The type of discourse Rhode and Eisenstein advance paves the way for legal reforms that give law an advocacy role in reducing disadvantages centering on race, sex, and class.

Because law is a force that institutionalizes as well as challenges inequality, there are limits to its utility in reducing sexual coercion. While the removal of legal barriers is necessary for reducing sexual coercion, it is not sufficient. Nevertheless, laws and legal practices that focus on gender disadvantage provide the basis for legal discourses capable of altering social perceptions of sexual coercion. Continued litigation in the area of sexual coercion can only help validate the injuries of victims and publicly expose those engaging in practices that disadvantage women. Moreover, litigation often provides the framework for educational and regulatory guidelines.

The history of reforms in rape and sexual harassment laws suggests that legal remedies to sexual coercion are open to change and new constructions. Hence the contradictions posed by the liberal legal reforms should not be interpreted as an impasse to feminist legal reforms in this area. Rather they should sensitize us to the need for legal discourses that place gender disadvantage rather than abstract equal rights at the center. Only with this type of approach can we hope to decenter the male referent so closely associated with previous laws and legal practices.

13
Preventing Sexual Coercion: A Feminist Agenda for Economic Change

Heidi Gottfried

his chapter seeks to define a feminist agenda for economic change aimed at preventing sexual coercion. Any program for reform posed exclusively at the economic level is necessarily partial and incomplete, however. Defining a unified feminist policy agenda is also problematic; feminism represents multiple theoretical frameworks from which different policy responses can be formulated, and women's experiences of sexual coercion differ depending on their position within overlapping relations of domination based on race, class, sexual preference, and national context. These caveats suggest caution in any attempt to pose general prescriptions on variable experiences of sexual coercion.

The Economic Dimension of Sexual Coercion

Male violence against women represents a regular feature of male domination throughout history and under capitalism (Edwards 1987) and constitutes a mechanism of social control: "Force and its threat is the basis for the extraction of benefits (e.g., economic, sexual, and prestige) that men engender from their domination of women" (Hammer 1978: 219). In addition to an economic basis for the perpetuation of sexual coercion, violence reinforces women's economic dependence on a male wage.

Sexual coercion of women by men encompasses all forms of abuse, coercion, and force arrayed along a continuum, including domestic violence, child sexual abuse, sexual harassment, and rape (Kelly 1987). Starting with domestic violence, scholars emphasize either economic or political reasons that men batter women. Stark, Flitcraft, and Frazier (1979) provide an economic determinist view, arguing that men's loss of control over women's labor power in the household, partly due to women's participation in the wage labor force, is the main impetus for battering. Breines and Gordon (1983) criticize this perspective for its economic reductionism. Dobash and Dobash (1979) recast the argument, linking male violence against individual women to men's desire to maintain power and privilege.

Whether men use sexual violence principally out of political or economic motives, women living in a battering relationship confront economic realities affecting their ability to leave an abusive situation. Many women depend on male wages for their economic security; even middle- and upper-class women experience a more significant decline in their standard of living and status than men do as a result of a divorce or a separation (Baca-Zinn and Eitzen 1987). Further, women with young children may fear a loss of child support if they demand a separation from their partner or if their partner threatens to leave. This economic jeopardy looms large for women who lack skills valued in the labor market and in the context of weak enforcement of child support laws. Michelle Fine summarizes the effect of economic dependence on the perpetuation of sexual coercion: "A social structure which deprives women of alternatives is a social structure likely to keep the violence closeted and privatized (in the 'privacy' of the family), encourage self-blame by the women . . . and perpetuate social abuse" (1981: 48–49).

Women most likely to leave abusive situations are those who possess the most resources—job skills, money, and social supports—and those who have not been exposed to violence as children (Fine 1981). This suggests that a range of possible remedies, including economic subsidies, vocational training, and safe, long-term shelters with child care, will enable some women to leave abusive relationships. "Options need to be available and viable to stimulate a sense of injustice and induce the decision to leave or challenge the domestic situation" (Fine 1981: 57).

Like spouse battering, child sexual abuse is widespread. Girls are mostly likely to be the victims and men the perpetrators in cases of child sexual abuse. Over the past decade researchers have related unemployment and the incidence of child abuse in general and child sexual abuse in particular. In one of the earliest studies on family violence, Gelles and Straus (1979) reported a higher rate of physical abuse of children in families with an unemployed father (22 percent) compared to families without an unemployed father (14 percent). Similarly, David Gil (1979) links violence against children to stress resulting from economic deprivation. "[These] data indicate that unemployment (particularly the husband's), social isolation (often a result of poverty), and unwanted pregnancies create stressful situations for parents, and thus create conditions leading to possible abuse and neglect" (Breines and Gordon 1983: 501).

On a cultural level, Herman suggests that asymmetry in the incest taboo in a male-dominant family system and culture helps explain the gender composition of both the population at risk and the perpetrators: "In patriarchal societies the rights of ownership and exchange of women within the family are vested in the father; because men make the rules, the taboo against sexual contact with the daughter does not carry the same force as that which prohibits incest with the mother" (Herman, cited by Breines and Gordon 1983: 525–526).

These studies suggest that a right to and creation of gainful employment opportunities will help stem the tide of domestic violence against both wives and female children. A set of guidelines enacted by the government could ensure equity in the distribution of jobs between men and women. As long as men retain the status of breadwinner, women will remain economically dependent on and vulnerable to acts of violence by men.

Over the past decade, the ubiquity of sexual harassment has been increasingly acknowledged. Sexual harassment is a way men silence and intimidate with the purpose of controlling women. These behaviors are usually repeated, unreciprocated, and offensive. According to Kelly (1987), sexual attention in the context of an unequal power relationship like that of teacher and student or supervisor and employee is inherently coercive regardless of the motives of the individual making the advances. Even if the male superior does not explicitly threaten the female subordinate, the woman must tolerate or ignore unwanted sexual attention in the context of fear that a negative response will affect the evaluation of her work.

In contrast to battering and child sexual abuse, the locus of sexual harassment is not principally found privatized in intimate relations but rather in public places. The function of "sex harassment is to manage ongoing male and female interactions according to accepted sex status norms, and to maintain male dominance occupationally and therefore economically, by intimidating, discouraging, or precipitating removal of women from work" (Tangri, Burt, and Johnson 1982: 40). Along these lines, Lin Farley (1978) argues that men use particular forms of sexual harassment to discourage women from entering male preserves in the labor market.

Litigation has been one of the primary tools for enforcing prohibitions against sexual harassment in the workplace. However, labeling sexual harassment must precede the formulation of reforms. It becomes difficult for women to name this form of sexual coercion because of its "taken for grantedness." As one survivor noted, "It's something that happens so much you just experience it in the street all the time, it's almost background of what's going on out of doors" (respondent cited by Kelly 1987: 53). Labeling sexual harassment transforms the private and personal experiences into a general problem for working women in a patriarchal society. The term *sexual harassment* enables women to see these personal encounters as part of an institutionalized system of male domination and thereby to struggle against it (Ramazanoglu 1987).

Current sexual harassment policies need to be strengthened at both the individual institutional (Robertson, Dyer, and Campbell 1988) and the federal governmental levels. Specifically, the reward structure of organizations should include economic sanctions (forfeiting pay increases, risking the loss of a job) against sexual harassment (Gutek 1985). These economic sanctions would attach a financial penalty to sexual harassment and thereby remove any perception that there is no cost to engaging in sexual harassing behaviors. In addition, sexual harassment policies should empower women collectively. Such policies therefore should be connected consciously to broader efforts to address gender inequality, increasing the number, status, and authority of women to challenge gender-based hierarchies (Kwitko and O'Hagan 1989).

Economic dependence on men (as an individual, as a kin group, or as a surrogate male represented by the state) locks women into a cycle of violence. Breaking this cycle requires dismantling all institutional supports of sexual violence. The examples provide some specific remedies for creating an economic climate that can reverse the pattern of economic dependence, thereby enabling women to resist abusive encounters. An agenda for preventing sexual coercion should enlarge the social options available to women by providing better support services and reducing economic dependence on men. Policies must address the economic basis and economic consequences of sexual coercion.

Preventing Sexual Coercion through Economic Changes

Models exist that promote concrete reforms for economic change. The past decade has been a period of experimentation with a new repertoire of policies emerging out of diffuse impulses, ranging from single-issue remedies by local women's committees in trade unions to judicial and legislative efforts by national unions and women's groups. The first set of examples here highlights the strategies of unions with a large share of female membership and local women's committees in male-dominated unions aimed at a particular workplace, firm, or industry using regular dispute resolution machinery (such as grievance procedures and collective bargaining). In the second example, comparable worth, the courts serve as the chief mechanism of reform. Finally, I identify efforts at the national level to enact legislation or negotiate child care and medical and family leave.

Unions and Women's Committees

In capitalist societies, particularly in the United States, unions are one of the major vehicles organizing the collective power of workers. They potentially play an important role in promoting an agenda for the improvement of women's economic well-being in general and for the prevention of sexual coercion in particular. A range of mechanisms is available to women in unions: the use of grievance procedures, the initiation of suits, the dissemination of information, the mobilization of their membership for support of women who experience sexual harassment, and the negotiation of contract provisions for child care, parental leave, and other supportive services.

The American Federation of State, County and Municipal Employees (AFSCME) has used litigation—including the San Jose city government suit in 1981 (Lynch 1986) and the state of Washington suit in 1983 (Blum 1987)—to promote pay equity. In addition the predominantly female local 9-to-5 of the Service Employees International Union (SEIU) has sponsored annual conventions addressing topics like pay equity and sexual harassment (Cameron 1986).

Women in male-dominated unions have created local women's committees and initiated campaigns directed toward women's rights both on and off the job. District 31 of the United Steel Workers of America (USWA) held a women's convention in the early 1980s to address the concerns of women steel workers. One of the workshops, dealing with sexual harassment, served three purposes: to name the problem, including the extent and incidence of sexual harassment; to provide a forum for women to discuss their own experiences of sexual abuse; and to identify remedies (informal support networks, grievance procedures, legal remedies).

The Women's Committee of the International Union of Electrical (IUE) workers local 201, in an overwhelmingly male work force employed by General Electric (GE) manufacturing plants located in the greater Boston area, articulated a multi-issue approach. The committee fought for training and entry into skilled, predominantly male jobs, for comparable-worth adjustments in traditionally female jobs, and for pregnancy disability benefits and parental leave. In addition, the committee assisted women in the filing of grievances on sexual harassment (Brown and Sheridan 1988).

One of the IUE Women's Committee's most successful and innovative campaigns was what became known as the Krikorian suit, filed in response to a flawed 1978 consent decree between the Equal Employment Opportunities Commission and GE. After four years, the union won an increase of wage rates, maternity benefits, and unpaid parental leave for 353 people in predominantly female job classifications (Brown and Sheridan 1988). Unfortunately, with the expiration of the Krikorian agreement in 1987, GE eliminated the parental leave policy, showing the precariousness of hard-won gains.

A final example of women's self-activity within a male-dominated union comes from the mining industry. Women, who constitute 2 percent of membership in the United Mine Workers of America (UMWA), developed a campaign for parental leave. This project was proposed by the Coal Employment Project (CEP), a nonprofit organization founded in 1977 to end discrimination against women in the mining industry. The CEP brought class-action sex discrimination suits against mine operators, documented problems of sexual harassment, helped women form support groups, and began sponsoring a national conference of women miners to define an agenda and formulate strategies for action (Totten, Totten, and Rostan, 1988). The women miners' parental leave campaign won support from the union and became part of the official bargaining agenda in the 1984 negotiation for a national coal contract (Totten, Totten, and Rostan 1988). Totten and coworkers attribute the failure to adopt the contract language on parental leave to the coal operators' resistance. In an eleventh-hour settlement, the union and the operators agreed to establish a joint committee charged with the responsibility for studying the issue (Totten, Totten, and Rostan 1988).

Several lessons can be drawn from these examples. First, organized efforts by women's committees within male-dominated unions or by a female leadership associated with some female-dominated unions have the organizational resources to pursue and to win support for women's concerns. Second, the unions most receptive to women's concerns tend to have a history of progressive political involvement. (Many of the unions discussed participated in the civil rights movement and supported noninterventionist U.S. foreign policy during the Vietnam War and more recently in Central America.) However, putting women's issues on the agenda will meet with some resistance, particularly in unions with a long history of excluding women from their ranks.

Comparable Worth and Job Integration

Many feminists propose comparable worth (Treiman and Hartmann 1981; Feldberg 1984; Steinberg 1987) or a combination of comparable worth and job integration (Bielby 1985) to end women's economic dependence on men and to undo gender inequality. Comparable worth aims to upgrade wage scales for jobs employing large numbers of women. "While affirmative action challenges the allocation of jobs on the basis of stereotypical gender traits, comparable worth challenges the allocation of rewards on the basis of such traits" (Blum 1987: 382). A comparable-worth strategy broadens the concept of discrimination to include the systematic undervaluation and low wages of traditional women's jobs.

Unions have pioneered the idea of comparable worth, promoting this agenda primarily through the courts. Probably the most important legal case was a pay equity suit brought in federal court against the state of Washington by AFSCME in behalf of 15,000 state employees. At first the court ruled in favor of the union; in 1983 Judge Jack E. Tanner directed the state to distribute nearly $1 billion to the affected women for damages and back pay and to a 30-percent pay adjustment for jobs in which women predominated. Two years later this decision was overturned by a federal appeals court. Nevertheless, Washington State agreed to spend $42 million for pay equity adjustments in the next contract year and to pay over $100 million in future adjustments (Blum 1987).

Subsequently many cities have agreed to implement wage adjustments, including Chicago, Los Angeles, and San Francisco. All but four states have taken some form of action in the public sector. In 1986 New York City locals of AFSCME negotiated a three-year contract that allocated funds for comparable worth adjustments to more than 50,000 employees in jobs predominantly held by women (Blum 1987).

These apparent success stories, however, hide limits to comparable worth as a means of increasing the value of women's work and eliminating the gender-based wage gap (Brenner 1987; Blum 1987; Reskin 1988). First, comparable worth has been confined to the public sector because workers are more likely to be unionized and the state is less likely to resist such a campaign (Brenner 1987). Second, the actual pay increases (ranging from 5 to 15 percent) fall below the projected necessary adjustments (10 to 30 percent) (Steinberg 1987). Third, comparable worth is framed in a liberal discourse of equal treatment that reinforces the "validity of meritocratic hierarchy, rather than questioning the market as the arbiter of wages" (Brenner 1987: 457). Blum (1987) summarizes the problems with comparable worth: it assumes a common interest among all women, it produces antagonisms between working-class men and women, and it falls short of attacking class- and gender-based inequality.

Some suggest combining comparable worth with job integration strategies. Whereas comparable worth redresses the devaluation of work done by women, job integration provides opportunities to women in areas heretofore closed to them (Bielby 1985). There is evidence linking sex-integrated work environments with low levels of sexual harassment (Gutek 1985). A minority of women can be isolated from a work group dominated by men, but such a strategy becomes less efficacious in a sex-integrated workplace. The experience of working together can demonstrate to men that women are partners in a collective enterprise.

The history of women's integration into predominantly male jobs, however, is replete with examples of women's entrance resulting in or being the result of the declining status of that job (clerical work, bank telling, typesetting). Once occupations are integrated, the occupation is often resegregated whereby men remain concentrated in the highest-status and best-paying jobs within the occupation (Reskin 1988). For example, male factory workers typically work in higher-paid positions classified as operatives, while women occupy lower-paid positions classified as assemblers (Bernstein 1988).

Men may tolerate women in predominantly male work settings if women work in female jobs and accept women doing men's jobs in traditionally female settings, but they resist women in traditionally male jobs in male work settings. Physical proximity per se is not threatening as long as another form of differentiation sets women apart from men. Since men benefit from sex segregation of occupations, one of the central mechanisms determining the wage gap, they will resist the implementation of comparable worth and integration strategies (Reskin 1988).

A more radical strategy would call into question gender, race, and class hierarchies. Following the experience of the Swedish labor movement, a solidaristic wage policy targets low-wage workers—mainly women and people of color—for the largest wage adjustments based on a principle of social need (Brenner 1987; Blum 1967). Brenner presents another strategy, less divisive than comparable worth, which was adopted by striking female clerical workers at Yale. These clerical workers demanded wage adjustments commensurate with the intrinsic value of their work instead of through comparisons with male blue-collar workers. During the strike, both the blue-collar and clerical unions supported the other's collective bargaining efforts (Brenner 1987).

Child Care Services

Child care has become an important part of the national political agenda. Until recently, state support of child care services has been severely limited in the United States. Such policies can be characterized as a nonsystem; always underfunded, and for the most part left to the marketplace (Gottfried 1988–1989). In the 1989 legislative session, Congress passed the Family Leave Act only to have the bill vetoed by President Bush. Even if the Family Leave Act had been enacted, it would have touched only the surface of a growing crisis in the provision of child care.

Unions have joined women's groups and civil rights organizations in promoting child care for working parents. The American Federation of Labor and Congress of Industrial Organization (AFL-CIO) called for "national comprehensive quality child care legislation" at their conventions during the 1960s and 1970s (Cornfield 1989). More recently, the AFL-CIO has supported and lobbied for legislation on family and medical leave.

Unions also have pursued child care benefits through collective bargaining. Between 1968 and 1975, the Amalgamated Clothing and Textile Workers Union (ACTWU) established union-operated multiemployer day care centers in Baltimore, Chicago, and small towns in the East (Cornfield 1989). In New York's Chinatown, a local of the International Ladies

Garment Workers Union (ILGWU) negotiated the establishment of a day care center. Some of these day care centers have since closed because of insufficient funding (Cornfield 1989).

An employer-provided benefit is a more common type of child care arrangement bargained by locals of the ILGWU, the ACTWU, the SEIU, the American Federation of Government Employees (AFGE), the Office and Professional Employees International Union (OPEIU), the USWA, the Newspaper Guild, and the Farm Labor Organizing Committee (FLOC). Two public sector unions, AFSCME and SEIU, have a strong record of contractual provisions for child care. Of AFSCME contracts covering 1,000 or more workers, 88 percent of the 754,000 workers enjoy maternity or parental leave contractual benefits. AFSCME members living in New York State can participate in the statewide day care system established in 1979, the first of its kind (Cornfield 1989). Further, AFSCME employs a women's rights coordinator who conducts workshops, disseminates information, and encourages locals to bargain child care benefits. The recent successful campaign to organize clerical and technical workers at Harvard University by AFSCME included child care as one of the bargaining issues (Cornfield 1989).

Taking the collective bargaining route presents some drawbacks. First, the extent of union contract coverage in the United States is low, reaching only 20 percent of the total working population and 13 percent of the eligible female workers, although 37 percent of eligible workers in the public sector belong to unions (U.S. Department of Commerce 1989). Unions, facing declining membership, could raise the banner of child care to attract new members and facilitate greater participation by existing female members, who make up an increasing proportion of the union movement (about 35 percent). Male union members who have benefited from gender hierarchies in the past will make uncertain, yet necessary, allies.

Elsewhere I have argued for a socialized child care policy as the most effective way to achieve the goals of an egalitarian social organization of the household and the empowerment of women (Gottfried 1988–1989). Both the funding for and the development of child care services could be linked to the educational system, making child care services more than way-stations for the custodial care of children.

Family and Medical Leave

A national policy is needed that creates a new minimum standard for family and medical leave. Recently the Institute for Women's Policy Research estimated the costs associated with the lack of family and medical leave at the national level. They found that all women workers, particularly minority women, bear a disproportionate share of this cost. According to a publication issued by the institute:

> A national leave policy would reduce the costs to workers and society of the socially necessary tasks of child birth, child care, and elder care, or of illness, because having the right to return to their jobs would reduce unemployment and income loss for workers who must be absent for these reasons. (Spalter-Roth and Hartmann 1988: 1)

A family and medical leave would help workers balance family responsibilities with employment demands. Workers would be entitled to take parental or medical leave without the risk of losing their job. Spalter-Roth and Hartmann describe the importance of this entitlement:

> This policy moves beyond the protective legislation that sets women workers apart from the rest of the work force and it moves beyond the equal treatment language of the Civil Rights Act. It does this by mandating a new kind of minimum labor standard that assumes that the average worker does not choose between family responsibilities and wage labor, but does both. (1988: 2)

Spalter-Roth and Hartmann (1988) estimate financial losses to working women and to taxpayers as six times greater than the cost to business for granting family and medical leaves. The General Accounting Office projects $102 million in annual costs to business in the current House version of the bill or $340 million in the Senate version compared to a $715 million annual loss to working women and men, their families, and taxpayers because of the lack of family and medical leave (Spalter-Roth and Hartmann 1988).

This severe economic impact on families may convince the Congress to pass legislation mandating a family and medical leave policy, but the form the bill takes may be less than satisfactory. The state often reinforces woman as a dependent; for example, income maintenance and employment policies make it difficult for women to leave marriage since a woman's entitlement is often filtered through a man (Hanmer 1978). A broad coalition is necessary to carry out such an agenda; women's groups, civil rights organizations, and unions could be mobilized to ensure that a national family and medical leave policy reflects the needs of women.

The Effect of Macroeconomic Level Changes on Sexual Coercion

Policies aimed at the macroeconomic level affect sexual coercive practices at the microsocial level. First, by formulating economic sanctions, policies establish a punitive consequence—financial costs—against men who engage in sexually coercive behaviors. These sanctions act as a deterrent and convey a message that sexual coercion will not be tolerated. The courts as well as individual organizations could promote and enforce these economic sanctions.

Second, economic reforms have a positive impact on reducing sexual coercion. Comparable worth would increase the earning potential of women, and support services like child care and family and medical leave would ensure that women did not lose income or income-generating opportunities. Such reforms would increase the economic independence of women as a group, thereby enabling individual women to escape abusive situations.

Third, unions or other forms of collective organization are vehicles for raising awareness about sexual coercion and formulating organizational mechanisms for preventing sexual coercion. In the workplace, unions can negotiate the separation of sex from work to create a professional work environment.

Long-Term Goals

The initial step in the process of developing an agenda for economic change is labeling the forms of sexual coercion. Labeling makes visible what was invisible, defining as unacceptable what was acceptable, and insisting that what was naturalized is problematic (Kelly 1988). Letting women speak for themselves—gaining a voice—is an important part of the political process directed at economic change. The efficacy of a policy should be measured according to whether it empowers women, both individually and collectively. This means the process, as well as the outcome, of policy formation must be considered and debated.

Economic reforms alone cannot do away with sexual coercion. To eliminate sexual coercion, we need to change economic institutions and structures (Bart and O'Brien 1985). We can envision a "society in which the right to contribute and the right to be cared for are equally shared by men and women. This depends on a reformulation of individual and collective responsibilities and the redistribution of material resources" (Brenner 1987: 451). In general, this restructuring would revise hierarchic structures and control approaches, experimenting with new collaborative and democratic types of organization (see Skinner 1988).

IV
Conclusion

14

What Is Known and Not Known about Sexual Coercion

Elizabeth Grauerholz
Mary A. Koralewski

S exual coercion is a multidimensional phenomenon, consisting of legal, sociocultural, interpersonal, and psychological aspects. As such, it is difficult to obtain an overall picture of the problem and to understand its complexity, particularly because, as Burkhart and Fromuth commented, research typically is event specific and researchers are separated by their different disciplinary contexts and their research focus. In this chapter, we draw upon information presented in previous chapters and other research to discuss what is known and not known about the nature, causes, and prevention of sexual coercion.

On the Nature of Sexual Coercion

Sexual coercion emerges in many forms. The act of forcing, pressuring, or tricking another individual into engaging in a sexual act may occur within the family, public, workplace, classroom, or a variety of other settings or groups. The means used to coerce sex may be physical, financial, or psychological. The actors may be adults or children, males or females. Yet despite this diversity, there are several commonalities among various sexually coercive acts.

First, sexual coercion is relatively commonplace: as many as 40 percent of girls may be sexually coerced during childhood, about half of the women on college campuses or in the workplace will experience sexual harassment, as many as one in four women may be raped during their lives, and almost all women and girls experience the threat of sexual violence (Kelly 1988; Stock, Krause, and Vaughan, 1988). The actual experience of coercion or the fear of violation is a fact of life for women and girls in our society. Current research also indicates that men and boys sometimes experience sexual coercion.

Second, it is apparent that sexual coercion is primarily a unidirectional phenomenon: it is perpetrated by men against women. This is certainly the case with rape, but as Harney and Muehlenhard suggest, this may be partly a function of how some researchers and lawmakers regard rape—as penile-vaginal contact with penetration. Prostitutes are usually female and patrons male, and although male prostitutes exist, they generally service men, not women. Male brothels for women are virtually nonexistent (Sandford 1975). In the case of sexual harassment, the same pattern appears, although a significant minority of men claimed to have been sexually harassed, as McKinney and Maroules suggest. The gender effect is less pronounced in child sexual abuse; women represent a surprisingly large proportion of perpetrators, as Knudsen and Burkhart and Fromuth discuss. Moreover, both boys and girls are subjected to sexual advances from adults and adolescents. This suggests that there is an interaction between gender and age; younger males are more likely to be sexually victimized than older males.

It is also clear that neither victims nor perpetrators are likely to be deviates. Rape, sexual harassment, and child sexual abuse are more likely to be perpetrated by acquaintances and intimates than by strangers or "crazed perverts." Even prostitutes, who are often viewed as deviates in our society, are not very different from other women. As Silverman (1977: 20) suggests, women workers are engaged in a type of prostitution-patron system since "in work situations . . . men provide the jobs through hiring and promotion, set salary levels and work conditions, and can terminate employment by firing." Others assert that there is little difference between a wife who is supported financially by her husband in exchange for sex and domestic labor and the prostitute who exchanges sex for money (de Beauvoir 1952). The same may be said for traditional dating relationships in which the male pays for the date with the expectation that the woman will grant sexual favors in return.

The many negative and pervasive effects of sexual coercion are evident. The personal, social, and financial costs associated with sexual harassment have been well documented, as have the personal and interpersonal effects of rape. Similarly, child sexual abuse is frequently traumatic, although it is not possible to determine its long-term effects. The effects extend to women and girls who have not actually been sexually victimized but who experience a generalized fear of being victimized. Stock suggests that women develop seemingly pathological symptoms (such as checking doors frequently) as a result of living in fear of sexual assault.

In sum, we know from studies of sexual coercion that it is relatively commonplace and unidirectional, usually involves psychological and socially normal individuals, and may have serious and pervasive effects. At the same time, several issues related to these points are not so well understood.

The actual incidence and prevalence of sexual coercion have not been determined, in large part because such crimes are underreported and because there is no single definition or measure employed across studies. A major task for researchers is to develop better measures of these phenomena, a difficult but achievable goal, as witnessed by recent developments in the area of date rape (Koss and Oros 1982). To some degree, before we are able to quantify measures, we must deal with conceptual issues more carefully. Knudsen notes, for instance, that even professionals disagree about what constitutes child sexual abuse. Also, as we have seen in this book, there is overlap among various acts, and many acts may be coercive but not be labeled as rape or sexual harassment, for example. These experiences remain untapped by researchers who focus on only particular acts. Thus, it would be helpful to measure experiences across the continuum of sexual coercion rather than focus on one particular act.

Despite different estimates of sexual coercion, we also know that the incidence rates from official statistics have been increasing during the past several decades, but it is not known whether this increase is due to actual increases in incidence or the rate of reporting. There is reason to believe that the latter is true. Women must first label their experience before they can report it, and many forms of sexual coercion have only recently been labeled as social and legal problems (for example, sexual harassment and date or marital rape). Thus, rate increases may be due to women's increased ability to label these experiences and then to seek help from professionals or to acknowledge these acts on self-report questionnaires. On the other hand, if sexual violence is a means to control women's lives and actions, as Stock suggests, then sexual coercion against women may be increasing as women challenge male power. In her study of English women from 1870 to 1950, Lewis (1984: 222) suggests that sexual violence increased "in tandem with the growth in both women's personal freedom and their ability to dispense with a male social and economic protector." However, Sanday (1981b) found that male aggression, including institutionalized rape, is less likely to occur in societies where females have economic and political power or authority than in those where women have no power or authority. As measures become more sensitive and reliable and we understand more fully the roots of sexual coercion, we may be able to determine whether the incidence rates are in fact increasing and whether the changing status of women is likely to correspond to increased levels of violence against them.

It also is not clear whether differences in victimization rates for males and females reflect actual differences in experiences, reporting, detection, or perceptions of what constitutes abuse. As Knudsen points out, young males do not necessarily view sexual experiences by older women as abusive, and as a culture, we tend to glamorize such behavior. In general, we do not fully understand the effects of sexual coercion on male victims and how these are related to gender identity, relative power, societal response, or age. Research on all types of male victimization needs further investigation, including rape by women, as Harney and Muehlenhard discussed.

In terms of effects, we need to explore more carefully the effects of prostitution on women, a topic lacking in the research but that could be enlightened by drawing on the research on the effects of other forms of sexual coercion as reviewed here. Also, we do not fully understand the varied outcomes of sexual coercion, the social costs of rape, child sexual abuse, and prostitution (in terms of lost potential or costs for therapy, for example), or the extent to which victimization may contribute to revictimization by rendering an individual more vulnerable to similar or different forms of sexual assault.

More generally, researchers need to continue to explore the ways in which various sexually coercive acts are related to one another. If sexual violence exists along a continuum, what is the dimension on which the points vary? At first, it seems reasonable to order these points along a continuum of noxiousness in terms of the degradation, hurtfulness, coerciveness, and/or injury involved. Many of us have an implicit rank ordering of the severity of each of these acts. However, as Leidig (1981) points out, while observers are in agreement about the end points of the continuum (obscene telephone calls, for example, are consistently rated as less noxious than rape with injury), there is considerable disagreement about the level of noxiousness involved in intermediate forms. For example, one act of forced intercourse perpetrated by a stranger may be less devastating to the survivor than several years of fondling by a parent.

Kelly (1988: 76) rejects ordering acts in terms of severity because "the degree of impact cannot be simplistically inferred from the form of sexual violence women experience or its place within a continuum." Instead Kelly arranges acts along a continuum of prevalence, ranging from threat of violence (experienced by virtually all women and girls) to incest.

Although sexually coercive acts can be conceptualized in terms of prevalence, to do so solely is to ignore other underlying dimensions of sexual violence. In fact, sexual violence is a complex and multidimensional problem, and attempts to define a single dimension along which these acts can be organized may be futile. Instead there may be several defining dimensions of the continuum.

For instance, points along the continuum may vary according to powerlessness or the ability one has in a situation to give or withhold consent or to exert one's own will. Because of the power differential involved with child sexual abuse, children are not capable of giving or withholding consent freely; hence child sexual abuse would rest at one end of the continuum along with instances of rape in which the rapist wields a weapon or is physically stronger. Similarly, if one is subjected to street hassling (such as "cat-calls"), the event is usually terminated before the victim has the opportunity to consent or withhold consent. The most one is able to do is ignore an offense or fight back, but both of these responses are done in reaction to the coercive act, which has already taken place. The same holds for people who are subjected to exhibitionists and frotteurs. At the other end are events such as obscene telephone calls. Although the receiver is initially subjected to the abuse without being given the opportunity to consent to listening, he or she has the ability to terminate the interaction (withhold further consent) by hanging up. Also, assuming that prostitutes have some job alternatives (if not adequate ones), the degree of powerlessness could be said to be less.

Yet another way these acts may vary concerns the relative directness of the event. Rape, for example, involves direct, overt expressions of violence. Some forms of sexual harassment, as McKinney and Maroules note, are more indirect and ambiguous, such as undue attention or sexist jokes. (We could include in this analysis acts such as sexist advertising.) Directness may also be related to effects on victims. While some acts may traumatize the survivor immediately upon impact, other acts may combine in an additive or multiplicative function, taking years to manifest themselves and making it more difficult over time to resist more overt acts of aggression. Prostitutes, for instance, might not experience many effects until months or years after prostituting.

In short, no single variable can account for the nature of sexual coercion. To understand this problem, we must explore the multitude of ways that sexually coercive acts are related.

On the Causes of Sexual Coercion

Attempts to understand the roots of sexual coercion are hampered somewhat by the fact that most theorists explain only one type of act. Few attempts have been made to develop models that can account for the many forms of sexual violence observed in our society.

Feminist theory is perhaps best able to account for all forms of sexual violence against women. According to Stock, this theory asserts that sexual violence is the result of power inequality between males and females and is an attempt to maintain this inequality. Child sexual abuse also can be understood as an outcome of the power difference between adults and children. Feminist theory cannot as easily explain violence against men by women. For this, we turn to the psychological or social psychological explanations of sexual coercion.

We see from Burkhart and Fromuth's discussion that child abuse perpetrators demonstrate an oversexualization of emotional needs, a pattern of sexual arousal to subordination, and a lack of empathy for children. Similarly, perpetrators of adult rape demonstrate misogynist beliefs and attitudes, aggressive motives, a rape-supportive personality profile, and characteristic patterns of sexual arousal. These attitudinal, personological, and motivational factors combine to form a psychological profile most descriptive of perpetrators. Interestingly, very little research has been done on the psychological and social psychological characteristics of sexual harassers. Instead most researchers focus on the organizational factors contributing to sexual harassment. Future research may determine whether the factors discussed by Burkhart and Fromuth apply to perpetrators of sexual harassment and even prostitution.

Thornhill and Thornhill put forth a sociobiological explanation of sexual coercion. Although this perspective has been criticized (Harding 1985), it provides a provocative thesis. A psychological adaption to rape may help to explain why sexual coercion appears to be universal (Palmer 1989). It also addresses the confusion concerning whether sexual coercion is motivated by power or sex by suggesting that it may be motivated by both. If one acknowledges that sexually coercive individuals may have both sexual and power motivations, it is easier to understand the range of behaviors and types of victims observed in studies of sexual coercion. Still, if a primary motive is reproduction, it is harder to understand instances of child sexual abuse, homosexual rape, or sexual harassment that occur without sexual intercourse.

Another important area to consider in terms of contributing factors is the role that social institutions play in causing or permitting sexual coercion. It is within institutions that sexually coercive attitudes and behavior are learned and manifested, and social institutions provide legitimation of certain behaviors (such as male dominance) that are related to sexual violence. The key to understanding the link between sexual violence and social institutions is to understand that all institutions in the United States are stratified by sex; that men, not women, historically and contemporarily, occupy most positions of power within institutions; and that men, not women, reap the rewards that flow from these positions. This power differential increases women's dependency on men, making violence more difficult to resist. Also, because institutions are dominated by men, some institutional norms and practices may facilitate, allow, and perhaps even encourage violence against women.

Within the educational system, for instance, Enke and Sudderth suggest that certain practices, especially differential socialization of males and females, contribute to the development of sexually coercive attitudes and behaviors. McKinney and Maroules also review research suggesting that the structure and norms within universities (such as diffused institutional authority and tolerance of eccentricity) may help perpetuate sexual coercion within their walls. Others suggest that certain institutions within the educational system, such as fraternities, encourage and foster violence against women (Martin and Hummer 1989).

A similar pattern is found for other social institutions, such as the legal institution, which contributes to the problem of sexual coercion in part by its ineffectiveness in dealing with victims and perpetrators. The economic institution is structured in such a way that women's dependency on men is reinforced, thereby making it more difficult for women to escape oppression and victimization. The media institution, especially the pornography industry, objectifies women and may perpetuate sexual violence.

In addition to these institutions, the extremely high incidence of sexual violence within the family suggests that the structure of the family itself may give rise to sexual coercion. One contributing factor is the dependency of women and children created by an unequal distribution of power and traditional division of labor. Women and children receive disproportionately fewer resources (income, goods, services) and possess less power and authority than men (Brannen and Wilson 1987; Szinovacz 1984). Because housework and child care are devalued and unpaid in our society, women's status within the family and society is diminished, reinforcing their social and economic dependence on husbands. Frieze (1983) found that marital rape victims tended to be more economically dependent on their husbands than were women who had not experienced wife rape. The dependence of women on men, and children on adults, makes it very difficult, perhaps even impossible, for victims to escape their attackers or to report abuse.

Another factor related to the division of labor within families that may have implications for understanding sexual coercion is men's lack of participation in child care (Coverman 1989). Parker and Parker (1986) found that the more involved fathers were in the care of their children, the less likely they were to abuse them sexually. This supports Herman and Hirschman's (1977) theory that because women are more involved in the care of children, they are in a better position than men to understand children's needs, the difference between affectionate and erotic involvement, and the boundaries of parental love.

Similarly, the dating relationship is structured along explicit social exchange principles (men pay for activities and in return, women are expected to provide sexual favors), which make sexual exploitation more likely. In return for economic rewards, women may feel pressured to have sexual relations, and men may feel entitled to demand them. As Box (1983: 152) suggests, for this economic support "many of these males may occasionally demand a sexual price beyond the level the female is willing to go without feeling it to be coerced from her rather than given freely."

Thus, it can be argued that the structure of social institutions serves to keep women in relatively powerless positions and therefore dependent on men. This, combined with the fact that most interactions within social institutions, particularly the family, are hidden from public view, and that inherent within social institutions are norms and practices that may give rise to sexual coercion, suggests that social institutions provide environments ripe for victimization. It would be useful for researchers to investigate carefully how social institutions such as these and others (for example, religious and health institutions) contribute to the problem.

The roots of sexual coercion and the factors contributing to its existence are complex, possibly with biological, psychological, interpersonal, sociocultural, and institutional elements. To some extent, we will probably never completely understand its causes, although research can provide insight into these processes. Perhaps the most important direction research can take toward this end is to explore sexual coercion in a cross-cultural context.

Cross-cultural research can help to identify the factors and conditions relevant to understanding the causes of sexual coercion. If societies vary considerably in terms of the incidence and prevalence of sexual coercion, we may be able to identify those factors at the root of sexual coercion.

Unfortunately, the cross-cultural work dealing with gender roles makes only passing reference to sexual violence. In Levinson's (1989: 12) analysis of ninety preliterate peasant societies, he does not address sexual violence within the family: "There is simply not enough data in the ethnographic literature to make the study of . . . [incest and marital rape] productive." The few accounts of sexual coercion that do exist suggest that such acts occur in a wide variety of cultures with different social, economic, and political systems.

Some attempt has been made to study unofficial victims in other countries (Hall 1985; Wilson 1978), but in general, no standard measure of sexual victimization is used, making comparisons difficult. Even the use of official statistics is difficult because in many countries, such as Britain, reporting is not mandatory (Nash and West 1985). Furthermore, given the dangers present in some cultures to women who lose their virginity through rape or other means, many victims remain silent (Hershatter 1986; Mandebaum 1988). For example, Mandebaum claims that in Arab societies, an unmarried pregnant woman may be killed by her father or brothers. Nevertheless, attempts to gain information in such cultures can be successful. Saadawi (1980) found that approximately 40 percent of Egyptian women had experienced sexual abuse as children.

Furthermore, some sexually violent acts are so ingrained in the culture that they are not defined as sexual coercion (for example, genital mutilation in some Arab cultures; Saadawi 1980). Perhaps, as Morgan (1987) suggests, in some societies, cultural legitimation is so effective that an act is not viewed as violent. For instance, in Elam's (1973) study of nomadic tribes in Uganda, an act of symbolic rape occurs at marriage in which the bride screams and fights vigorously to resist sexual intercourse. Interesting, Elam (1973: 180) later states, "Throughout my time in Himaland . . . I can state that rape is almost unheard of."

Such factors make it extremely difficult to derive objective and reliable measures that can be used in cross-cultural research. If we are to understand the causes of sexual coercion, however, researchers would do well to develop such measures and investigate sexual coercion within different cultural contexts.

On the Prevention of Sexual Coercion

To eliminate or reduce the occurrence of sexual coercion, intervention should begin early in life, continue throughout, and extend itself into some new areas not currently thought of as being relevant. This intervention should approach the problem at each of three levels: the institutional, the interpersonal, and the individual.

The most encompassing is an institutional or sociocultural level. Even in institutions that claim to promote justice and equality, such as marriages and families, men occupy positions of authority and control most resources, reinforcing women's dependency on men and making sexual coercion more possible. In addition, many institutions are racist, and this bias is also structured into organizations and into the groups' norms. Consequently women of color who are sexually harassed, raped, molested, or abused face additional problems in redressing their grievances.

Social institutions are intertwined so that attempts to change one will inevitably create disruption and probably resistance from another. As Bart and associates (1989: 432) suggest, "We have learned how institutions, when not facilitating or ideologically supporting the violence and covering it up when it occurs, obdurately resist change."

On the other hand, efforts to eliminate sexual violence may be best directed at social institutions. Stockard and Johnson (1980: 278) maintain that

> because individuals live and mature within social institutions, one way to alter their motivations and self-definitions is to change these institutions.

Because cultural symbols ultimately reflect existing social reality, they may eventually alter to reflect institutional changes. It must also be recognized that societies may more easily legislate changes in institutions than in individual attitudes, thus making institutions the easiest area in which to intervene.

The most obvious strategies include a better-informed educational, law enforcement, and judicial system. Changes must occur within the economic system, for, as Gottfried pointed out, as long as an unequal system of wage earnings is allowed to exist and women are subsequently financially dependent on men, men can abuse their power by forcing women to submit to sexual coercion.

Within the health institution, mental health professionals can play a vital role in the prevention of sexual coercion. Instead of labeling women as neurotic and thus deviant, attention should be paid to society's pathological acceptance of violence and its tolerance of male socialization, which permits it. It has been much more convenient to view women's response to victimization as pathological instead of male perpetration as reprehensible (for example, we do not diagnose perpetrators of abuse as having an exploitative personality disorder, but victims may be diagnosed as having masochistic features).

Children and adults need to acquire different values about interpersonal relationships. Couples need to adopt better methods of communicating, along the lines of the informed consent method Allgeier and Royster discussed. Another important area of change concerns therapy and counseling for survivors and perpetrators. Clinicians should avoid the potential abuse of power in the therapy relationship. This abuse can take many forms, ranging from outright sexual contact between clients and therapists to a paternalistic therapist who subtly undermines the client's efforts and encourages an unhealthy dependence on her or him. Although estimates of the frequency of sexual contact between therapists and clients are difficult to obtain, Holroyd and Brodsky (1977) found that in a sample of licensed psychologists, 5.5 percent of the male and 0.6 percent of the female therapists reported having sexual intercourse with their clients. Another example of how the therapy situation has the potential for further abuse concerns conjoint therapists whose belief system dictates an intolerance of divorce, even in cases of battering or sexual violence. Feminist therapists have long known the value of empowerment for women and thus are less likely to mimic the authoritarian, didactic, patriarchal medical-model approach and are more likely to give clients respect for their own experience and feelings (treating survivors as clients and not victims as patients).

Also, therapists should constantly be aware of the potential for further victim blaming. It is likely that survivors will already have experienced blame from family, friends, and the legal and medical communities, and thus it is crucial not to perpetuate this abuse in the therapy situation. For example, when obtaining a detailed history of the abuse, it is important to obtain information without suggesting the survivor was at fault (for example, it is appropriate to assess whether alcohol was involved but not to say, "You know, you shouldn't have been drinking.") There can be a fine line between blaming the victim by suggesting she was at fault for making certain decisions and empowering her to make changes in her life in order to minimize her level of risk.

At the individual level, assertiveness and self-defense training, as well as remedial therapy, will equip individual women with the skills necessary to minimize their level of risk and to cope with coercion should it occur. Self-defense training also empowers individuals and provides a community of support, as Thompson discusses.

An empowering exercise that can be used with students and children is to attempt to create in writing a utopia free of violence. A quotation from Monique Wittig (quoted in Griffin 1979: 102) can serve as inspiration: "There was a time when you were not a slave, remember that. You walked alone, full of laughter you bathed barebellied. You say you have lost all recollection of it, remember . . . you say there are no words to describe it, you say it does not exist. But remember. Make an effort to remember. Or, failing that, invent." If one assumes that only that which can be envisioned can be realized, as we begin to envision our utopia, we come closer to transforming the fantasy into a reality.

Summary

Sexual coercion is a complex problem, but it is clear that our understanding of it has increased significantly during the past two decades. We are much closer to understanding sexual coercion as a multidimensional construct than we were even a decade ago, when most researchers focused solely on a particular act and saw no relationship between the act and other forms of sexual coercion. A unidimensional approach to understanding the causes and prevention of sexual coercion still predominates, however; most theories and models fail to account for multiple acts or situations involving sexual coercion. We hope that the issues explored in this book will propel researchers and practitioners forward in their efforts to uncover the complex nature, causes, and prevention of sexual coercion.

References

Abarbanel;. G. 1986. Rape and resistance. *Journal of Interpersonal Violence* 1: 100–105.

Abbey, A 1982. Sex differences in attributions for friendly behavior: Do males misperceive females' friendliness? *Journal of Personality and Social Psychology* 42: 830–838.

Abbey, A. 1987. Misperceptions of friendly behavior as sexual interest: A survey of naturally occurring incidents. *Psychology of Women Quarterly* 11: 173–194.

Abbey, A., and C. Melby. 1986. The effects of nonverbal cues on gender differences in perceptions of sexual intent. *Sex Roles* 15: 283–298.

Abel, G., D.H. Barlow, E.B. Blanchard, and D. Guild. 1977. The components of rapists' sexual arousal. *Archives of General Psychiatry* 34: 895–903.

Adams, C., J. Fay, and J. Loreen-Martin. 1984. *NO is not enough: Helping teenagers avoid sexual assault.* San Luis Obispo, Calif.: Impact Publishers.

Adams, J.W., J.L. Kottke, and J.S. Padgitt. 1983. Sexual harassment of university students. *Journal of College Personnel* (November): 484–491.

Adams-Tucker, C. 1984. The unmet psychiatric needs of sexually abused youths: Referrals from a child protection agency and clinical evaluations. *Journal of the American Academy of Child Psychiatry* 23: 659–667.

Adams-Tucker, C. 1985. Defense mechanisms used by sexually abused children. *Children Today* 14: 9–12, 34.

Ageton, S.S. 1983. *Sexual assault among adolescents.* Lexington, Mass.: Lexington Books.

Ageton, S.S. 1985. *A research report for teenagers: Facts about sexual assault.* Rockville, Md.: U.S. Department of Health and Human Services.

Aizenman, M., and G. Kelley. 1988. The incidence of violence and acquaintance rape in dating relationships among college men and women. *Journal of College Student Development* 29: 305–311.

Akers, R.L. 1985. *Deviant behavior: A social learning approach.* 3d ed. Belmont, Calif.: Wadsworth.

Alexander, P.C., and S.L. Lupfer. 1987. Family characteristics and long term consequences associated with sexual abuse. *Archives of Sexual Behavior* 16: 235–245.

Alexander, R.D. 1979. *Darwinism and human affairs.* Seattle: University of Washington Press.

Alexander, R.D. 1987. *The biology of moral systems.* New York: Aldine de Gruyter.

Allgeier, E.R. 1989. Pleasure and danger in sexual relationships: Risks in taking positions about sexual issues. Invited plenary presentation at the Annual Meeting of the Society for the Scientific Study of Sex, Toronto.

Allgeier, E.R., and M.W. Wiederman. 1990. The association between love and marriage: Kephart (1967) thrice revisited. Paper presented at the Midcontinent Region Meeting of the Society for the Scientific Study of Sex, Toledo, Ohio.

American Humane Association. 1988. *Highlights of official child neglect and abuse reporting 1986*. Denver: American Humane Association.

American Psychiatric Association. 1987. *Diagnostic and statistical manual III— Revised*. New York: American Psychiatric Press.

Amir, M. 1971. *Patterns in forcible rape*. Chicago: University of Chicago Press.

Anonymous. 1989. MM graduates speak. *Model Mugging News* 3: 6.

Araji, S., and D. Finkelhor. 1986. Abusers: A review of the research. In D. Finkelhor and Associates (eds.), *Sourcebook on child sexual abuse*, pp. 89–118. Beverly Hills: Sage.

Armentrout, J.A. and A.L. Hauer. 1978. MMPIs of rapists of adults, rapists of children, and non-rapist sex offenders. *Journal of Clinical Psychology* 34: 330–332.

Atkeson, B.M., K.S. Calhoun, P.A. Resick, and E.M. Ellis. 1982. Victims of rape: Repeated assessment of depressive symptoms. *Journal of Consulting and Clinical Psychology* 50: 96–102.

Attias, R., and J. Goodwin. 1985. Knowledge and management strategies in incest cases: A survey of physicians, psychologists and family counselors. *Child Abuse and Neglect* 9: 527–533.

Baca-Zinn, M., and D.S. Eitzen. 1987. *Diversity in American families*. New York: Harper & Row.

Backhouse, C., and L. Cohen. 1982. *Sexual harassment on the job*. Englewood Cliffs, N.J.: Prentice-Hall.

Bagley, C., and L. Young. 1987. Juvenile prostitution and child sexual abuse: A controlled study. *Canadian Journal of Community Mental Health* 6: 5–26.

Barry, K. 1979. Female sexual slavery. Englewood Cliffs, N.J.: Prentice-Hall.

Barry, K. 1985. Social etiology of crimes against women. *Victimology* 10: 1–4, 164–178.

Bart, P.B. 1981. A study of women who both were raped and avoided rape. *Journal of Social Issues* 37: 123–137.

Bart, P.B., P. Miller, E. Moran, and E. Stanko. 1989. Guest editor's introduction. *Gender and Society* 3: 429–436.

Bart, P.B., and P.H. O'Brien. 1985. *Stopping rape: Successful survival strategies*. New York: Pergamon.

Bass, E., and L. Davis. 1988. *The courage to heal*. New York: Harper.

Batelle Law and Justice Study Center. 1978. *Forcible rape: An analysis of legal issues*. Washington, D.C.: U.S. Government Printing Office.

Bateman, P. 1986. Let's get out from between the rock and the hard place. *Journal of Interpersonal Violence* 1: 105–111.

Baxter, R.H. 1985. *Sexual harassment in the workplace*. New York: Executive Enterprises Publications.

Beavers, R.W. 1977. *Psychotherapy and growth: A family systems perspective*. New York: Brunner/Mazel Publishers.

Becker, J.V., J. Cunningham-Rathner, and M.S. Kaplan. 1986. Adolescent sexual offenders: Demographics, criminal and sexual histories and recommendations for reducing future offenses. *Journal of Interpersonal Violence* 1: 431–455.

Becker, J.V., L.J. Skinner, M.D. Abel, and E.C. Treacy. 1982. Incidence and types of sexual dysfunctions in rape and incest victims. *Journal of Sex and Marital Therapy* 8: 65–74.

Belknap, J. 1989. The sexual victimization of unmarried women by nonrelative acquaintances. In M.A. Pirog-Good and J.E. Stets (eds.), *Violence in dating relationships: Emerging social issues*, pp. 205–218. New York: Praeger.

Beneke, T. 1982. *Men on rape: What they have to say about sexual violence.* New York: St. Martin's Press.

Benjamin, J. 1988. *The bonds of love: Psychoanalysis, feminism, and the problem of domination.* New York: Pantheon.

Benson, D.J., and G.E. Thomas. 1982. Sexual harassment on a university campus: The confluence of authority relations, sexual interest and gender stratification. *Social Problems* 29: 236–251.

Benson, K.A. 1984. Comment on Crocker's "An analysis of university definitions of sexual harassment." *Signs* 9: 516–519.

Berliner, L. 1987. Commentary editor's introduction, commentary I and II. *Journal of Interpersonal Violence* 2: 106–108, 118–120.

Berliner, L. 1989. Child abuse prevention education: How can we make it work? *Journal of Interpersonal Violence* 4: 251–253.

Berliner, L., and J.R. Conte. 1990. The process of victimization: The victims' perspective. *Child Abuse and Neglect* 14: 29–40.

Berliner, L., and J.R. Wheeler. 1987. Treating the effects of sexual abuse on children. *Journal of Interpersonal Violence* 2: 415–434.

Bernstein, A. 1988. So you think you've come a long way, baby? *Business Week,* February 29.

Best, R. 1983. *We all have scars: What boys and girls learn in elementary school.* Bloomington: Indiana University Press.

Betzig, L. 1985. *Despotism and differential reproduction: A Darwinian view of history.* New York: Aldine de Gruyter.

Betzig, L., M.B. Mulder, and P. Turke (eds). 1988. *Human reproductive behavior: A Darwinian perspective.* New York: Cambridge University Press.

Bielby, W. 1985. Undoing discrimination: Comparable worth and job integration. Paper presented at the Conference on Ingredients for Women's Employment Policy, State University of New York, Albany.

Binder, R.L., and D.E. McNiel. 1987. Evaluation of a school-based sexual abuse prevention program: Cognitive and emotional effects. *Child Abuse and Neglect* 11: 497–506.

Bixler, R.H. 1983. The multiple meanings of "incest." *Journal of Sex Research* 19: 197–201.

Black, H.C. 1968. *Black's law dictionary.* St. Paul: West Publishing Company.

Blader, J.C., and W.L. Marshall. 1989. Is assessment of sexual arousal in rapists worthwhile? A critique of current methods and the development of a response compatibility approach. *Clinical Psychology Review* 9: 569–587.

Blau, P. 1964. *Exchange and power in social life.* New York: Wiley.

Blum, L. 1987. Possibilities and limits of comparable worth. *Gender and Society* 1: 380–399.

Boat, B.W., and M.D. Everson. 1988. Interviewing young children with anatomical dolls. *Child Welfare* 67: 337–352.

Bond, J.C., and P. Peery. 1970. Is the black male castrated? In T. Cade (ed.), *The black woman*, pp. 113–118. New York: Signet.

Borkin, J., and L. Frank. 1986. Sexual abuse prevention for preschoolers: A pilot program. *Child Welfare* 65: 75–82.

Box, S. 1983. *Power, crime, and mystification.* London: Tavistock.

Bracey, D. 1979. *Baby pros.* New York: John Jay Press.

Brannen, J., and G. Wilson. 1987. *Give and take in families: Studies in resource distribution.* London: Allen & Unwin.

Breines, W., and L. Gordon. 1983. The new scholarship on family violence. *Signs* 8: 490–531.

Brenner, J. 1987. Feminist political discourse: Radical versus liberal approaches to the feminization of poverty and comparable worth. *Gender and Society* 1: 447–465.

Brewer, M.B., and R.A. Berk (eds.). 1982. Beyond nine to five: Sexual harassment on the job. *Journal of Social Issues* 38.

Briere, J. 1984. Effects of childhood sexual abuse on latter psychiatric functioning: post sexual abuse syndrome. Third National Conference on Sexual Victimization of Children, Washington, D.C.

Briere, J. 1989. *Therapy for adults molested as children: Beyond survival.* New York: Springer.

Briere, J., and M. Runtz. 1987. Post sexual abuse trauma: Data and implications for clinical practice. *Journal of Interpersonal Violence* 2: 367–379.

Briere, J., and M. Runtz. 1989. Symptomatology associated with childhood sexual victimization in a nonclinical adult sample. *Child Abuse and Neglect* 12: 51–59.

Briere, J., D. Evans, M. Runtz, and T. Wall. 1988. Symptomology in men who were molested as children: A comparison study. *American Journal of Orthopsychiatry* 58: 457–461.

Bristow, E. 1983. *Prostitution and prejudice: The Jewish fight against white slavery.* New York: Schocken Books.

Brodsky, C. 1976. *The harassed worker.* Lexington, Mass.: D.C. Heath.

Brodyaga, L., M. Gates, S. Singer, M. Tucker, and R. White. 1975. *Rape and its victims: A report for citizens, health facilities, and criminal justice agencies.* National Institute of Law Enforcement and Criminal Justice, Law Enforcement Assistance Administration, U.S. Department of Justice. Washington, D.C.: U.S. Government Printing Office.

Brown, A., and L. Sheridan. 1988. Pioneering women's committee: Struggles with hard times. *Labor Research Review* 11: 63–78.

Brown, M. 1979. Teenage prostitution. *Adolescence* 14: 665–679.

Browne, A., and D. Finkelhor. 1986. The impact of sexual abuse: A review of the research. *Psychological Bulletin* 91: 66–77.

Brownmiller, S. 1975. *Against our will: Men, women, and rape.* New York: Simon & Schuster.

Bryant, M.A. 1977. Prostitution and the criminal justice system. *Journal of Police Science and Administration* 5: 379–389.

Budin, L.E., and C.F. Johnson. 1989. Sex abuse prevention programs: Offenders' attitudes about their efficacy. *Child Abuse and Neglect* 13: 77–87.

Bularzik, M. 1978. Sexual harassment at the workplace: Historical notes. *Radical America* (July–August): 24–43.

Bulkley, J. 1985. Analysis of civil child protection statutes dealing with sexual abuse. In J. Bulkley, (ed.), *Child sexual abuse and the law*, pp. 81–88. Washington, D.C.: American Bar Association.

Bureau of Labor Statistics. 1989. *Union membership in 1988*. Washington, D.C.: U.S. Department of Labor.

Burgess, A.W., and L.L. Holmstrom. 1974. Rape trauma syndrome. *American Journal of Psychiatry* 131: 981–986.

Burgess, A.W., and L.L. Holmstrom. 1979. Rape: Sexual description and recovery. *American Journal of Orthopsychiatry* 49: 648–657.

Burkhart, B.R., and C. Bohmer. In press. Hidden rape and the legal crucible: Analyses and implications of epidemiological, social and legal factors. *Journal for the Expert Witness, the Trial Attorney and the Trial Judge.*

Burkhart, B.R., and A.L. Stanton. 1988. Acquaintance rape. In G.W. Russell (ed.), *Violence in intimate relationships*, pp. 43–65. New York: PMA Press.

Burnam, M.A., J.A. Stein, J.M. Golding, J.M. Siegel, S.B. Sorenson, A.B. Forsythe, and C.A. Telles, 1988. Sexual assault and mental disorders in a community population. *Journal of Consulting and Clinical Psychology* 56: 843–850.

Burt, M. 1980. Cultural myths and supports for rape. *Journal of Personality and Social Psychology* 38: 217–230.

Burt, M. 1983. Justifying personal violence: A comparison of rapists and the general public. *Victimology* 8: 131–150.

Burt, M., and R. Estep. 1981. Apprehension and fear: Learning a sense of sexual vulnerability. *Sex Roles* 7: 511–522.

Buss, D.M. 1987. Sex differences in human mate selection criteria: An evolutionary perspective. In C. Crawford, M. Smith, and D. Krebs (eds.), *Sociobiology and psychology: Ideas, issues, and applications*, pp. 335–351. Hillsdale, N.J.: Erlbaum.

Buss, D.M. 1989. Sex differences in human mate preferences: Evolutionary hypotheses tested in 37 cultures. *Behavioral and Brain Sciences* 12: 1–14.

Caignon, D., and G. Groves. 1987. *Her wits about her: Self defense success stories by women*. New York: Harper & Row.

Calhoun, K., S. Kelley, A. Amick, and R. Gardner. 1986. Factors differentiating sexually coercive and noncoercive college males. Paper presented at the meeting of the Southeastern Psychological Association, Orlando, Florida.

Calhoun, L.G., J.W. Selby, and L.J. Warring. 1976. Social perception of the victim's causal role in rape: An exploratory examination of four factors. *Human Relations* 29: 517–526.

Cameron, C. 1986. Noon at nine to five: Reflections on a decade of organizing. *Labor Research Review* 8: 103–108.

Cancian, F.M. 1987. *Love in America: Gender and self-development*. New York: Cambridge University Press.

Cann, A., L.G. Calhoun, and J.W. Selby. 1979. Attributing responsibility to the victim of rape: Influence of information regarding past sexual experience. *Human Relations* 32: 57–67.

Cantwell, H.B. 1988. Child sexual abuse: Very young perpetrators. *Child Abuse and Neglect* 12: 579–582.

Caplan, G. 1964. *Principles of preventive psychiatry.* New York: Basic Books.

Caputi, J. 1987. *The age of sex crime.* Bowling Green, Ohio: Bowling Green State University Press.

Caputi, J. 1989. The sexual politics of murder. *Gender and Society* 3: 437–456.

Carlson, M.I., S. Julsonnet, and C.L. Muehlenhard. 1988. Sexual assertiveness: Increasing women's ability to refuse unwanted sexual advances. Paper presented at the Annual Meeting of the Association for the Advancement of Behavior Therapy, New York.

Carmody, D. 1989. Increasing rapes on campus spur college to fight back. *New York Times*, January 1.

Carson, D.K., J.R. Council, and M.A. Volk. 1988. Temperament, adjustment and alcoholism in adult female incest victims. *Violence and Victims* 3: 205–216.

Carter, J. 1974. Problems of professional belief. In J. Carter (ed.), *The maltreated child*, pp. 51–57. Hove, England: Priory Press.

Cavaiola, A.A., and M. Schiff. 1988. Behavioral sequelae of physical and/or sexual abuse in adolescents. *Child Abuse and Neglect* 12: 181–188.

Chappell, D., and J. James. 1976. Victim selection and apprehension from the rapist's perspective: A preliminary investigation. Paper presented to the Second International Symposium on Victimology, Boston.

Chappell, D., and S. Singer. 1977. Rape in New York City: A study of material in the police files and its meaning. In D. Chappell, R. Geis, and R. Geis (eds.), *Forcible rape: The crime, the victim, and the offender*, pp. 245–271. New York: Columbia University Press.

Check, J.V.P., and N.M. Malamuth. 1983. Sex role stereotyping and reactions to depictions of stranger versus acquaintance rape. *Journal of Personality and Social Psychology* 45: 344–356.

Chisholm, S. 1970. Black women and politics. *Black Scholar* 1: 40–45.

Clark, L., and D. Lewis. 1977. *Rape: The price of coercive sexuality.* Toronto: Women's Press.

Cohen, C. 1987. Legal dilemmas in sexual harassment cases. *Labor Law Journal* (November): 681–688.

Cohn, A.H., and D. Daro. 1987. Is treatment too late: What ten years of evaluative research tells us. *Child Abuse and Neglect* 11: 433–442.

Cohn, E.S., L.H. Kidder, and J. Harvey. 1979. Crime prevention vs. victimization prevention: The psychology of two different reactions. *Victimology* 3: 285–296.

Cole, E. 1982. Sibling incest: The myth of benign sibling incest. *Women and Therapy* 1: 79–89.

Cole, J.A. 1988. Predictors of sexually coercive and aggressive behavior in college males. Ph.D. dissertation, Auburn University.

Coleman, J.S. 1966. *The adolescent society.* New York: Free Press.

Coles, F. 1986. Forced to quit: Sexual harassment complaints and agency response. *Sex Roles* 14: 81–95.

Collins, E., and T. Blodgett. 1981. Sexual harassment . . . some see it . . . some won't. *Harvard Business Review* 59: 76–94.

Conte, J.R. 1985. An evaluation of a program to prevent the sexual victimization of young children. *Child Abuse and Neglect* 9: 319–328.

Conte, J.R. 1986. Sexual abuse and the family: A critical analysis. *Journal of Psychotherapy and the Family* 2: 113–126.

Conte, J.R. 1987. Ethical issues in evaluation of prevention programs. *Child Abuse and Neglect* 11: 171–172.

Conte, J.R., and J.R. Schuerman. 1987. Factors associated with an increased impact of child sexual abuse. *Child Abuse and Neglect* 11: 201–211.

Conte, J.R., C. Rosen, and L. Saperstein. 1986. An analysis of programs to prevent the sexual victimization of children. *Journal of Primary Prevention* 6: 141–155.

Conte, J.R., C. Rosen, L. Saperstein, and R. Shermack. 1985. An evaluation of a program to prevent the sexual victimization of young children. *Child Abuse and Neglect* 9: 319–328.

Conte, J.R., S. Wolf, and T. Smith. 1989. What sexual offenders tell us about prevention strategies. *Child Abuse and Neglect* 13: 293–301.

Cornfield, D. 1989. Labor unions, corporations, and families: Institutional competition in the provision of social welfare. Unpublished manuscript.

Corsaro, W.A. 1985. *Friendship and peer culture in the early years.* Norwood, N.J.: Ablex.

Cosmides, L., and J. Tooby. 1987. From evolution to behavior: Evolutionary psychology as the missing link. In J. Dupre (ed.), *The latest on the best: Essays on evolution and optimality,* pp. 277–306. Cambridge, Mass.: MIT Press.

Courtois, C.A. 1988. *Healing the incest wound: Adult survivors in therapy.* New York: Norton.

Coverman, S. 1989. Women's work is never done: The division of domestic labor. In J. Freeman (ed.), *Women: A feminist perspective,* pp. 356–368. Mountain View, Calif.: Mayfield Publishing Co.

Craig, M.E. In press. Coercive sexuality in dating relationships: A situational model. *Clinical Psychology Review.*

Craig, M.E., S.C. Kalichman, and D.R. Follingstad. 1989. Coercive sexual behavior among college students: Relationship characteristics and affective experiences. *Archives of Sexual Behavior* 18: 421–434.

Crocker, P.L. 1983. An analysis of university definitions of sexual harassment. *Signs* 8: 696–707.

Cunningham, J., T. Pearce, and P. Pearce. 1988. Childhood sexual abuse and medical complaints in adult women. *Journal of Interpersonal Violence* 3: 131–144.

Cupoli, J.M., and P.M. Sewell. 1988. One thousand fifty-nine children with a chief complaint of sexual abuse. *Child Abuse and Neglect* 12: 151–162.

D'Emilio, J., and E.B. Freedman. 1988. *Intimate matters: A history of sexuality in America.* New York: Harper & Row.

Daly, Mary 1973. *Beyond God the Father: Toward a theory of women's liberation.* Boston: Beacon Press.

Daly, Martin, and M. Wilson. 1983. *Sex, evolution, and behavior.* 2d ed. North Scituate, Mass.: Duxbury Press.

Daly, Martin, and M. Wilson. 1988. *Homicide*. New York: Aldine de Gruyter.

Daly, Martin, M. Wilson, and S.J. Weghorst. 1982. Male sexual jealousy. *Ethology and Sociobiology* 3: 11–27.

Davis, G.E., and H. Leitenberg. 1987. Adolescent sex offenders. *Psychology Bulletin* 101: 417–427.

Davis, K. 1937. The sociology of prostitution. *American Sociological Review* 2: 746–755.

de Beauvoir, S. 1952. *The second sex*. New York: Alfred A. Knopf.

Deblinger, E., S.V. McLeer, M.S. Atkins, D. Ralphe, and E. Foa. 1989. Post-traumatic stress in sexually abused, physically abused, and nonabused children. *Child Abuse and Neglect* 13: 403–408.

Deegan, M.J. 1988. *Jane Addams and the men of the Chicago school, 1892–1918*. New Brunswick, N.J.: Transaction Press.

Deitz, S.R., K.T. Blackwell, P.C. Daley, and B.J. Bentley. 1982. Measurement of empathy toward rape victims and rapists. *Journal of Personality and Social Psychology* 43: 372–384.

DeJong, A.R. 1989. Sexual interactions among siblings and cousins: Experimentation or exploitation? *Child Abuse and Neglect* 13: 271–279.

DeJong, A.R., G.A. Emmett, and A.R. Hervada. 1982. Epidemiological factors in sexual abuse of boys. *American Journal of Diseases of Children* 136: 990–993.

deMause, L. 1974. *The history of childhood*. New York: Psychohistory Press.

deYoung, M. 1987. Toward a theory of child sexual abuse. *Journal of Sex Education and Therapy* 13: 17–21.

deYoung, M. 1988a. Issues in determining the veracity of sexual abuse allegations. *Children's Health Care* 17: 50–57.

deYoung, M. 1988b. The good touch/bad touch dilemma. *Child Welfare* 67: 60–68.

Diamond, I. 1980. Pornography and repression: A reconsideration. *Signs* 5: 686–701.

Dickemann, M. 1981. Paternal confidence and dowry competition: A biocultural analysis of purdah. In R.D. Alexander and D.W. Tinkle (eds.), *Natural selection and social behavior*, pp. 417–438. New York: Chiron Press.

Dietz, P.E., and B. Evans. 1982. Pornographic imagery and prevalence of paraphilia. *American Journal of Psychiatry* 139: 1439.

Dimock, P.T. 1988. Adult males sexually abused as children: Characteristics and implications for treatment. *Journal of Interpersonal Violence* 3: 203–221.

DiPietro, S.B. 1987. The effects of intrafamilial child sexual abuse on the adjustment and attitudes of adolescents. *Violence and Victims* 2: 59–78.

Dobash, R.E., and R. Dobash. 1979. *Violence against wives: A case against the patriarchy*. New York: Free Press.

Dolinko, D. 1986. Supreme Court review: Foreword: How to criticize the death penalty. *Journal of Criminal Law and Criminology* 77: 546–601.

Donnerstein, E. 1980. Aggressive erotica and violence against women. *Journal of Personality and Social Psychology* 39: 269–277.

Downer, A. 1986. Training teachers to be partners. In M. Nelson and K. Clark (eds.), *An evaluator's guide to preventing child sexual abuse*, pp. 80–86. Santa Cruz, Calif.: Network Publications.

Dube, R., and M. Hebert. 1988. Sexual abuse of children 12 years of age: A review of 511 cases. *Child Abuse and Neglect* 12: 321–330.

Duffee, S.B., and J.W. Bascuas. 1987. MMPI profile types of sexual abusers of children: An empirical classification. Paper presented at the National Family Violence Conference, University of New Hampshire, Durham, July.

Dworkin, A. 1976. *Our Blood: Prophecies and discourses on sexual politics.* New York: Harper & Row.

Dworkin, A. 1981. *Pornography: On men possessing women.* New York: Perigee Books.

Dworkin, A. 1987. *Intercourse.* New York: Free Press.

Dworkin, R. 1977. *Taking rights seriously.* Cambridge, Mass.: Harvard University Press.

Dzeich, B.W., and L. Weiner. 1984. *The lecherous professor.* Boston: Beacon Press.

Eckenrode, J., J. Munsch, J. Powers, and J. Doris. 1988. The nature and substantiation of official sexual abuse reports. *Child Abuse and Neglect* 12: 311–319.

Eder D., and S. Parker. 1987. The cultural production and reproduction of gender: The effect of extracurricular activities on peer-group culture. *Sociology of Education* 60: 200–213.

Edwards, A. 1987. Male violence in feminist theory: An analysis of the changing conceptions of sex/gender violence and male dominance. In J. Hanmer and M. Maynard (eds.), *Women, violence and social control,* pp. 13–29. Atlantic Highlands, N.J.: Humanities Press International.

Einbender, A.J., and W.N. Friedrich. 1989. Psychological functioning and behavior of sexually abused girls. *Journal of Consulting and Clinical Psychology* 57: 155–157.

Eisenberg, N., R.G. Owens, and M.E. Dewey. 1987. Attitudes of health professionals to child sexual abuse and incest. *Child Abuse and Neglect* 11: 109–116.

Eisenstein, Z. 1988. *The female body and the law.* Berkeley: University of California Press.

Eitzen, D.S. 1975. Athletics in the status system of male adolescents: A replication of Coleman's "the adolescent society." *Adolescence* 10: 267–276.

Elam, Y. 1973. *The social and sexual roles of Hima women: A study of nomadic cattle breeders in Nyabushozi County, Ankole, Uganda.* Manchester: Manchester University Press.

Ellerstein, N., and J.W. Canavan. 1980. Sexual abuse of boys. *American Journal of Diseases of Children* 134: 255–257.

Ellis, E.M., B.M. Atkeson, and K.S. Calhoun. 1981. An assessment of long-term reaction to rape. *Journal of Abnormal Psychology* 90: 263–266.

Ellis, L. 1989. *Theories of rape: Inquiries into the causes of sexual aggression.* New York: Hemisphere Publishing Co.

Elwell, M.E., and P.H. Ephross. 1987. Initial reactions of sexually abused children. *Social Casework* 68: 109–116.

Erway, K.L. 1990. Comorbidity of sexual and physical aggression in college males: Defining a typology of violence toward women. Ph.D. dissertation. Auburn University.

Estrich, S. 1987. *Real rape.* Cambridge: Harvard University Press.

Evans, L.J. 1978. Sexual harassment: Women's hidden occupational hazard. In J.R. Chapman and M. Gates (eds.), *The victimization of women,* pp. 203–233. Beverly Hills, Calif.: Sage Publications.

Everson, M.D., and B.W. Boat. 1989. False allegations of sexual abuse by children and adolescents. *Journal of the American Academy of Child and Adolescent Psychiatry* 28: 230–235.

Fain, T., and D. Anderton. 1987. Sexual harassment: Organizational context and diffuse status. *Sex Roles* 16: 291–311.

Faller, K.C. 1988. Criteria for judging the credibility of children's statements about their sexual abuse. *Child Welfare* 67: 389–401.

Faller, K.C. 1989. Characteristics of a clinical sample of sexually abused children: How boy and girl victims differ. *Child Abuse and Neglect* 13: 281–289.

Farley, L. 1978. *Sexual shakedown: The sexual harassment of women on the job.* New York: McGraw-Hill.

Fehrenbach, P.A., and C. Monastersky. 1988. Characteristics of female adolescent sexual offenders. *American Journal of Orthopsychiatry* 58: 148–151.

Fehrenbach, P.A., W. Smith, C. Monastersky, and R.W. Deisher. 1986. Adolescent sexual offenders: Offender and offense characteristics. *American Journal of Orthopsychiatry* 56: 225–233.

Feild, H.S. 1978. Attitudes toward rape: A comparative analysis of police rapists, crisis counselors, and citizens. *Journal of Personality and Social Psychology* 36: 156–179.

Feinauer, L.L. 1988. Relationship of long term effects of childhood sexual abuse to identity of the offender: Family, friend or stranger. *Women and Therapy* 7: 84–107.

Feinauer, L.L. 1989. Comparison of long-term effects of child abuse by type of abuse and by relationship of the offender to the victim. *American Journal of Family Therapy* 17: 48–56.

Feinberg, J. 1988. Hard cases for the harm principle. In R.M. Baird and S.E. Rosenbaum (eds.), *Morality and the law,* pp. 55–66. Buffalo, N.Y.: Prometheus Books.

Feinman, C. 1986. *Women in the criminal justice system.* 2d ed. New York: Praeger.

Feldberg, R. 1984. Comparable worth: Toward theory and practice in the United States. *Signs* 10: 311–328.

Fine, M. 1981. An injustice by any other name. *Victimology* 6: 48–58.

Fine, M. 1988. Sexuality, schooling, and adolescent females: The missing discourse of desire. *Harvard Educational Review* 58: 29–53.

Finkelhor, D. 1979a. What's wrong with sex between adults and children? Ethics and the problem of sexual abuse. *American Journal of Orthopsychiatry* 49: 692–697.

Finkelhor, D. 1979b. *Sexually victimized children.* New York: Free Press.

Finkelhor, D. 1981. The sexual abuse of boys. *Victimology* 6: 76–84.

Finkelhor, D. 1984. *Child sexual abuse: New theory and research.* New York: Free Press.

Finkelhor, D. 1986. Abusers: Special topics. In D. Finkelhor and Associates (eds.), *Sourcebook on child sexual abuse,* pp. 119–142. Beverly Hills, Calif.: Sage.

Finkelhor, D. 1987. The trauma of child sexual abuse: Two models. *Journal of Interpersonal Violence* 2: 348–366.

Finkelhor, D., and L. Baron. 1986a. Risk factors for child sexual abuse. *Journal of Interpersonal Violence* 1: 43–71.

Finkelhor, D., and L. Baron. 1986b. High-risk children. In D. Finkelhor and Associates (eds.), *Sourcebook on child sexual abuse*, pp. 60–88. Beverly Hills, Calif.: Sage.

Finkelhor, D., and I.A. Lewis, 1988. An epidemiologic approach to the study of child molestation. In R.A. Prentky and V.L. Quinsey (eds.), *Human sexual aggression: Current perspectives*, pp. 64–78. New York: New York Academy of Sciences.

Finkelhor, D., and K. Yllo. 1985. *License to rape: Sexual abuse of wives*. New York: Holt, Rinehart, and Winston.

Finkelhor, D., G. Hotaling, I.A. Lewis, and C. Smith. 1990. Sexual abuse in a national survey of adult men and women: Prevalence, characteristics and risk factors. *Child Abuse and Neglect* 14: 19–28.

Fitzgerald, L.F., L.M. Weitzman, Y. Gold, and M. Ormerod. 1988. Academic harassment: Sex and denial in scholarly garb. *Psychology of Women Quarterly* 12: 329–340.

Flarity-White, L.A., and C.L. Muehlenhard. 1988. Self-report, behavioral role-play, and cognitive measures of women's ability to refuse unwanted sexual advances. Paper presented at the Annual Meeting of the Association for the Advancement of Behavior Therapy, New York.

Flinn, M.V. 1988. Mate guarding in a Caribbean village. *Ethology and Sociobiology* 9: 1–28.

Freire, P. 1968. *Pedagogy of the oppressed*. Translated by M.B. Ramos. New York: Seabury Press.

Freund, K., and R. Blanchard. 1989. Phallometric diagnosis of pedophilia. *Journal of Consulting and Clinical Psychology* 57: 100–105.

Friedan, B. 1974. *The feminine mystique*. New York: Dell.

Friedan, B. 1981. *The second stage*. New York: Summit.

Friedrich, W.N., R.L. Beilke, and A.J. Urquiza. 1987. Children from sexually abusive families: A behavioral comparison. *Journal of Interpersonal Violence* 2: 391–402.

Frieze, I. 1983. Investigating the causes and consequences of marital rape. *Signs* 8: 532–553.

Frieze, I.H., J.E. Parsons, P.B. Johnson, D.N. Ruble, and G.L. Zellman. 1978. *Women and sex roles: A social psychological perspective*. New York: W.W. Norton.

Fritz, G.S., K. Stoll, and N.N. Wagner. 1981. A comparison of males and females who were sexually molested as children. *Journal of Sex and Marital Therapy* 7: 54–59.

Fromuth, M.E. 1986. The relationship of childhood sexual abuse with later psychological and sexual adjustment in a sample of college women. *Child Abuse and Neglect* 10: 5–15.

Fromuth, M.E., and B.R. Burkhart. 1987. Childhood sexual victimization among college men: Definitional and methodological issues. *Violence and Victims* 2: 241–253.

Frude, N. 1982. The sexual nature of sexual abuse: A review of the literature. *Child Abuse and Neglect* 6: 211–223.

Fryer, G.E., Jr., S.K. Kraizer, and T. Miyoshi. 1987a. Measuring actual reduction of risk to child abuse: A new approach. *Child Abuse and Neglect* 2: 173–179.

Fryer, G.E., Jr., S.K. Kraizer, and T. Miyoshi. 1987b. Measuring children's retention of skills to resist stranger abduction: Use of the simulation technique. *Child Abuse and Neglect* 11: 181–185.

Galliher, J.F., and J.R. Cross. 1985. *Morals legislation without morality.* New Brunswick, N.J.: Rutgers University Press.

Galvin, J., and K. Polk. 1983. Attrition in case processing: Is rape unique? *Journal of Research in Crime and Delinquency* 20: 126–154.

Gaulier, B., S.K. Travis, and E.R. Allgeier. 1986. Proceptive behavior and the use of behavioral cues in heterosexual courtship. Paper presented in the symposium, Miscommunication between Male and Female Students, Annual Meeting of the Midcontinent Region of the Society for the Scientific Study of Sex, Madison, Wisconsin.

Gelles, R., and M. Straus. 1979. Determinants of violence in the family. In Wesley R. Burr et al. (eds.), *Contemporary theories about the family,* 1: 549–581, New York: Free Press.

George, W.H., and G.A. Marlatt. 1986. The effects of alcohol and anger on interest in violence, erotica and deviance. *Journal of Abnormal Behavior* 95: 150–158.

Gibson-Ainyette, I., D. Templer, R. Brown, and L. Veaco. 1988. Adolescent female prostitutes. *Archives of Sexual Behavior* 17: 431–439.

Gil, D. 1979. Unraveling child abuse. In D. Gil (ed.), *Child abuse and violence,* pp. 3–17. New York: AMS Press.

Gilbert, N. 1988. Teaching children to prevent sexual abuse. *Public Interest* (Fall): 3–15.

Gilgun, J.F. 1988. Self-centeredness and the adult male perpetrator of child sexual abuse. *Contemporary Family Therapy* 10: 216–234.

Gilgun, J.F., and S. Gordon. 1985. Sex education and the prevention of child sexual abuse. *Journal of Sex Education and Therapy* 11: 46–52.

Gilmartin-Zena, P. 1988. Gender differences in students' attitudes toward rape. *Sociological Focus* 21: 279–292.

Ginsberg, G., J. Koreski, and J. Galloway. 1977. Sexual advances by an employee's supervisor: A sex discrimination violation of Title VII? *Employee Relations Law Journal* 3: 83–93.

Giovannoni, J.M., and R.M. Becerra. 1979. *Defining child abuse.* New York: Free Press.

Glendon, M.A. 1987. *Abortion and divorce in Western law: American failures, European challenges.* Cambridge: Harvard University Press.

Goodchilds, J.D., G.L. Zellman, P.B. Johnson, and R. Giarrusso. 1988. Adolescents and their perceptions of sexual interactions. In A.W. Burgess (ed.), *Rape and sexual assault* 2: 245–270. New York: Garland Publishing.

Goode, W.J. 1971. Force and violence in the family. *Journal of Marriage and the Family* 33: 624–636.

Gordon, M. 1989. The family environment of sexual abuse: A comparison of natal and stepfather abuse. *Child Abuse and Neglect* 13: 121–130.

Gordon, M.T., and S. Riger. 1989. *The female fear.* New York: Free Press.

Gordon, R. 1984. Critical legal histories. *Stanford Law Review* 36: 57–125.

Gottfried, H. 1988–1989. In defense of socialized child care: A comparison of child care policies in the United States and Sweden. *National Women Studies Association Journal* 1: 336–346.

Grauerholz, E. 1987. Balancing the power in dating relationships. *Sex Roles* 17: 563–571.

Grauerholz, E. 1989. Sexual harassment of women professors by students: Exploring the dynamics of power, authority, and gender in a university setting. *Sex Roles* 21: 789–801.

Grauerholz, E. 1990. Sexual harassment in the academy: The experiences of faculty women. Unpublished manuscript.

Greer, J.G., and I.R. Stuart (eds.). 1983. *The sexual aggressor: Current perspectives on treatment.* New York: Van Nostrand Reinhold.

Griffin, S. 1971. Rape: The all-American crime. *Ramparts* (September): 26–35.

Griffin, S. 1979. *Rape: The power of consciousness.* New York: Harper & Row.

Griffin, S. 1981. *Pornography and silence: Culture's revenge against nature.* New York: Harper & Row.

Groth, A.N. 1979a. *Men who rape: The psychology of the offender.* New York: Plenum.

Groth, A.N. 1979b. Sexual trauma in the life histories of rapists and child molesters. *Victimology* 4: 10–16.

Groth, A.N. 1982. The incest offender. In S.M. Sgroi (ed.), *Handbook of clinical intervention in child sexual abuse,* pp. 215–239. Lexington, Mass.: Lexington Books.

Groth, A.N., and A. Burgess. 1980. Male rape: Offenders and victims. *American Journal of Psychiatry* 137: 807–810.

Gruber, K.J., and R.J. Jones. 1983. Identifying determinants of risk of sexual victimization of youth: A multivariate approach. *Child Abuse and Neglect* 7: 17–24.

Gutek, B. 1985. *Sex and the workplace: The impact of sexual behavior and harassment on women, men and organizations.* San Francisco: Jossey-Bass.

Gutek, B., and V. Dunwoody-Miller. 1986. Understanding sex in the workplace. In A.H. Stromberg, L. Larwood, and B. Gutek (eds.), *Women and Work: An Annual Review,* Volume 2, pp. 249–269. Beverly Hills, Calif.: Sage.

Gutek, B., B. Morasch, and A.G. Cohen. 1983. Interpreting social sexual behavior in a work setting. *Journal of Vocational Behavior* 22: 30–48.

Gutek, B., C.Y. Nakamura, M. Gahart, I. Handschumacher, and D. Russell. 1980. Sexuality and the workplace. *Basic and Applied Social Psychology* 1: 255–265.

Hagan, J. 1985. *Modern criminology: Crime, criminal behavior, and its control.* New York: McGraw-Hill.

Hale, M. 1678. *Pleas of the crown.* London: Emelyn.

Hall, G.C.N. 1990. Prediction of sexual aggression. *Clinical Psychology Review* 10: 229–246.

Hall, R. 1985. *Ask any woman: A London inquiry into rape and sexual assault.* Bristol, England: Falling Wall Press.

Hanmer, J. 1978. Violence and the social control of women. In G. Littlejohn, B. Smart, J. Wakeford, and N. Yuval-Davis (eds.), *Power and the state,* pp. 217–238. London: Croom Helm.

Hansen, R. 1987. The unpopular victim. *Journal of Interpersonal Violence* 2: 123–125.

Harding, C. 1985. Sociobiological hypotheses about rape: A critical look at the data behind the hypotheses. In S. Sunday and E. Tobach (eds.), *Violence against women: A critique of the sociobiology of rape,* pp. 23–59. New York: Gordian.

Harshbarger, S. 1987. Prosecution is an appropriate response in child sexual abuse cases. *Journal of Interpersonal Violence* 2: 108–112.

Hart, B. 1986. Lesbian battering: An examination. In K. Lobel (ed.), *Naming the violence: Speaking out about lesbian battering,* pp. 173–189. Seattle, Wash.: Seal Press.

Harter, S., P.C. Alexander, and R.A. Neimeyer. 1988. Longterm effects of incestuous child abuse in college women: Social adjustment, social cognition and family characteristics. *Journal of Consulting and Clinical Psychology* 56: 5–8.

Harvard Law Review. 1984. Sexual harassment claims of abusive work environment under Title VII. *Harvard Law Review* 97: 1449–1467.

Harvey, P., R. Forehand, C. Brown, and T. Holmes. 1988. The prevention of sexual abuse: Examination of the effectiveness of a program with kindergarten age children. *Behavior Therapy* 19: 429–435.

Hatfield, E. 1983. What do women and men want from love and sex? In E.R. Allgeier and N.B. McCormick (eds.), *Changing boundaries: Gender roles and sexual behavior,* pp. 106–134. Palo Alto, Calif.: Mayfield.

Haugaard, J.J., and R.E. Emery. 1989. Methodological issues in child sexual abuse research. *Child Abuse and Neglect* 13: 89–100.

Haugaard, J.J., and N.D. Reppucci. 1988. *The sexual abuse of children.* San Francisco: Jossey Bass.

Haugaard, J.J., and C. Tilly. 1988. Characteristics predicting children's responses to sexual encounters with other children. *Child Abuse and Neglect* 12: 209–218.

Heath, L., and L. Davidson. 1988. Dealing with the threat of rape: Reactance or learned helplessness? *Journal of Applied Social Psychology* 18: 1334–1351.

Herman, J.L. 1981. *Father/daughter incest.* Cambridge: Harvard University Press.

Herman, J.L., and L. Hirschman. 1977. Father-daughter incest. *Signs* 2: 735–756.

Hershatter, G. 1986. *The workers of Tianjin, 1900–1949.* Stanford: Stanford University Press.

Holmstrom, L.L., and A.W. Burgess. 1978. *The victim of rape: Institutional reactions.* New York: Wiley.

Holroyd, J.C., and A.M. Brodsky. 1977. Psychologists' attitudes and practices regarding erotic and nonerotic physical contact with patients. *American Psychologist* 32: 843–849.

Howells, K. 1981. Adults' sexual interest in children: Considerations relevant to theories of etiology. In M. Cook and K. Howells (eds.), *Adult sexual interest in children,* pp. 55–94. New York: Academic Press.

Hutchins, L.D. 1986. Pornography: The prosecution of pornographer under prostitution statutes—A new approach. *Syracuse Law Review* 37: 977–1002.

Iowa State University. 1982. Sexual harassment of students at Iowa State University. Subcommittee report of the University Committee on Women, 2–33.

Jackson, S. 1978. How to make babies: Sexism in sex education. *Women's Studies International Quarterly* 1: 341–352.

Jackson, T.L., and W.P. Ferguson. 1983. Attribution of blame in incest. *American Journal of Community Psychology* 11: 313–322.

James, J. 1976. Motivations for entrance into prostitution. In L. Crites (ed.), *The female offender*, pp. 177–206. Lexington, Mass.: D.C. Heath.

James, P. 1981. Do it yourself self-defense. In F. Delacosta and F. Newman (eds.), *Fight back!* pp. 201–205. Minneapolis: Cleis Press.

Janoff-Bulman, R. 1985. The aftermath of victimization: Rebuilding shattered assumptions. In C.R. Figley (ed.), *Trauma and its wake: The study and treatment of post-traumatic stress disorder*, pp. 15–35. New York: Brunner/Mazel.

Jensen, I., and B. Gutek. 1982. Attributions and assignments of responsibility for sexual harassment. *Journal of Social Issues* 38: 121–136.

Johnson, J.D., and L.A. Jackson. 1988. Assessing the effects of factors that might underlie the differential perception of acquaintance and stranger rape. *Sex Roles* 19: 37–45.

Johnson, M.P., and S. Shuman. 1983. Sexual harassment of students at the Pennsylvania State University. *Report*, 2–32.

Johnson, T.C. 1989. Child perpetrators—Children who molest other children: Preliminary findings. *Child Abuse and Neglect* 12: 219–229.

Johnston, A.J. 1987. Women fight sexual assault. *Progressive* (September): 12–13.

Jones, D.P.H., and J.M. McGraw. 1987. Reliable and fictitious accounts of sexual abuse to children. *Journal of Interpersonal Violence* 2:27–45.

Kalichman, S.C., M.E. Craig, and D.R. Follingstad. 1988. Mental health professionals and suspected cases of child abuse: An investigation of factors influencing reporting. *Community Mental Health Journal* 24: 43–51.

Kalven, H., and H. Zeisel. 1966. *The American jury.* Boston: Little, Brown.

Kanin, E.J. 1965. Male sex aggression and three psychiatric hypotheses. *Journal of Sex Research* 1: 221–231.

Kanin, E.J. 1967a. Reference groups and sex conduct norm violations. *Sociological Quarterly* 8: 495–504.

Kanin, E.J. 1967b. An examination of sexual aggression as a response to sexual frustration. *Journal of Marriage and the Family* 29: 428–433.

Kanin, E.J. 1969. Selected dyadic aspects of male sex aggression. *Journal of Sex Research* 5: 12–28.

Kanin, E.J. 1984. Date rape: Unofficial criminals and victims. *Victimology* 9: 95–108.

Kanin, E.J. 1985. Date rapists: Differential sexual socialization and relative deprivation. *Archives of Sexual Behavior* 14: 219–231.

Kaufman, A., P. DiVasto, R. Jackson, D. Voorhees, and J. Christy. 1980. Male rape victims: Noninstitutionalized assault. *American Journal of Psychiatry* 137: 221–223.

Kelley, G. 1957. Hostility. Presidential address to the Clinical Division, American Psychological Association.

Kelly, L. 1987. The continuum of sexual violence. In J. Hanmer and M. Maynard (eds.), *Women, violence and social control*, pp. 46–60. Atlantic Highlands, N.J.: Humanities Press International.

Kelly, L. 1988. *Surviving sexual violence.* Minneapolis: University of Minnesota Press.

Kendall-Thackett, K.A., and A.F. Simon. 1987. Perpetrators and their acts: Data from 365 adults molested as children. *Child Abuse and Neglect* 11: 237–245.

Kenig, S., and J. Ryan. 1986. Sex differences in levels of tolerance and attribution of blame for sexual harassment on a university campus. *Sex Roles* 15: 535–549.

Kephart, W.M. 1967. Some correlates of romantic love. *Journal of Marriage and the Family* 29: 470–474.

Kessler, S., D.J. Ashenden, R.W. Connell, and G.W. Dowsett. 1985. Gender relations in secondary schooling. *Sociology of Education* 58: 34–48.

Kidder, L.H., J.L. Boell, and M.M. Moyer. 1983. Rights consciousness and victimization prevention: Personal defense and assertiveness training. *Journal of Social Issues* 39: 155–170.

Kilbourne, J. 1986. The child as a sex object. In M. Nelson and K. Clark (eds.), *An educator's guide to preventing child sexual abuse,* pp. 40–46. Santa Cruz, Calif.: Network Publications.

Kilpatrick, A.C. 1987. Childhood sexual experiences: Problems and issues in studying long-range effects. *Journal of Sex Research* 23: 173–196.

Kilpatrick, D.G., L.J. Veronen, and P.A. Resick. 1979. The aftermath of rape: Recent empirical findings. *American Journal of Orthopsychiatry* 49: 658–669.

Kilpatrick, D.G., L.J. Veronen, and P.A. Resick. 1982. Psychological sequelae to rape: Assessment and treatment strategies. In D.M. Doleys, R.L. Meredith, and A.R. Ciminero (eds.), *Behavioral medicine: Assessment and treatment strategies,* pp. 473–498. New York: Plenum.

Kirkendall, L.A. 1961. *Premarital intercourse and interpersonal relationships.* New York: Julian Press.

Kirkland, K.D., and C.A. Bauer. 1982. MMPI traits of incestuous fathers. *Journal of Clinical Psychology* 38: 645–649.

Klein, D. 1981. Violence against women: Some considerations regarding its causes and its elimination. *Crime and Delinquency* 27: 64–81.

Klein, J. 1978. Born again porn. *Mother Jones* (February): 14–20.

Klemmack, S.H., and D.L. Klemmack. 1976. The social definition of rape. In M.J. Waler and S.L. Brodsky (eds.), *Sexual assault,* pp. 135–147. Lexington, Mass.: Lexington Books.

Knight, R.A. 1989. An assessment of the concurrent validity of a child molester typology. *Journal of Interpersonal Violence* 4: 131–150.

Knight, R.A., D.L. Carter, and R.A. Prentky. 1989. A system for the classification of child molesters: Reliability and application. *Journal of Interpersonal Violence* 4: 3–23.

Knight, R.A., R. Rosenberg, and B.A. Schneider. 1985. Classification of sexual offenders: Perspectives, methods, and validation. In A.W. Burgess (ed.), *Rape and sexual assault: A research handbook,* pp. 222–293. New York: Garland.

Knox, D., and K. Wilson. 1981. Dating behaviors of university students. *Family Relations* 30: 255–258.

Knudsen, D.D. 1988. *Child protective services: Discretion, decisions, dilemmas.* Springfield, Ill.: Charles C. Thomas.

Knudsen, D.D. 1989. Duplicate reports of child maltreatment: A research note. *Child Abuse and Neglect* 13: 41–43.

Kolko, D.J. , J.T. Moser, and S.R. Weldy. 1988. Behavioral/emotional indicators of sexual abuse in child psychiatric inpatients: A controlled comparison with physical abuse. *Child Abuse and Neglect* 12: 529–541.

Komarovsky, M. 1985. *Women in college.* New York: Basic Books.

Koss, M.P. 1988. The method used in the Ms. Project on campus sexual assault. In R. Warshaw, *I never called it rape*, pp. 189–210. New York: Harper & Row.

Koss, M.P. 1989. Is there a rape epidemic? Paper presented at the annual meeting of the American Association for the Advancement of Science, San Francisco.

Koss, M.P. 1989. Criminal Victimization among women: Impact on health and medical utilization. Paper presented at the University of Kansas, Lawrence, March 29.

Koss, M.P. 1990. The women's mental health agenda: Violence against women. *American Psychologist* 45: 374–380.

Koss, M.P., and B.R. Burkhart. 1989. A conceptual analysis of rape victimization: Long-term effects and implications for treatment. *Psychology of Women's Quarterly* 13: 27–40.

Koss, M.P., and T.E. Dinero. 1988. Predictors of sexual aggression among a national sample of male college students. In R.A. Prentky and V.L. Quinsey (eds.), *Human sexual aggression: Current perspectives*, pp. 133–147. New York: New York Academy of Sciences.

Koss, M.P., T.E. Dinero, C.A. Siebel, and S.L. Cox. 1988. Stranger and acquaintance rape: Are there differences in the victim's experience? *Psychology of Women Quarterly* 12: 1–24.

Koss, M.P., C.A. Gidycz, and N. Wisniewski. 1987. The scope of rape: Incidence and prevalence of sexual aggression and victimization in a national sample of higher education students. *Journal of Consulting and Clinical Psychology* 55: 162–170.

Koss, M.P., K.E. Leonard, D.A. Beezley, and C.J. Oros. 1985. Nonstranger sexual aggression: A discriminant analysis of the psychological characteristics of undetected offenders. *Sex Roles* 12: 981–992.

Koss, M.P., and C.J. Oros. 1982. Sexual experiences survey: A research instrument investigating sexual aggression and victimization. *Journal of Consulting and Clinical Psychology* 50: 455–457.

Kraizer, S.K. 1985. *The safe child book.* New York: Dell.

Kraizer, S.K. 1986. Rethinking prevention. *Child Abuse and Neglect* 10: 259–261.

Kraizer, S., G.E. Fryer, and M. Miller. 1988. Programming for preventing sexual abuse and abduction: What does it mean when it works? *Child Welfare* 67: 69–78.

Krulewitz, J.E. 1981. Sex differences in evaluations of female and male victims' response to assault. *Journal of Applied Social Psychology* 11: 460–474.

Kwitko, L., and P. O'Hagan. 1989. Mobilizing reforms for sexual harassment in an academic institution. Paper presented at the Society for the Study of Social Problems, San Francisco, California.

L'Armand, K., and A. Pepitone. 1982. Judgments of rape: A study of victim-rapist relationship and victim sexual history. *Personality and Social Psychology Bulletin* 8: 134–139.

Lafontaine, E., and L. Tredeau. 1986. The frequency, sources, and correlates of sexual harassment among women in traditional male occupations. *Sex Roles* 15: 433–442.

LaFree, G.D. 1980. Variables affecting guilty pleas and convictions in rape cases: Toward a social theory of rape processing. *Social Forces* 58: 833–850.

LaFree, G. 1989. *Rape and criminal justice: The social construction of rape.* Belmont, Calif.: Wadsworth.

LaFree, G.D., Reskin, B.F., and C.A. Visher. 1985. Jurors' responses to victims' behavior and legal issues in sexual assault trials. *Social Problems* 32: 389–407.

Landis, C., A.T. Landis, M.M. Bolles, H.F. Metzger, M.W. Pitts, D.A. D'Esopo, N.C. Moloy, S.J. Kleegman, and R.L. Dickenson. 1940. *Sex in development.* New York: Paul B. Hoebert.

Langevin, R. 1983. *Sexual strands: Understanding and treating sexual anomalies in men.* Hillsdale, N.J.: Lawrence Erlbaum Associates.

LaPlante, M.N., N. McCormick, and G.G. Brannigan. 1980. Living the sexual script: College students' views of influence in sexual encounters. *Journal of Sex Research* 16: 338–355.

Largen, M.A. 1988. Rape reform law: An analysis. In A.W. Burgess (ed.), *Rape and sexual assault* 2: 271–292. New York: Garland.

Lazarus, R.S., and S. Folkman. 1984. *Stress, appraisal, and coping.* New York: Springer.

Lee, L.A. 1987. Rape prevention: Experiential training for men. *Journal of Counseling and Development* 66: 100–101.

Lees, S. 1986. *Losing out: Sexuality and adolescent girls.* London: Hutchinson.

Lehne, G.K. 1976. Homophobia among men. In D.S. David and R. Brannon (eds.), *The forty-nine percent majority: The male sex role*, pp. 66–88. Reading, Mass.: Addison-Wesley.

Leidholdt, D. Some notes on objectification: From objectification to violence. Unpublished paper.

Leidig, M. 1981. Violence against women: A feminist-psychological analysis. In S. Cox, *Female psychology*, pp. 190–205. New York: St. Martin's Press.

Lemert, E. 1951. *Social pathology.* New York: McGraw-Hill.

Leonard, E.B. 1982. *Women, crime, and society: A critique of criminology theory.* New York: Longman.

Leslie, C., D.L. Gonzalez, N. Abbott, S. Hutchison, and T. Namuth. 1988. Listening, feeling, helping: In a dozen states, peer counseling comes of age. *Newsweek* (October 31): 79.

Leventhal, J.M. 1987. Programs to prevent sexual abuse: What outcomes should be measured? *Child Abuse and Neglect* 11: 169–171.

Lever, J. 1978. Sex differences in the complexity of children's play and games. *American Sociological Review* 43: 471–483.

Levine, E.M., and E.J. Kanin. 1987. Sexual violence among dates and acquaintances: Trends and their implications for marriage and family. *Journal of Family Violence* 2: 55–65.

Levinson, D. 1989. *Family violence in cross-cultural perspective.* Newbury Park, Calif.: Sage Publications.

Lewin, M. 1985. Unwanted intercourse: The difficulty of saying no. *Psychology of Women Quarterly* 9: 184–192.

Lewis, J. 1984. *Women in England: 1870–1950: Sexual divisions and social change.* Bloomington: Indiana University Press.

Lindberg, F.H., and L.J. Distad. 1985. Survival responses to incest: Adolescents in crisis. *Child Abuse and Neglect* 9: 521–526.

Lindsey, L.L. 1990. *Gender roles: A sociological perspective.* Englewood Cliffs, N.J.: Prentice-Hall.

Livingston, J.A. 1982. Responses to sexual harassment on the job: Legal, organizational and individual actions. *Journal of Social Issues* 38: 5–22.

Livingston, R. 1987. Sexually and physically abused children. *Journal of the American Academy of Child and Adolescent Psychiatry* 26: 413–415.

Lobel, K. 1986. *Naming the violence: Speaking out about lesbian battering.* Seattle, Wash.: Seal Press.

Longo, R.E. 1982. Sexual learning and experience among adolescent sexual offenders. *International Journal of Offender Therapy and Comparative Criminology* 26: 235–241.

Longo, R.E., and A.N. Groth. 1983. Juvenile sexual offenses in the histories of adult rapists and child molesters. *International Journal of Offender Therapy and Comparative Criminology* 21: 249–254.

Lott, B., M.E. Reilly, and D. Howard. 1982. Sexual assault and harassment: A campus community case study. *Signs* 8: 296–319.

Lowman, J. 1987. Taking young prostitutes seriously. *Canadian Review of Sociology and Anthropology* 24: 99–116.

Loy, P., and L.P. Stewart. 1984. The extent and effect of the sexual harassment of working women. *Sociological Focus* 17: 31–43.

Luria, Z., S. Friedman, and M. Rose. 1987. *Human sexuality.* New York: Wiley.

Lynch, R. 1986. Organizing clerical workers: Problems and prospects. *Labor Research Review* 8: 91–102.

McCahill, T.W., L.C. Meyer, and A.M. Fishman. 1979. *The aftermath of rape.* Lexington, Mass.: Lexington.Books

McConahay, S.A., and J.B. McConchay. 1977. Sexual permissiveness, sex-role rigidity, and violence across cultures. *Journal of Social Issues* 33: 134–143.

McCormick, N.B. 1979. Come-ons and put-offs: Unmarried students' strategies for having and avoiding sexual intercourse. *Psychology of Women Quarterly* 4: 194–211.

McCormick, N.B., and C.J. Jesser. 1983. The courtship game: Power in the sexual encounter. In E.R. Allgeier and N.B. McCormick (eds.), *Changing boundaries: Gender roles and sexual behavior*, pp. 64–86. Palo Alto, Calif.: Mayfield Publishing Co.

McDermott, M.J. 1979. *Rape victimization in 26 American cities.* National Crime Survey Victimization and Attitude Data. Washington, D.C.: U.S. Government Printing Office.

McIvor, D.L., and B. Duthie. 1986. MMPI profiles of incest offenders: Men who molest younger children and men who molest older children. *Criminal Justice and Behavior* 13: 450–452.

McKinney, K. 1990. Attitudes toward sexual harassment and perceptions of blame: Views of male and female graduate students. *Free Inquiry into Creative Sociology* 18: 73–76.

McKinney, K. In Press. Sexual harassment of University faculty by students and colleagues. *Sex Roles.*

McKinney, K., and C. Howard. 1986. Coerced intimacy: The case of sexual harassment on a college campus. Paper presented at the Illinois Sociological Association Meetings, October, Chicago.

McKinney, K., C. Olson, and A. Satterfield. 1988. Graduate students' experiences with and responses to sexual harassment. *Journal of Interpersonal Violence* 3: 319–325.

MacKinnon, C. 1979. *Sexual harassment of working women.* New Haven: Yale University Press.

MacKinnon, C. 1982a. Sexual harassment: The experience. In B.R. Price and N.J. Sokoloff (eds.), *The criminal justice system and women*, pp. 353–370. New York: Clark Boardman.

MacKinnon, C. 1982b. Feminism, Marxism, method, and the state: An agenda for theory. *Signs* 7: 15–44.

MacKinnon, C. 1986. Pornography: Not a moral issue. *Women's Studies International Forum* 9: 63–78.

MacKinnon, C.A. 1987. *Feminism unmodified: Discourses on life and law.* Cambridge: Harvard University Press.

McLeer, S.V., E. Deblinger, M.S. Atkins, and E.B. Foa. 1988. Post traumatic stress disorder in sexually abused children. *Journal of the American Academy of Child and Adolescent Psychiatry* 27: 650–654.

Mahoney, E.R. 1982. Male sexual access rights. In S. deAlcorn (ed.), *Sourcebook for educators: Sexual assault prevention for adolescents*, pp. 241–250. Tacoma, Wash.: Pierce County Rape Relief.

Mahoney, E.R., M.D. Shively, and M. Traw. 1986. Sexual coercion and assault: Male socialization and female risk. *Sexual Coercion and Assault* 1: 2–8.

Malamuth, N.M. 1981a. Rape fantasies as a function of exposure to violent sexual stimuli. *Archives of Sexual Behavior* 10: 33–45.

Malamuth, N. 1981b. Rape proclivity among males. *Journal of Social Issues* 37: 138–157.

Malamuth, N.M. 1984. Aggression against women: Cultural and individual causes. In N.M. Malamuth and E. Donnerstein (eds.), *Pornography and sexual aggression*, pp. 19–52. New York: Academic Press.

Malamuth, N.M. 1986. Predictors of naturalistic sexual aggression. *Journal of Personality and Social Psychology* 50: 953–962.

Malamuth, N.M. 1988. A multidimensional approach to sexual aggression: Combining measures of past behavior and present likelihood. In R.A. Prentsky and V.L. Quinsey (eds.), *Human sexual aggression: Current perspectives*, pp. 123–132. New York: New York Academy of Science.

Malamuth, N.M., and J.V.P. Check. 1981. The effects of mass media exposure on acceptance of violence against women: A field experiment. *Journal of Research in Personality* 15: 436–446.

Malamuth, N.M., and J.V.P. Check. 1983. Sexual arousal to rape depictions: Individual differences. *Journal of Abnormal Psychology* 92: 55–67.

Malamuth, N.M., and J.V.P. Check. 1985. The effects of aggressive pornography on beliefs in rape myths: Individual differences. *Journal of Research in Personality* 19: 299–320.

Malamuth, N.M., S. Haber, and S. Feshbach. 1980. Testing hypotheses regarding rape: Exposure to sexual violence, sex differences, and the "normality" of rapists. *Journal of Research in Personality* 14: 121–137.

Malamuth, N.M., and B. Spinner. 1980. A longitudinal content analysis of sexual violence in the best-selling erotic magazines. *Journal of Sex Research* 226–237.

Mandoki, C.A., and B.R. Burkhart. 1989. Coping and adjustment to rape. Paper presented at the Ninety-seventh Annual Meeting of the American Psychological Association, New Orleans.

Mandoki, C.A., and B.R. Burkhart. In press. Women as victims: Antecedents and consequences. In A. Parrot and L. Beckhofer (eds.), *Hidden rape: Sexual assault among acquaintances, friends and intimates.* New York: Wiley.

Mandebaum, D.G. 1988. *Women's seclusion and men's honor: Sex roles in North India, Bangladesh, and Pakistan.* Tucson: University of Arizona Press.

Mann, C.R. 1984. *Female crime and delinquency.* University: University of Alabama Press.

Mannarino, A.P., and J. Cohen. 1987. Psychological symptoms of sexually abused children. Paper presented at the National Conference on Family Violence, University of New Hampshire, Durham.

Marolla, J., and D. Scully. 1982. *Attitudes toward women, violence, and rape: A comparison of convicted rapists and other felons.* Rockville, Md.: National Institute of Mental Health.

Marshall, W.L., H.E. Barbaree, and J. Butt. 1988. Sexual offenders against male children: Sexual preferences. *Behavioral Research and Therapy* 26: 383–391.

Marshall, W.L., H.E. Barbaree, and D. Christophe. 1986. Sexual offenders against female children: Sexual preference for age of victims and type of behavior. *Canadian Journal of Behavioural Science* 18: 424–439.

Martin, P., and R. Hummer. 1989. Fraternities and rape on campus. *Gender and Society* 3: 457–473.

Marx, K., and F. Engels. 1975 *Collected works.* New York: International Publishers.

Maxwell, C. 1989. Attitudes surrounding date rape on a college campus: The situation at Indiana University. Unpublished manuscript.

Maxwell, C. 1990. High school students' attributions of responsibility in rape cases: Pilot study. Unpublished manuscript.

Mazer, D.B., and E.F. Percival. 1989. Ideology or experience? The relationships among perceptions, attitudes, and experiences of sexual harassment in university students. *Sex Roles* 20: 135–147.

Medea, A., and K. Thompson. 1984. *Against rape.* New York: Farrar, Straus & Giroux.

Mensch, E. 1982. The history of mainstream legal thought. In D. Kairys (ed.), *The politics of law: A progressive critique,* pp. 18–39. New York: Panthenon.

Mehrhof, B., and P. Kearon. 1973. Rape: An act of terror. In A. Koedt, E. Levine, and A. Rapone (eds.), *Radical feminism*, pp. 228–233. New York: Quadrangle.

Messner, M. 1987. The life of a man's seasons: Male identity in the life course of the jock. In M.S. Kimmel (ed.), *Changing men: New directions in research on men and masculinity*, pp. 53–67. Newbury Park, Calif.: Sage Publications.

Metha, A., and J. Nigg. 1983. Sexual harassment on campus: An institutional response. *Journal of the National Association for Women Deans, Administrators, and Counselors* 46: 23–29.

Mian, M., W. Wehrspann, H. Klagner-Diamond, D. LeBaron, and C. Winder. 1986. Review of 125 children 6 years of age and under who were sexually abused. *Child Abuse and Neglect* 10: 223–229.

Miller, B.A., W.R. Downs, D.M. Gondoli, and A. Keil. 1987. The role of childhood sexual abuse in the development of alcoholism in women. *Violence and Victims* 2: 157–172.

Miller-Perrin, C.L., and S.K. Wurtele. 1988. The child sexual abuse prevention movement: A critical analysis of primary and secondary approaches. *Clinical Psychology Review* 8: 313–329.

Millett, K. 1971. Prostitution: A quartet for female voices. In V. Gornick and B.K. Moran (eds.), *Woman in a sexist society*, pp. 21–69 New York: New American Library.

Moon, R., L.B. Tanner, and S. Pascale. 1970. Karate as self defense for women. In L.B. Tanner (ed.), *Voices from women's liberation*, pp. 256–264. New York: Signet.

Moore, M.M. 1985. Nonverbal courtship patterns in women: Context and consequences. *Ethology and Sociobiology* 6: 201–212.

Morgan, D.H.J. 1987. Masculinity and violence. In J. Hanmer and M. Maynard (eds.), *Women, violence and social control*, pp. 180–192. Atlantic Highlands, N.J.: Humanities Press International.

Mosher, D.L. 1970. Sex callousness toward women. In *Technical report of the Commission on Obscenity and Pornography*, vol. 7: *Erotica and antisocial behavior*, pp. 313–325. Washington, D.C.: U.S. Government Printing Office.

Mosher, D.L., and R.D. Anderson. 1986. Macho personality, sexual aggression, and reactions to guided imagery of realistic rape. *Journal of Research in Personality* 20: 77–95.

Mosher, D.L., and S.S. Tomkins. 197. Scripting the macho man: Hypermasculine socialization and enculturation. Unpublished manuscript.

Muehlenhard, C.L. 1981. Dating initiation from a woman's perspective. *Behavior Therapy* 12: 682–691.

Muehlenhard, C.L. 1988a. Misinterpreted dating behaviors and the risk of date rape. *Journal of Social and Clinical Psychology* 6: 20–37.

Muehlenhard, C.L. 1988b. "Nice women" don't say yes and "real men" don't say no: How miscommunication and the sexual double standard can cause sexual problems. *Women and Therapy* 7: 95–108.

Muehlenhard, C.L. 1989. Young men pressured into having sex with women. *Medical Aspects of Human Sexuality* 23: 50–62.

Muehlenhard, C.L., and S.W. Cook. 1988. Men's self-reports of unwanted sexual activity. *Journal of Sex Research* 24: 58–72.

Muehlenhard, C.L., and P.L. Falcon. In press. Men's heterosocial skill and attitudes toward women as predictors of verbal sexual coercion and forceful rape. *Sex Roles.*

Muehlenhard, C.L., S. Julsonnet, M.I. Carlson, and L.A. Flarity-White. 1989. A cognitive-behavioral program for preventing sexual coercion. *Behavior Therapist* 12: 211–214.

Muehlenhard, C.L., and M.A. Linton. 1987. Date rape and sexual aggression in dating situations: Incidence and risk factors. *Journal of Counseling Psychology* 34: 186–196.

Murphy, S.M., D.G. Kilpatrick, A. Amick-McMullan, L.J. Veronen, J. Poduhovich, C.L. Best, L.A. Villeponteaux, and B.E. Saunders. 1988. Current psychological functioning of child sexual assault survivors. *Journal of Interpersonal Violence* 3: 55–79.

Nadelson, C., M. Notman, H. Jackson, and J. Gornick. 1982. A follow-up study of rape victims. *American Journal of Psychiatry* 139: 1266–1270.

Nash, C.L., and D.J. West. 1985. Sexual molestation of young girls: A retrospective survey. In D. J. West (ed.), *Sexual victimization*, pp. 1–92. Aldershot, England: Gower.

National Incidence Study. 1981. *National study of the incidence and severity of child abuse and neglect.* Washington, D.C.: U.S. Department of Health and Human Services, National Center on Child Abuse and Neglect.

National Incidence Study. 1988. *Study of national incidence and prevalence of child abuse and neglect.* Washington, D.C.: U.S. Department of Health and Human Services, National Center on Child Abuse and Neglect.

Nelson, M., and K. Clark (eds.). 1986. *The educator's guide to preventing child sexual abuse.* Santa Cruz, Calif.: Network Publications.

Nettler, G. 1989. *Criminology lessons: Arguments about crime, punishment, and the interpretation of conduct with advice for individuals and prescriptions for public policy.* Cincinnati: Anderson Publishing Co.

Neugarten, D.A., and J.M. Shafritz (eds.). 1980. *Sexuality in organizations: Romantic and coercive behaviors at work.* Oak Park, Ill.: Moore.

Newberger, E.H. 1987. Prosecution: A problematic approach to child abuse. *Journal of Interpersonal Violence* 2: 112–117.

Newman, F., and E. Cohen, with P. Tobin and G. Macpherson. 1985. Historical perspectives on the study of female prostitution. *International Journal of Women's Studies* 8: 80–86.

Normand, G. 1989. Madman shoots 14 women. *La Presse* (December 7): 1.

O'Toole, R., J.P. Turbett, J. Sargent, and A.W. O'Toole. 1987. Recognizing and reacting to child abuse: Physicians, nurses, teachers, social workers, law enforcement officers and community residents. Paper presented at the National Family Violence Conference, University of New Hampshire, Durham, July.

Off Our Backs. 1990. Letters (March): 36–37.

Overall, C. 1987. *Ethics and human reproduction: A feminist analysis.* Boston: Allen and Unwin.

Overholser, J.C., and S. Beck. 1986. Multimethod assessment of rapists, child molesters and three control groups on behavioral and psychological measures. *Journal of consulting and Clinical Psychology* 54: 682–687.

Ozer, E.M., and A. Bandura. 1990. Mechanisms governing empowerment effects: A self-efficacy analysis. *Journal of Personality and Social Psychology,* 58: 472–486.

Palmer, C. 1989. Is rape a cultural universal? A reexamination of the ethnographic data. *Ethnology* 28: 1–16.

Parker, H., and S. Parker. 1986. Father-daughter sexual abuse: An emerging perspective. *American Journal of Orthopsychiatry* 56: 531–549.

Parrot, A. 1986. Parent's role in sexual assault prevention. Paper presented at the 1986 National Convention of the Society for the Scientific Study of Sex, St. Louis, Missouri.

Parrot, A. 1987. *Stop date rape: How to get what you want, but not more than you bargained for.* Ithaca, N.Y.: Cornell Coalition Advocating Rape Education.

Parrot, A. 1988. *Coping with date rape and acquaintance rape.* New York: Rosen Publishing Group.

Pascale, S., R. Moon, and L.B. Tanner. 1970. Self-defense for women. In R. Morgan (ed.), *Sisterhood is powerful,* pp. 469–477. New York: Vintage.

Pasewark, R.A., and D.A. Albers. 1972. Crisis intervention: Theory in search of a paradigm. *Social Work* 17: 70–77.

Paul, E.F. 1989. *Equity and gender: The comparable worth debate.* New Brunswick, N.J.: Transaction Books.

Paveza, G.J. 1988. Risk factors in father-daughter child sexual abuse: A case-control study. *Journal of Interpersonal Violence* 3: 290–306.

Peplau, L.A., Z. Rubin, and C.T. Hill. 1977. Sexual intimacy in dating relationships. *Journal of Social Issues* 33: 86–109.

Perper, T. 1985. *Sex signals: The biology of love.* Philadelphia: ISI Press.

Perper, T., and V.S. Fox. 1980. Flirtation behavior in public settings. Paper presented at the Eastern Region meeting of the society for the Scientific Study of Sex, Philadelphia.

Perper, T., and D.L. Weis. 1987. Proceptive and rejective strategies of U.S. and Canadian college women. *Journal of Sex Research* 23: 455–480.

Peters, S.D., G.E. Wyatt, and D. Finkelhor. 1986. Prevalence. In D. Finkelhor, S. Araji, L. Baron, A. Brown, S.D. Peters, and G.E. Wyatt (eds.), *A Sourcebook on Child Sexual Abuse,* pp. 15–59. Beverly Hills, Calif.: Sage.

Pierce, R., and L.H. Pierce. 1985. The sexually abused child: A comparison of male and female victims. *Child Abuse and Neglect* 9: 191–199.

Pierce, R., and L.H. Pierce. 1987. Incestuous victimization by juvenile sex offenders. *Journal of Family Violence* 2: 351–364.

Pirog-Good, M.A., and J.A. Stets (eds.). 1989. *Violence in dating relationships: Emerging social issues.* New York: Praeger.

Plummer, C. 1986. Child sexual abuse prevention: Keys to program success. In M. Nelson and K. Clark (eds.), *An educator's guide to preventing child sexual abuse,* pp. 69–79. Santa Cruz, Calif.: Network Publications.

Poche, C., R. Brouwer, and M. Swearingen. 1981. Teaching self-protection to young children. *Journal of Applied Behavioral Analysis* 14: 169–176.

Pollis, C.A. 1988. An assessment of the impact of feminism on sexual science. *Journal of Sex Research* 25: 85–105.

Porter, E. 1986. *Treating the young male victim of sexual assault.* Syracuse: Safer Society Press.

Powell, G. 1986. Effects of sex role identity and sex on definitions of sexual harassment. *Sex Roles* 14: 9–19.

President's Commission on Obscenity and Pornography. 1970. *The report of the President's Commission on Obscenity and Pornography.* New York: Bantam Books.

Project on the Status and Education of Women. 1985. *When sex becomes a crime.* Washington, D.C.: Association of American Colleges.

Pryor, J.B. 1985. The lay person's understanding of sexual harassment. *Sex Roles* 13: 273–286.

Pryor, J.B. 1987. Sexual harassment proclivities in men. *Sex Roles* 17: 269–289.

Pryor, J.B., and J.D. Day. 1988. Interpretations of sexual harassment: An attributional analysis. *Sex Roles* 18: 405–417.

Quinn, K.M. 1988. The credibility of children's allegation of sexual abuse. *Behavioral Sciences and the Law* 6: 181–189.

Quinsey, V.L., G. Marion, D. Upfold, and K.T. Popple. 1986. Issues in teaching physical methods of resisting rape. *Sexual Coercion and Assault* 1: 125–130.

Quinsey, V., and D. Upfold. 1985. Rape completion and victim injury as a function of female resistance strategy. *Canadian Journal of Behavioral Science* 17: 40–50.

Rada, R.T. 1978. *Clinical aspects of the rapist.* New York: Grune & Stratton.

Rader, C.M. 1977. MMPI profile types of exposers, rapists, and assaulters in a court services population. *Journal of Consulting and Clinical Psychology* 45: 61–69.

Ramazanoglu, C. 1987. Sex and violence in academic life or you can keep a good woman down. In J. Hanmer and M. Maynard (eds.), *Women, violence and social control*, pp. 61–74. Atlantic Highlands, N.J.: Humanities Press International.

Randolph, M.K., and G.R. Gredler. 1985. Prevention of child sexual assault. *Techniques: A Journal for Remedial Education and Counseling* 1: 399–402.

Rapaport, K., and B.R. Burkhart. 1984. Personality and attitudinal characteristics of sexually coercive college males. *Journal of Abnormal Psychology* 93: 216–221.

Rapaport, K., and B.R. Burkhart. 1987. Sexually coercive males' responses to rape depictions. Paper presented at the Thirtieth Annual Meeting of the Society for the Scientific Study of Sex, Atlanta.

Reilly, M.E., B. Lott, and S.M. Gallogly. 1986. Sexual harassment of university students. *Sex Roles* 15: 333–358.

Reilly, M.E., S. Carpenter, V. Dull, and K. Bartlett. 1982. The factorial survey: An approach to defining sexual harassment on campus. *Journal of Social Issues* 38: 99–110.

Reinhart, M. 1987. Sexually abused boys. *Child Abuse and Neglect* 11: 229–235.

Remick, H. 1984. *Comparable worth and wage discrimination: Technical possibilities and political realities.* Philadelphia: Temple University Press.

Resick, P.A., Calhoun, K.S., Atkeson, B.M., and B.M. Ellis. 1981. Social adjustment in victims of sexual assault. *Journal of Consulting and Clinical Psychology* 49: 705–712.

Resick, P.H. 1983. The rape reaction: Research findings and implications for intervention. *Behavior Therapy* 6: 129–132.

Reskin, B. 1988. Bringing men back in: Sex differentiation and the devaluation of women's work. *Gender and Society* 2: 58–81.

Reynolds, H. 1986. *The economics of prostitution.* Springfield, Ill.: Charles C. Thomas.

Rhode, D. 1989. *Gender justice.* Cambridge: Harvard University Press.

Richardson, L. 1989. Secrecy and status: The social construction of forbidden relationships. In B.J. Risman and P. Schwartz (eds.), *Gender in intimate relationships: A microstructural approach,* pp. 108–119. Belmont, Calif.: Wadsworth Publishing Co.

Richler, M. 1989. Editorial. *New York Times* (December 9): A3.

Riger, S., and M. Gordon. 1981. The fear of rape: A study in social control. *Journal of Social Issues* 37: 71–92.

Riger, S., M. Gordon, and R. LeBailly. 1982. Coping with urban crime: Women's use of precautionary behaviors. *American Journal of Community Psychology* 10: 369–386.

Risin, L.I., and M.P. Koss. 1987. The sexual abuse of boys: Childhood victimizations reported by a national sample. *Journal of Interpersonal Violence* 2: 309–323.

Roark, M.L. 1987. Preventing violence on college campuses. *Journal of Counseling and Development* 65: 367–371.

Robertson, C., C. Dyer, and D. Campbell. 1988. Campus harassment: Sexual harassment policies and procedures at institutions of higher learning. *Signs* 13: 792–812.

Roche, J.P. 1986. Premarital sex: Attitudes and behavior by dating stage. *Adolescence* 21: 107–121.

Rosenbaum, M. 1982. Work and the addicted prostitute. In N.H. Rafter and E. Stankon (eds.), *Judge, lawyer, victim, thief,* pp. 131–150. Boston: Northeastern University Press.

Rosenberg, F., and R.G. Simmons. 1975. Sex differences in the self-concept in adolescence. *Sex Roles* 1: 147–159.

Rosenthal, J.A. 1988. Patterns of reported child abuse and neglect. *Child Abuse and Neglect* 12: 263–271.

Rossi, P.W., and E. Weber-Burdin. 1983. Sexual harassment on campus. *Social Science Research* 12: 131–158.

Roth, G. 1987. Your body is your ally. *Model Mugging News* 1: 1, 3.

Rozee-Koker, P. 1987. Effects of self-efficacy, fear of rape and perceived risk on intention to take a self-defense class. Paper presented to the Midwest Society for Feminist Studies, Akron, Ohio.

Rozee-Koker, P. 1988. The effects of fear of rape on working women. Paper presented at the American Psychological Association, Atlanta.

Rubin, Z., C.T. Hill, L.A. Peplau, and C. Dunkel-Schetter. 1980. Self disclosure in dating couples: Sex roles and the ethic of openness. *Journal of Marriage and the Family* 42: 305–317.

Russell, A.B., and C.M. Trainor. 1984. *Trends in child abuse and neglect: A national perspective*. Denver: American Humane Association.

Russell, D.E.H. 1975. *The politics of rape: The victim's perspective*. New York: Stein and Day.

Russell, D.E.H. 1982. *Rape in Marriage*. New York: Macmillan.

Russell, D.E.H. 1984. *Sexual exploitation*. Beverly Hills, Calif.: Sage.

Russell, D.E.H. 1988. Pornography and rape: A causal model. *Political Psychology* 9: 41–73.

Russell, D., and J. Caputi. 1990. Canadian massacre: It was political. *New Directions for Women* (March–April): 17.

Russell, D.E.H., and D. Finkelhor. 1984. The gender gap among perpetrators of child sexual abuse. In D.E.H. Russell, *Sexual exploitation: Rape, child sexual abuse, and workplace harassment*, pp. 215–231. Beverly Hills, Calif.: Sage Publications.

Saadawi, N. 1980. *The hidden face of Eve: women in the Arab world*. Translated and edited by S. Hetata. Boston: Beacon Press.

Safran, C. 1976. What men do to women on the job: A shocking look at sexual harassment. *Redbook* 149: 217–223.

Sanday, P.R. 1981a. The socio-cultural context of rape: A cross-cultural study. *Journal of Social Issues* 37: 5–27.

Sanday, P.R. 1981b. *Female power and male dominance: On the origins of sexual inequality*. Cambridge: Cambridge University Press.

Sandford, J. 1975. *Prostitutes: Portraits of people in the sexploitation business*. London: Secker and Warburg.

Sanford, L.T. 1980. *The silent children*. New York: McGraw-Hill.

Sarrel, P.M., and W.H. Masters. 1982. Sexual molestation of men by women. *Archives of Sexual Behavior* 11: 117–131.

Saunders, E.J. 1988. A comparative study of attitudes toward child sexual abuse among social work and judicial system professionals. *Child Abuse and Neglect* 12: 83–90.

Savitz, L., and L. Rosen. 1988. The sexuality of prostitutes: Sexual enjoyment reported by "streetwalkers." *Journal of Sex Research* 24: 200–208.

Scheppele, K., and P. Bart. 1983. Through women's eyes: Defining danger in the wake of sexual assault. *Journal of Social Issues* 39: 63–81.

Schlafly, P. 1981. A clash over worker sexual harassment. *San Francisco Chronicle* (August): 13.

Schneider, B.E. 1987. Graduate women, sexual harassment and university policy. *Journal of Higher Education* 58: 46–65.

Schultz, L.G. 1980. The sexual abuse of children and minors: A short history of legal control efforts. In L.G. Schultz (ed.), *Sexual victimology of youth*, pp. 3–17. Springfield, Ill.: Charles C. Thomas.

Schur, E. 1988. *The Americanization of sex*. Philadelphia: Temple University Press.

Scully, D., and J. Marolla 1984. Convicted rapists' vocabulary of motive: Excuses and justifications. *Social Problems* 31: 530–544.

Segal, Z.V., and W.L. Marshall. 1985. Heterosexual social skills in a population of rapists and child molesters. *Journal of Consulting and Clinical Psychology* 53: 55–63.

Seghorn, T.K., R.A. Prentky, and R.J. Boucher. 1987. Childhood sexual abuse in the lives of sexually aggressive offenders. *Journal of the American Academy of Child and Adolescent Psychiatry* 26: 262–267.

Seidner, A.L., and K.S. Calhoun. 1984. Childhood sexual abuse: Factors related to differential adult adjustment. Paper presented at the National Family Violence Research Conference, University of New Hampshire, Durham.

Seng, M.J. 1986. Sexual behavior between adults and children: Some issues of definition. *Journal of Offender Counseling, Services and Rehabilitation* 11: 47–61.

Seymour, W.C. 1979. Sexual harassment: Finding a cause of action under Title VII. *Labor Law Journal* 30: 139–156.

Sgroi, S.M., L.C. Blick, and F.S. Porter. 1982. A conceptual framework for child sexual abuse. In S.M. Sgroi (ed.), *Handbook of clinical intervention in child sexual abuse*, pp. 9–37. Lexington, Mass.: Lexington Books.

Sheffield, C. 1984. Sexual terrorism. In J. Freeman (ed.), *Women: A feminist perspective*, pp. 3–19. Palo Alto, Calif.: Mayfield.

Shields, W.M., and L.M. Shields. 1983. Forcible rape: An evolutionary perspective. *Ethology and Sociobiology* 4: 115–136.

Shrage, L. 1989. Should feminists oppose prostitution? *Ethics* 99: 347–361.

Sidel, R. 1990. *On her own: Growing up in the shadow of the American dream.* New York: Viking.

Silbert, M.H. 1982. Prostitution and sexual assault: Summary of results. *International Journal for Biosocial Research* 3: 69–71.

Silbert, M.H. 1988. Compounding factors in the rape of street prostitutes. In A.W. Burgess (ed.), *Rape and sexual assault*, pp. 75–90. New York: Garland Publishers.

Silverman, D. 1977. Sexual harassment: Working women's dilemma. *Quest* 3: 15–24.

Simmons, R.G., F. Rosenberg, and M. Rosenberg. 1973. Disturbance in the self-image at adolescence. *American Sociological Review* 38: 553–568.

Simpson, J.A., B. Campbell, and E. Berscheid. 1986. The association between romantic love and marriage: Kephart (1967) twice revisited. *Personality and Social Psychology Bulletin* 12: 363–372.

Sink, F. 1987. Studies of true and false allegation: A critical review. Paper presented at the Family Violence Conference, University of New Hampshire, Durham.

Skelton, C.A., and B.R. Burkhart. 1980. Sexual assault: Determinants of victim disclosure. *Criminal Justice and Behavior* 7: 229–236.

Skinner, J. 1988. Who's changing whom? Women, management and work organization. In A. Coyle and J. Skinner (eds.), *Women and work: Positive action for change*, pp. 152–168. London: Macmillan.

Smith, D.D. 1976. The social content of pornography. *Journal of Communication* 26: 16–24.

Smith, R.E., J.P. Keating, R.K. Hester, and H.E. Mitchell. 1976. Role and justice considerations in the attribution of responsibility to a rape victim. *Journal of Research in Personality* 10: 346–357.

Smith, R.L. 1984. Human sperm competition. In R.L. Smith (ed.), *Sperm competition and the evolution of animal mating systems*, pp. 601–659. New York: Academic Press.

Smith, S.E. 1986. *Fear or freedom*. Racine, Wis.: Mother Courage Press.

Snyder, J.C., and E.H. Newberger. 1986. Consensus and difference among hospital professionals in evaluating child maltreatment. *Violence and Victims* 1: 125–139.

Somers, A. 1982. Sexual harassment in academe: Legal issues and definitions. *Journal of Social Issues* 38: 23–32.

Sommerfeldt, T., B.R. Burkhart, and C.A. Mandoki. 1989. In her own words: Victim's descriptions of hidden rape effects. Poster presented at the ninety-seventh Annual Meeting of the American Psychological Association, New Orleans.

Spalter-Roth, R., and H. Hartmann. 1988. *Unnecessary losses: costs to Americans of the lack of family and medical leave*. Washington D.C.: Institute for Women's Policy Research.

Sprecher, S. 1984. Sex differences in bases of power in dating relationships. *Sex Roles* 12: 449–462.

Spreitzer, E., and M. Pugh. 1973. Interscholastic athletics and educational expectations. *Sociology of Education* 46: 171–182.

Stark, E., A. Flitcraft, and W. Frazier. 1979. Medicine and patriarchal violence: The social construction of a "private" event. *International Journal of Health Services* 9: 461–493.

Steinberg, R. 1987. Radical challenges in a liberal world: The mixed success of comparable worth. *Gender and Society* 1: 466–475.

Steiner, G. 1985. *Constitutional inequality: The political fortunes of the equal rights amendment*. Washington, D.C.: Brookings Institution.

Stock, W., D. Krause, and K. Vaughan. 1988. Generalized fear of rape among women: Pathological or sane? Paper presented at the Midwestern Regional Meeting of the Society for the Scientific Study of Sex, Chicago.

Stockard, J., and M.M. Johnson. 1980. *Sex roles*. Englewood Cliffs, N.J.: Prentice-Hall.

Storaska, F. 1975. *How to say no to a rapist and survive*. New York: Random House.

Struckman-Johnson, C. 1988. Forced sex on dates: It happens to men, too. *Journal of Sex Research* 24: 234–241.

Summit, R.C. 1983. The child sexual abuse accommodation syndrome. *Child Abuse and Neglect* 7: 177–193.

Swan, H.L., A.N. Press, and S.L. Briggs. 1985. Child sexual abuse prevention: Does it work? *Child Welfare* 64: 395–405.

Swift, C.F. 1985. The prevention of rape. In A.W. Burgess (ed.), *Rape and sexual assault: A research handbook*, pp. 413–426. New York: Garland Publishing.

Symons, D. 1979. *The evolution of human sexuality*. Oxford: Oxford University Press.

Symons, D. 1987a. If we're all Darwinians, what's the fuss about? In C. Crawford, M. Smith, and D. Krebs (eds.), *Sociobiology and psychology: Ideas, issues and applications*, pp. 121–146. Hillsdale, N.J.: Erlbaum.

Symons, D. 1987b. An evolutionary approach: Can Darwin's view of life shed light on human sexuality? In J.H. Greer and W.T. O'Donahue (eds.), *Theories of human sexuality*, pp. 91–125. New York: Plenum Press.

Szinovacz, M.E. 1984. Changing family roles and interactions. In B.B. Hess and M.B. Sussman (eds.), *Women and the family: Two decades of change*, pp. 163–202. New York: Haworth Press.

Szirom, T. 1988. *Teaching gender?* Sydney: Allen and Unwin.

Tangri, S.S., M.R. Burt, and L.B. Johnson. 1982. Sexual harassment at work: Three explanatory models. *Journal of Social Issues* 38: 33–54.

Tavris, C., and C. Wade. 1984. *The longest war: Sex differences in perspective.* New York: Harcourt Brace Jovanovich.

Taylor, S.E. 1983. Adjustment to threatening events: A theory of cognitive adaptation. *American Psychologist* 38: 1161–1173.

Tedesco, J.F., and S.V. Schnell. 1987. Children's reactions to sex abuse investigations and litigation. *Child Abuse and Neglect* 11: 267–272.

Telsey, N. 1981. Karate and the feminist resistance movement. In F. Delacoste and F. Newman (eds.), *Fight back!* pp. 101–103. Minneapolis: Cleis.

Terpstra, D.E., and D.D. Baker. 1986. A framework for the study of sexual harassment. *Basic and Applied Social Psychology* 7: 17–34.

Terpstra, D.E., and D.D. Baker. 1988. Outcomes of sexual harassment charges. *Academy of Management Journal* (March): 185–194.

Territo, L., J. Halsted, and M. Bromley. 1989. *Crime and justice in America: A human perspective.* St Paul: West.

Tesoro, M. 1988. Model mugging: The rape you prevent may be your own. *Black Belt* (May): 32–37.

Tharinger, D.J., J.J. Krivacska, M. Laye-McDonough, L. Jamison, G.G. Vincent, and A.D. Hedlund. 1988. Prevention of child sexual abuse: An analysis of issues, educational programs, and research findings. *School Psychology Review* 17: 614–634.

Thompson, M.E. 1990. Quotations from model mugging graduates, 1987–1990. Unpublished manuscript.

Thornburg, H.D. 1981. Adolescent sources of information on sex. *Journal of School Health* 51: 274–277.

Thorne, B. 1986. Girls and boys together . . . but mostly apart: Gender arrangements in elementary schools. In W. Hartup and Z. Rubin (eds.), *Relationships and development*, pp. 167–184. Hillsdale, N.J.: Lawrence Erlbaum.

Thorne, B., and Z. Luria. 1986. Sexuality and gender in children's daily worlds. *Social Problems* 33: 176–190.

Thornhill, N.W. In press. Human inbreeding. In N.W. Thornhill and W.M. Shields (eds.), *The natural history of inbreeding and outbreeding: Theoretical and empirical perspectives.* Chicago: University of Chicago Press.

Thornhill, N.W., and R. Thornhill. 1990. An evolutionary analysis of psychological pain following rape: The effect of the nature of the sexual act. Unpublished manuscript.

Thornhill, R. In press. The study of adaptation. In M. Bekoff and D. Jamieson (eds.), *Interpretation and explanation in the study of behavior*, vol. 2. Boulder, Colo.: Westview Press.

Thornhill, R., and N.W. Thornhill. 1983. Human rape: An evolutionary analysis. *Ethology and Sociobiology* 4: 137–173.

Thornhill, R., and N.W. Thornhill. 1990. The evolutionary psychology of human rape. Unpublished manuscript.

Thornton, B., and R.M. Ryckman. 1983. The influence of a rape victim's physical attractiveness on observers' attributions of responsibility. *Human Relations* 36: 549–562.

Tong, R. 1984. *Women, sex, and the law.* Totowa, N.J.: Rowman and Littlefield.

Tooby, J., and L. Cosmides. 1989. Evolutionary psychology and the generation of culture, part I: Theoretical considerations. *Ethology and Sociobiology* 10: 29–50.

Totten, C., G. Totten, and J. Rostan. 1988. Women miners' fight for parental leave. *Labor Research Review* 11: 89–95.

Townsend, J.M. 1987. Sex differences in sexuality among medical students: Effects of increasing socioeconomic status. *Archives of Sexual Behavior* 16: 415–444.

Townsend, J.M. 1989. Mate selection criteria: A pilot study. *Ethology and Sociobiology* 10: 241–253.

Treiman, D., and H. Hartmann. 1981. *Women, work, and wages: Equal pay for jobs of equal value.* Washington, D.C.: National Academy Press.

Trivers, R.L. 1985. *Social evolution.* Menlo Park, Calif.: Benjamin/Cummings.

Trudell, B., and M.H. Whatley. 1988. School sexual abuse prevention: Unintended consequences and dilemmas. *Child Abuse and Neglect* 12: 103–113.

U.S. Department of Justice. 1987. *Felony laws of the 50 states and the District of Columbia, 1986.* Washington, D.C.: U.S. Department of Justice, Bureau of Justice Statistics.

U.S. Department of Justice. Federal Bureau of Investigation. 1988. *Structure and implementation plan for the enhanced UCR program.* Washington, D.C.: U.S. Department of Justice.

U.S. Merit Systems Protection Board. 1981. *Sexual harassment in the federal workplace: Is it a problem?* Washington, D.C.: Office of Merit Systems Review and Studies.

Vago, S. 1988. *Law and society.* Englewood Cliffs, N.J.: Prentice-Hall.

Vander Mey, B.J. 1988. The sexual victimization of male children: A review of previous research. *Child Abuse and Neglect* 12: 61–72.

Vhay, M.D. 1988. The harms of asking: Towards a comprehensive treatment of sexual harassment. *University of Chicago Law Review* 55: 328–362.

Vogel, L. 1983. *Marxism and the oppression of women: Toward a unitary theory.* New Brunswick, N.J.: Rutgers University Press.

Waller, W. 1938. *The family: A dynamic interpretation.* New York: Cordon.

Warr, M. 1985. Fear of rape among urban women. *Social Problems* 32: 238–250.

Warshaw, R. 1988. *I never called it rape.* New York: Harper & Row.

Washington Post, 1989. December 8, p. A58.

Waterman, C.K., and D. Foss-Goodman. 1984. Child molesting: Variables relating to attribution of fault to victims, offenders, and nonparticipating parents. *Journal of Sex Research* 20: 329–349.

Wattenberg, E. 1985. In a different light: A feminist perspective on the role of mothers in father-daughter incest. *Child Welfare* 64: 203–211.

WBAI Consciousness Raising. 1973. Men and violence. In A. Koedt, E. Levine, and A. Rapone (eds.), *Radical feminism*, pp. 63–71. New York: Quadrangle.

Webb, E.J., D.T. Campbell, R.D. Schwartz, and L. Sechrest. 1966. *Unobtrusive measures*. Chicago: Rand-McNally.

Weber-Burdin, E., and P.H. Rossi. 1982. Defining sexual harassment on campus: A replication and extension. *Journal of Social Issues* 38: 111–120.

Weis, K., and S. Borges. 1973. Victimology and rape: The case of the legitimate victim. *Issues in Criminology* 8: 71–115.

West, D. 1982. I was afraid to shut my eyes. In A.M. Scacco, Jr. (ed.), *Male rape: A casebook of sexual aggressions*, pp. 169–172. New York: AMS Press.

Whatley, M.H., and B. Trudell. 1988. The role of the family in child sexual abuse prevention programs. *Journal of Education* 170: 95–016.

White, S., B.M. Halpin, G.A. Strom, and G. Santilli. 1988. Behavioral comparisons of young sexually abused, neglected and nonreferred children. *Journal of Clinical Child Psychology* 17: 53–61.

Wigmore, J. 1934. *Evidence*. Boston: Little, Brown.

Williams, G.C. 1966. *Adaptation and natural selection*. Princeton: Princeton University Press.

Wilson, K.R., and L.A. Kraus. 1983. Sexual harassment in the university. *Journal of College Student Personnel* (May): 219–224.

Wilson, M., and Martin Daly. 1985. Competitiveness, risk taking, and violence: The young male syndrome. *Ethology and Sociobiology* 6: 69–73.

Wilson, P. 1978. *The other side of rape*. St. Lucia, Queensland: University of Queensland Press.

Winick, C., and P.M. Kinsie. 1971. *The lively commerce*. Chicago: Quadrangle Books.

Wolfgang, M., and M. Riedel. 1977. Race, rape and the death penalty. In D. Chappell, R. Geis, and G. Geis (eds.), *Forcible rape: The crime, the victim and the offender*, pp. 119–133. New York: Columbia University Press.

Wollitzer, R.I. 1988. Sixth Amendment—defendant's right to confront witnesses: Constitutionality of protective measures in child sexual assault cases: Coy v. Iowa, 108, S. Ct. 2798. *Journal of Criminal Law and Criminology* 29: 759–794.

Wurtele, S.K., S.R. Marrs, and C.L. Miller-Perrin. 1987. Practice makes perfect? The role of participant modeling in sexual abuse prevention programs. *Journal of Consulting and Clinical Psychology* 55: 599–602.

Wurtele, S.K., D.A. Saslawsky, C.L. Miller, S.R. Marrs, and J.C. Britcher. 1986. Teaching personal safety skills for potential prevention of sexual abuse: A comparison of treatments. *Journal of Consulting and Clinical Psychology* 54: 688–692.

Wyatt, G.E. 1985. The sexual abuse of Afro-American and white-American women in childhood. *Child Abuse and Neglect* 9: 507–519.

Wyatt, G.E., and M.R. Mickey. 1987. Ameliorating the effects of child sexual abuse: An exploratory study of support by parents and others. *Journal of Interpersonal Violence* 2: 403–414.

Wyatt, G.E., and S.D. Peters. 1986. Issues in the definition of child sexual abuse in prevalence research. *Child Abuse and Neglect* 10: 231–240.

Yates, A., and T. Musty. 1988. Preschool children's erroneous allegations of sexual molestation. *American Journal of Psychiatry* 145: 989–992.

Zillmann, D., and J. Bryant. 1984. Effects of massive exposure to pornography. In N. Malamuth and E. Donnerstein (eds.), *Pornography and sexual aggression*, pp. 115–136. Orlando, Fl.: Academic Press.

Zuravin, S. 1989. The ecology of child abuse and neglect: Review of the literature and presentation of data. *Violence and Victims* 4: 101–120.

Index

About the Contributors

Elizabeth Rice Allgeier obtained her Ph.D. in social/personality psychology at Purdue University in 1976. She is a professor of psychology at Bowling Green State University. A past president of The Society for the Scientific Study of Sex, she was named a G. Stanley Hall lecturer by the American Psychological Association in 1986 for exemplary undergraduate teaching and won the BGSU Alumni Association's Master Teacher Award in 1988. The coauthor of four books, she is currently working on the third edition of *Sexual Interactions*, a human sexuality text written with her husband. She is also presently involved in a number of projects examining variables associated with consensual and coercive sexual experience.

Barry R. Burkhart received his Ph.D. in clinical psychology from Florida State University in 1974. Currently a professor of psychology at Auburn University, he has served as a private practitioner and a consultant to numerous law enforcement agencies and as an editorial reviewer to several scientific journals. He has published extensively in the areas of child sexual abuse and acquaintance rape.

Jo Dixon received her Ph.D. from Indiana University and is currently an assistant professor of Sociology at New York University. She has published several articles on patterns of gun ownership and racial discrimination in criminal sentencing. She is currently engaged in research that explores the effects of gender on social and legal constructions of self-defense.

Janet Enke is a doctoral candidate in sociology at Indiana University. Her dissertation examines the conflict between competition and friendship among female athletes in a high school setting. Her main fields of interest are gender, qualitative methods, the sociology of education, and social psychology.

Mary Ellen Fromuth, Ph.D., is an assistant professor in the psychology department at Middle Tennessee State University. Her primary research interest is in child sexual abuse with a focus on epidemiological factors and long-term correlates.

Heidi Gottfried received her Ph.D. in sociology from the University of Wisconsin of Madison in 1987. She is an assistant professor of sociology at Purdue University. Her publications and research address issues in political economy from a feminist perspective. She is currently developing a book on gender, class, and the state in Sweden.

Patricia Harney is a doctoral student in clinical psychology at the University of Kansas. Her present area of interest is a study of theoretical issues that inform various definitions of sexual coercion, particularly in relation to nonphysical forms of coercion. Additionally, she is interested in the factors that influence the labeling of unwanted sexual activity as coercive, and women's perceptions of the social, cultural, and interpersonal factors that constrain their sexual autonomy.

Dean Knudsen is a professor in the department of sociology and anthropology at Purdue University. He received his Ph.D. from the University of North Carolina-Chapel Hill in 1964. His book *Child Protective Services: Discretion, Decisions and Dilemmas* was published in 1988. He is currently coediting a book with JoAnn Miller entitled *Abused and Battered: Social and Legal Responses to Family Violence.*

Nick Maroules earned his J.D. in 1979 from the Golden Gate School of Law, and his Ph.D. in 1986 in sociology from the University of California at San Diego. He currently teaches in the department of sociology, anthropology, and social work at Illinois State University. His research interests include the sociology of law, criminology, and delinquency; sociolinguistics; and qualitative and quantitative research methods.

Kathleen McKinney received her Ph.D. in sociology in 1982 from the University of Wisconsin at Madison and is currently in the department of sociology, anthropology, and social work at Illinois State University. She has published frequently in the areas of sexual harassment, sexual attitudes, and standards, contraceptive attitudes and behavior, and teaching issues and techniques. She is coeditor of a book entitled *Human Sexuality: The Societal and Interpersonal Context* and is currently coediting a book entitled *Sexuality in Close Relationships.*

JoAnn L. Miller completed the Ph.D. in sociology at the University of Massachusetts at Amherst in 1984. Her teaching and research pursuits fall broadly in the sociology-of-law field. She is especially interested in women and the law, focusing much of her recent work on the problems of violence against women, sexual harassment, and prostitution. She has coedited several books, including *Sentencing Reform: A Review and Annotated Bibliography*, and *Research in Social Problems and Public Policy, Volumes III and IV.*

Charlene L. Muehlenhard holds a joint appointment is psychology and women's studies at the University of Kansas. She received her Ph.D. in 1981 from the University of Wisconsin at Madison. While her research program initially focused on social-skills training and changing gender roles, these interests have led to her research on date rape and sexual coercion. She is especially interested in the relationship between sexual coercion and traditional gender roles.

Andrea Parrot received her Ph.D. at Cornell University in 1981 and is presently an assistant professor in the department of human service studies at Cornell. She has been a consultant to numerous colleges, universities, educational media producers, federal and state agencies, and crime prevention programs. Dr. Parrot teaches a course on human sexuality, and is a clinical assistant professor of psychiatry at the SUNY Health Sciences Center of Syracuse, New York, where she teaches a medical school course on acquaintance-rape prevention for college audiences called "STOP DATE RAPE!" and for high school audiences called "I Know You Said 'No' But I Thought You Meant 'Yes.'" Dr. Parrot's *Acquaintance Rape and Sexual Assault Prevention Manual* and her most recent book, *Coping with Date Rape and Acquaintance Rape*, are designed to help people avoid acquaintance rape and to help victims become survivors.

Betty J. Turner Royster received her Ph.D. in personality/social psychology from Kansas State University in 1988. She is an assistant professor of psychology at Bowling Green State University. Her primary research interests center around perceived loss of control and its impact upon behavior. She is currently involved in a series of studies on sexual harassment with particular emphasis on the personality and situational factors related to vulnerability to harass or be harassed. She teaches courses in the psychology of gender, personality theory, and human sexuality.

Wendy Stock, Ph.D., received her B.A. in psychology from the University of California at Berkeley in 1976, and her M.A. and Ph.D. from the State University of New York at Stony Brook. Dr. Stock is currently an assistant professor in psychology at Texas A&M University where she teaches graduate courses in psychopathology and treatment of sexual dysfunctions, and undergraduate courses in human sexuality and abnormal psychology. Dr. Stock's doctoral work was on effects of pornography on women, and she continues to conduct physiological and questionnaire research on the effects of pornography. She has published research articles and chapters in the areas of sexual dysfunction, sexual fantasy, pornography, and feminist therapy.

Lori K. Sudderth received her undergraduate degree from the University of Texas at Austin and is currently a doctoral student in sociology at Indiana University in Bloomington. Her primary interests include the sociology of gender roles, criminology, sexuality, and emotions, with a special focus on surviving and coping with sexual violence.

Martha E. Thompson is a professor of sociology and women's studies and the chair of the department of sociology at Northeastern Illinois University in Chicago. She is also an instructor for Model Mugging, a highly specialized self-defense course in which women learn a knockout defense against assailants of any size. She has been active in the women's movement since 1970. Most of her writing and research is on the application of feminist principles to everyday life; for example, in teaching, parenting, housework, relationships, and political organizing.

Nancy Wilmsen Thornhill is research assistant professor of biology and associate in anthropology at the University of New Mexico. She received her Ph.D. in anthropology in 1987 from the University of New Mexico. Her research interests include evolutionary studies of psychological pain, particularly that experienced by rape victims. Her major area of research involves the study of rules regulating human marriage patterns, particularly rules about incest and inbreeding. She is the editor of *The Natural History of Inbreeding and Outbreeding: Theoretical and Empirical Perspectives* (The University of Chicago Press, forthcoming).

Randy Thornhill is professor of biology at the University of New Mexico. His main research interest is sexual selection, particularly how this process has worked during the evolution of secondary sexual characteristics of animals. His current research includes studies of human sexuality and of the importance of female mate choice in the evolution of elaborate male traits in birds and insects. He is the coauthor with John Alcock of *The Evolution of Insect Mating Systems* (Harvard University Press 1983).

About the Editors

Elizabeth Grauerholz received her Ph.D. from Indiana University in 1985. She is currently an assistant professor of sociology at Purdue University, where she teaches courses on sexual coercion, marriage and family, and social psychology. Her research examines the relationship among gender, power, and sexuality.

Mary A. Koralewski is a doctoral candidate in the clinical psychology program at Purdue University. Her research interests include date rape, how alcohol affects the dating situation, and prevention of sexual coercion. She has been conducting therapy for survivors of rape and childhood sexual abuse for the past five years.

DATE DUE

Brodart Co.   Cat. # 55 137 001   Printed in USA